GOLF  RULES ILLUSTRATED

COMPILED BY
THE UNITED STATES GOLF ASSOCIATION

RULES INCIDENTS BY
GARY A. GALYEAN

ILLUSTRATIONS BY
SUDDEN IMPACT MEDIA

hamlyn

CONTENTS

In the Rules of Golf, the gender used in relation to any person is understood to include both genders.

FOREWORD

The Rules of Golf, although only 34 in number, can sometimes seem daunting, and illogical. There are Rules that are clear and simple and that make perfect sense, while others, dealing with complicated situations, can lose you in their logic. We all strive to find the threads of continuity in the Rules that will lead us to a fuller, more comfortable understanding of their application. That is the goal of this publication.

An understanding of the Rules, and the concepts behind them, can sometimes best be learned by studying incidents that actually took place, as well as the rulings that were made to resolve them. Hypothetical, "what-if" situations are not a part of these pages. In many cases, the incidents included here, following the recitation of each Rule, will be remembered as events you read about in sports reports, or saw on television. The narratives we have provided describe the detail and logic behind those rulings. Why was Tiger Woods permitted to have spectators move a boulder out of his line of play (Rule 23)? Why was not Robert De Vincenzo permitted to simply correct his score card at the 1968 Masters Tournament and accept the result of his athletic performance (Rule 6)? The answers are here.

Every four years, the United States Golf Association and The R&A in St. Andrews update the Rules in an effort to adapt them to new situations that may have come to light in competitions around the world.

It is with great pleasure that we provide to you the latest edition of *Golf Rules Illustrated* that includes the quadrennial Rules changes, as well as incidents that help to explain them. We hope that all golfers, regardless of their abilities, will gain a better understanding of the Rules from these pages and, thereby, a more enjoyable experience on the golf course. Thank you for your interest in the Rules of Golf, which serve all of us as the backbone of the game.

James T. Bunch
Chairman, Rules of Golf Committee
United States Golf Association

HOW TO USE THE RULES BOOK

UNDERSTAND THE WORDS

The Rules book is written in a very precise and deliberate fashion. You should be aware of and understand the following differences in word use:

may = optional

should = recommendation

must = instruction (and penalty if not carried out)

a ball = you may substitute another ball (e.g., Rules 26, 27 and 28)

the ball = you may not substitute another ball (e.g., Rules 24-2 and 25-1)

KNOW THE DEFINITIONS

There are over 50 defined terms and these form the foundation around which the Rules of Play are written. A good knowledge of the defined terms (which are italicized throughout the book) is very important to the correct application of the Rules.

WHAT IS THE RULING?

To answer any question on the Rules you must first establish the facts of the case.

To do so you should identify:

1 The form of play (e.g., match play or stroke play; single, foursome or four-ball?).

2 Who is involved (e.g., the player, his partner or caddie, an outside agency?).

3 Where the incident occurred (e.g., on the teeing ground, in a bunker or water hazard, on the putting green or elsewhere on the course?).

4 The player's intentions (e.g., what was he doing and what does he want to do?).

5 Any subsequent events (e.g., the player has returned his score card or the competition has closed).

REFER TO THE BOOK

It is recommended that you carry a Rules book in your golf bag and use it whenever a question arises. If in doubt, play the course as you find it and play the ball as it lies. Once back in the Clubhouse, reference to "Decisions on the Rules of Golf" should help resolve any outstanding queries.

The USGA publication entitled *A Modification of the Rules of Golf for Golfers with Disabilities* that contains permissible modifications to The Rules of Golf to accommodate disabled golfers is available through the USGA.

*For up-to-date information regarding Appendix II, Design of Clubs, please contact the USGA or refer to www.usga.org.

PRINCIPAL CHANGES

GENERAL

The changes to the Rules generally fall into two broad categories: (1) those that improve the clarity of the Rules and (2) those that reduce the penalties in certain circumstances to ensure that they are proportionate.

DEFINITIONS

Advice

Amended to allow the exchange of information on distance, as it is not considered to be "advice."

Lost Ball

Amended to clarify substituted ball issues and to include the concept of "stroke-and-distance" (see corresponding changes to Rules 18-1, 24-3, 25-1c, 26 and 27-1).

Matches

Definition withdrawn and replaced by two new Definitions, "Forms of Match Play" and "Forms of Stroke Play."

RULES

Rule 1-2. Exerting Influence on Ball

Note added to clarify what constitutes a serious breach of Rule 1-2.

Rule 4-1. Form and Make of Clubs

Amended to reduce the penalty for carrying, but not using, a non-conforming club or a club in breach of Rule 4-2, from disqualification to the same as carrying more than 14 clubs.

Rule 12-1. Searching for Ball; Seeing Ball

Amended to include searching for a ball in an obstruction.

Rule 12-2. Identifying Ball

Amended to allow a player to lift his ball for identification in a hazard (see corresponding change to Rule 15-3, removing the exemption from penalty for playing a wrong ball in a hazard).

Rule 13-4. Ball in Hazard; Prohibited Actions

Exception 1 amended for clarification; Exception 2 amended to refer to Rule 13-2; Exception 3 added to exempt a player from penalty under Rule 13-4a (testing the condition of the hazard) in certain circumstances.

Rule 14-3. Artificial Devices, Unusual Equipment and Unusual Use of Equipment

Amended to refer to the unusual use of equipment (see also new Exception on use of equipment in a traditionally accepted manner) and new Exception added for players with a legitimate medical reason to use an artificial device or unusual equipment.

Note added to clarify that a Local Rule may be introduced allowing the use of distance measuring devices; previously authorized by Decision only.

Rule 15-2. Substituted Ball

Exception added to avoid a "double penalty" when player incorrectly substitutes ball and plays from the wrong place (see corresponding change to Rule 20-7c).

Rule 15-3. Wrong Ball

Amended to remove the exemption from penalty for playing a wrong ball in a hazard (see corresponding change to Rule 12-2, allowing a player to lift a ball for identification in a hazard).

Rule 16-1e. Standing Astride or on Line of Putt

Exception added to apply no penalty if act was inadvertent or to avoid standing on another player's line of putt; previously authorized by Decision only.

Rule 18. Ball at Rest Moved

Penalty statement amended to avoid a "double penalty" when player lifts ball without authority and incorrectly substitutes a ball (see related changes to Rules 15-2 and 20-7c).

Rule 18-1. Ball at Rest Moved; By Outside Agency

Note added to clarify procedure when a ball might have been moved by an outside agency.

Rule 19-2. Ball in Motion Deflected or Stopped By Player, Partner, Caddie or Equipment

Amended to reduce the penalty in both match play and stroke play to one stroke.

Rule 20-3a. Placing and Replacing; By Whom and Where

Amended to reduce the penalty for having the wrong person place or replace a ball to one stroke.

Rule 20-7c. Playing from Wrong Place; Stroke Play

Note added to avoid a "double penalty" when player plays from a wrong place and incorrectly substitutes a ball (see corresponding change to Rule 15-2).

Rule 24-1. Movable Obstruction

Amended to allow a flagstick, whether attended, removed or held up, to be moved when a ball is in motion.

Rule 24-3. Ball in Obstruction Not Found; Rule 25-1c. Ball in Abnormal Ground Condition Not Found; Rule 26-1. Water Hazards (Including Lateral Water Hazards); Rule 27-1. Stroke and Distance; Ball Out of Bounds; Ball Not Found Within Five Minutes

The term "reasonable evidence" has been replaced by "known or virtually certain" when determining whether a ball that has not been found may be treated as lost in an obstruction (Rule 24-3), an abnormal ground condition (Rule 25-1) or a water hazard (Rule 26-1). See corresponding change to Definition of "Lost Ball" and Rule 18-1.

APPENDIX I
Seams of Cut Turf

New Specimen Local Rule added.

Temporary Immovable Obstruction

Clause II of the Specimen Local Rule amended to include an additional requirement that, for intervention relief to be granted, the temporary immovable obstruction must be on the player's line of play.

APPENDIX II
Adjustability

Amended to allow forms of adjustability other than weight adjustment, subject to evaluation by the USGA.

Clubhead; Plain in Shape

Amended to clarify meaning of "plain in shape" and list some of the features that are not permitted; previously detailed in guidelines on equipment Rules.

Clubhead; Dimensions, Volume and Moment of Inertia

Sections added on moment of inertia and putter head dimensions; previously detailed in guidelines on equipment Rules and test protocols.

Clubhead; Spring Effect and Dynamic Properties

New section added on spring effect. The limit, as detailed in the Pendulum Test Protocol, now applies to all clubs (except putters) and in all forms of the game; previously covered by condition of competition.

SECTION I
ETIQUETTE; BEHAVIOR ON THE COURSE

Introduction

This Section provides guidelines on the manner in which the game of golf should be played. If they are followed, all players will gain maximum enjoyment from the game. The overriding principle is that consideration should be shown to others on the course at all times.

The Spirit of the Game

Golf is played, for the most part, without the supervision of a referee or umpire. The game relies on the integrity of the individual to show consideration for other players and to abide by the Rules. All players should conduct themselves in a disciplined manner, demonstrating courtesy and sportsmanship at all times, irrespective of how competitive they may be. This is the spirit of the game of golf.

Safety

Players should ensure that no one is standing close by or in a position to be hit by the club, the ball or any stones, pebbles, twigs or the like when they make a stroke or practice swing.

Players should not play until the players in front are out of range.

Players should always alert greenstaff nearby or ahead when they are about to make a stroke that might endanger them.

If a player plays a ball in a direction where there is a danger of hitting someone, he should immediately shout a warning. The traditional word of warning in such situations is "fore."

Consideration for Other Players
No Disturbance or Distraction

Players should always show consideration for other players on the course and should not disturb their play by moving, talking or making unnecessary noise.

Players should ensure that any electronic device taken onto the course does not distract other players.

On the teeing ground, a player should not tee his ball until it is his turn to play.

Players should not stand close to or directly behind the ball, or directly behind the hole, when a player is about to play.

On the Putting Green

On the putting green, players should not stand on another player's line of putt or, when he is making a stroke, cast a shadow over his line of putt.

Players should remain on or close to the putting green until all other players in the group have holed out.

Scoring

In stroke play, a player who is acting as a marker should, if necessary, on the way to the next tee, check the score with the player concerned and record it.

Pace of Play
Play at Good Pace and Keep Up

Players should play at a good pace. The Committee may establish pace of play guidelines that all players should follow.

It is a group's responsibility to keep up with the group in front. If it loses a clear hole and it is delaying the group behind, it should invite the group behind to play through, irrespective of the number of players in that group. Where a group has not lost a clear hole, but it is apparent that the group behind can play faster, it should invite the faster moving group to play through.

Be Ready to Play

Players should be ready to play as soon as it is their turn to play. When playing on or near the putting green, they should leave their bags or carts in such a position as will enable quick movement off the green and towards the next tee. When the play of a hole has been completed, players should immediately leave the putting green.

Lost Ball

If a player believes his ball may be lost outside a water hazard or is out of bounds, to save time, he should play a provisional ball.

7

CARE OF THE COURSE

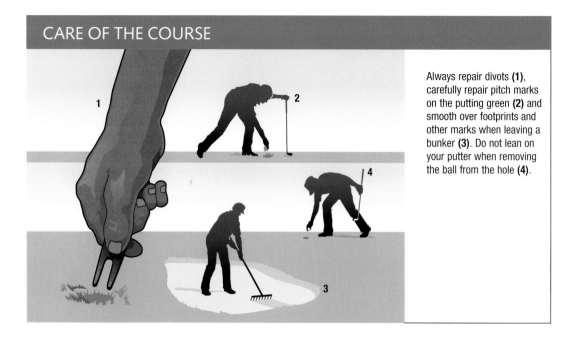

Always repair divots **(1)**, carefully repair pitch marks on the putting green **(2)** and smooth over footprints and other marks when leaving a bunker **(3)**. Do not lean on your putter when removing the ball from the hole **(4)**.

Players searching for a ball should signal the players in the group behind them to play through as soon as it becomes apparent that the ball will not easily be found. They should not search for five minutes before doing so. Having allowed the group behind to play through, they should not continue play until that group has passed and is out of range.

Priority on the Course

Unless otherwise determined by the Committee, priority on the course is determined by a group's pace of play. Any group playing a whole round is entitled to pass a group playing a shorter round. The term "group" includes a single player.

Care of the Course
Bunkers

Before leaving a bunker, players should carefully fill up and smooth over all holes and footprints made by them and any nearby made by others. If a rake is within reasonable proximity of the bunker, the rake should be used for this purpose.

Repair of Divots, Ball-Marks and Damage by Shoes

Players should carefully repair any divot holes made by them and any damage to the putting green made by the impact of a ball (whether or not made by the player himself). On completion of the hole by all players in the group, damage to the putting green caused by golf shoes should be repaired.

Preventing Unnecessary Damage

Players should avoid causing damage to the course by removing divots when taking practice swings or by hitting the head of a club into the ground, whether in anger or for any other reason.

Players should ensure that no damage is done to the putting green when putting down bags or the flagstick.

In order to avoid damaging the hole, players and caddies should not stand too close to the hole and should take care during the handling of the flagstick and the removal of a ball from the hole. The head of a club should not be used to remove a ball from the hole.

Players should not lean on their clubs when on the putting green, particularly when removing the ball from the hole.

The flagstick should be properly replaced in the hole before the players leave the putting green.

Local notices regulating the movement of golf carts should be strictly observed.

Conclusion; Penalties for Breach

If players follow the guidelines in this Section, it will make the game more enjoyable for everyone.

If a player consistently disregards these guidelines during a round or over a period of time to the detriment of others, it is recommended that the Committee consider taking appropriate disciplinary action against the offending player. Such action may, for example, include prohibiting play for a limited time on the course or in a certain number of competitions. This is considered to be justifiable in terms of protecting the interest of the majority of golfers who wish to play in accordance with these guidelines.

In the case of a serious breach of etiquette, the Committee may disqualify a player under Rule 33-7.

Frequently asked question

Q Does a single player have any standing on the golf course?

A The Etiquette section of the 2008 Rules of Golf suggests that, unless otherwise determined by the Committee, priority on the course is determined by a group's pace of play, and the term "group" includes a single player. The Pace of Play part of the Etiquette section also states, "It is a group's responsibility to keep up with the group in front. If a group loses a clear hole and this is delaying the group behind, it should invite the group behind to play through, irrespective of the number of players in that group. Where a group has not lost a clear hole, but it is apparent that the group behind can play faster, it should invite the faster moving group to play through." Therefore, a slow group should give way, where possible, to a faster group, and single golfers should have the same rights as all other players.

SECTION II
DEFINITIONS

The Definitions are listed alphabetically and, in the *Rules* themselves, defined terms are in *italics*.

Abnormal Ground Conditions An *"abnormal ground condition"* is any *casual water*, *ground under repair* or hole, cast or runway on the *course* made by a *burrowing animal*, a reptile or a bird.

Addressing the Ball A player has *"addressed the ball"* when he has taken his *stance* and has also grounded his club, except that in a *hazard* a player has *addressed the ball* when he has taken his *stance*.

Advice *"Advice"* is any counsel or suggestion that could influence a player in determining his play, the choice of a club or the method of making a *stroke*.

Information on the *Rules*, distance or matters of public information, such as the position of *hazards* or the *flagstick* on the *putting green*, is not *advice*.

Ball Deemed to Move See *"Move or Moved."*

Ball Holed See *"Holed."*

Ball Lost See *"Lost Ball."*

Ball in Play A ball is *"in play"* as soon as the player has made a *stroke* on the *teeing ground*. It remains *in play* until it is *holed*, except when it is *lost*, *out of bounds* or lifted, or another ball has been *substituted* whether or not the substitution is permitted; a ball so *substituted* becomes the *ball in play*.

If a ball is played from outside the *teeing ground* when the player is starting play of a hole, or when attempting to correct this mistake, the ball is not *in play* and Rule 11-4 or 11-5 applies. Otherwise, *ball in play* includes a ball played from outside the *teeing ground* when the player elects or is required to play his next *stroke* from the *teeing ground*.

Exception in match play: *Ball in play* includes a ball played by the player from outside the *teeing ground* when starting play of a hole if the opponent does not require the *stroke* to be canceled in accordance with Rule 11-4a.

9

ADDRESSING THE BALL

Except in a hazard, a player has addressed the ball when he has taken his stance and grounded his club.

In a bunker or water hazard a player has addressed the ball when he has taken his stance.

The player has decided not to ground his putter. Therefore, he has not "addressed the ball" and cannot be penalized under Rule 18-2b.

Best-Ball See *"Forms of Match Play."*

Bunker A *"bunker"* is a *hazard* consisting of a prepared area of ground, often a hollow, from which turf or soil has been removed and replaced with sand or the like.

Grass-covered ground bordering or within a *bunker*, including a stacked turf face (whether grass-covered or earthen), is not part of the *bunker*. A wall or lip of the *bunker* not covered with grass is part of the *bunker*. The margin of a *bunker* extends vertically downwards, but not upwards.

A ball is in a *bunker* when it lies in or any part of it touches the *bunker*.

Burrowing Animal A *"burrowing animal"* is an animal (other than a worm, insect or the like) that makes a hole for habitation or shelter, such as a rabbit, mole, groundhog, gopher or salamander. **Note:** A hole made by a non-burrowing animal, such as a dog, is not an *abnormal ground*

condition unless marked or declared as *ground under repair*.

Caddie A *"caddie"* is one who assists the player in accordance with the *Rules*, which may include carrying or handling the player's clubs during play.

When one *caddie* is employed by more than one player, he is always deemed to be the *caddie* of the player sharing the *caddie* whose ball (or whose *partner's* ball) is involved, and *equipment* carried by him is deemed to be that player's *equipment*, except when the *caddie* acts upon specific directions of another player (or the *partner* of another player) sharing the *caddie*, in which case he is considered to be that other player's *caddie*.

Casual Water *"Casual water"* is any temporary accumulation of water on the *course* that is not in a *water hazard* and is visible before or after the player takes his *stance*. Snow and natural ice, other than frost, are either *casual water* or

BUNKER

A bunker face consisting of stacked turf (whether grass covered or earthen) is not part of the bunker.

loose impediments, at the option of the player. Manufactured ice is an *obstruction*. Dew and frost are not *casual water*.

A ball is in *casual water* when it lies in or any part of it touches the *casual water*.

Committee The "*Committee*" is the committee in charge of the competition or, if the matter does not arise in a competition, the committee in charge of the *course*.

Competitor A "*competitor*" is a player in a stroke-play competition. A "*fellow-competitor*" is any person with whom the *competitor* plays. Neither is *partner* of the other.

In stroke-play *foursome* and *four-ball* competitions, where the context so admits, the word "*competitor*" or "*fellow-competitor*" includes his *partner*.

Course The "*course*" is the whole area within any boundaries established by the *Committee* (see Rule 33-2).

Equipment "*Equipment*" is anything used, worn or carried by the player or anything carried for the player by his *partner* or either of their *caddies*,

except any ball he has played at the hole being played and any small object, such as a coin or a *tee*, when used to mark the position of a ball or the extent of an area in which a ball is to be dropped. *Equipment* includes a golf cart, whether or not motorized.

Note 1: A ball played at the hole being played is *equipment* when it has been lifted and not put back into play.

Note 2: When a golf cart is shared by two or more players, the cart and everything in it are deemed to be the *equipment* of one of the players sharing the cart.

If the cart is being moved by one of the players (or the *partner* of one of the players) sharing it, the cart and everything in it are deemed to be that player's *equipment*. Otherwise, the cart and everything in it are deemed to be the *equipment* of the player sharing the cart whose ball (or whose *partner's* ball) is involved.

Fellow-Competitor See "*Competitor*."

Flagstick The "*flagstick*" is a movable straight indicator, with or without bunting or other material attached, which is centered in the *hole* to show its position. It must be circular in cross-section.

CADDIE

A caddie will carry a player's clubs and offer advice on club selection, the direction of play and line for putting.

CASUAL WATER

Casual water is an 'abnormal ground condition' and a player may take relief from such a condition under Rule 25-1.

Padding or shock absorbent material that might unduly influence the movement of the ball is prohibited.

Forecaddie A *"forecaddie"* is one who is employed by the *Committee* to indicate to players the position of balls during play. He is an *outside agency*.

Forms of Match Play
Single: A match in which one player plays against another player.
Threesome: A match in which one player plays against two other players, and each *side* plays one ball.
Foursome: A match in which two players play against two other players, and each *side* plays one ball.
Three-Ball: Three players play a match against one another, each playing his own ball. Each player is playing two distinct matches.
Best-Ball: A match in which one player plays against the better ball of two other players or the best ball of three other players.
Four-Ball: A match in which two players play their better ball against the better ball of two other players.

EQUIPMENT

Any small object, such as a coin or a tee, used to mark the extent of an area in which a ball can be dropped is not equipment of the player.

13

GROUND UNDER REPAIR

Forms of Stroke Play

Individual: A competition in which each *competitor* plays as an individual.

Foursome: A competition in which two *competitors* play as *partners* and play one ball.

Four-Ball: A competition in which two *competitors* play as *partners*, each playing his own ball. The lower score of the *partners* is the score for the hole. If one *partner* fails to complete the play of the hole, there is no penalty.

Note: For bogey, par and Stableford competitions, see Rule 32-1.

Four-Ball See "*Forms of Match Play*" and "*Forms of Stroke Play.*"

Foursome See "*Forms of Match Play*" and "*Forms of Stroke Play.*"

Ground Under Repair "*Ground under repair*" is any part of the *course* so marked by order of the *Committee* or so declared by its authorized representative. All ground and any grass, bush, tree or other growing thing within the *ground under repair* are part of the *ground under repair*. *Ground under repair* includes material piled for removal and a hole made by a greenkeeper, even if not so marked. Grass cuttings and other material left on the *course* that have been abandoned and are not intended to be removed are not *ground under repair* unless so marked.

When the margin of *ground under repair* is defined by stakes, the stakes are inside the *ground under repair*, and the margin of the *ground under repair* is defined by the nearest outside points of the stakes at ground level. When both stakes and lines are used to indicate *ground under repair*, the stakes identify the *ground under repair* and the lines define the margin of the *ground under repair*. When the margin of *ground under repair* is defined by a line on the ground, the line itself is in the *ground under repair*. The margin of *ground under repair* extends vertically downwards but not upwards.

A ball is in *ground under repair* when it lies in or any part of it touches the *ground under repair*.

Stakes used to define the margin of or identify *ground under repair* are *obstructions*.

Note: The *Committee* may make a Local Rule prohibiting play from *ground under repair* or an environmentally-sensitive area defined as *ground under repair*.

Hazards A "*hazard*" is any *bunker* or *water hazard*.

Hole The "*hole*" must be 4¼ inches (108 mm) in diameter and at least 4 inches (101.6 mm) deep. If a lining is used, it must be sunk at least 1 inch (25.4 mm) below the *putting green* surface, unless the nature of the soil makes it impracticable to do so; its outer diameter must not exceed 4¼ inches (108 mm).

Holed A ball is "*holed*" when it is at rest within the circumference of the *hole* and all of it is below the level of the lip of the *hole*.

Honor The player who is to play first from the *teeing ground* is said to have the "*honor*."

Lateral Water Hazard A "*lateral water hazard*" is a *water hazard* or that part of a *water hazard* so situated that it is not possible, or is deemed by the *Committee* to be impracticable, to drop a ball behind the *water hazard* in accordance with Rule 26-1b. All ground and water within the margin of a *lateral water hazard* are part of the *lateral water hazard*.

When the margin of a *lateral water hazard* is defined by stakes, the stakes are inside the *lateral water hazard*, and the margin of the *hazard* is defined by the nearest outside points of the stakes

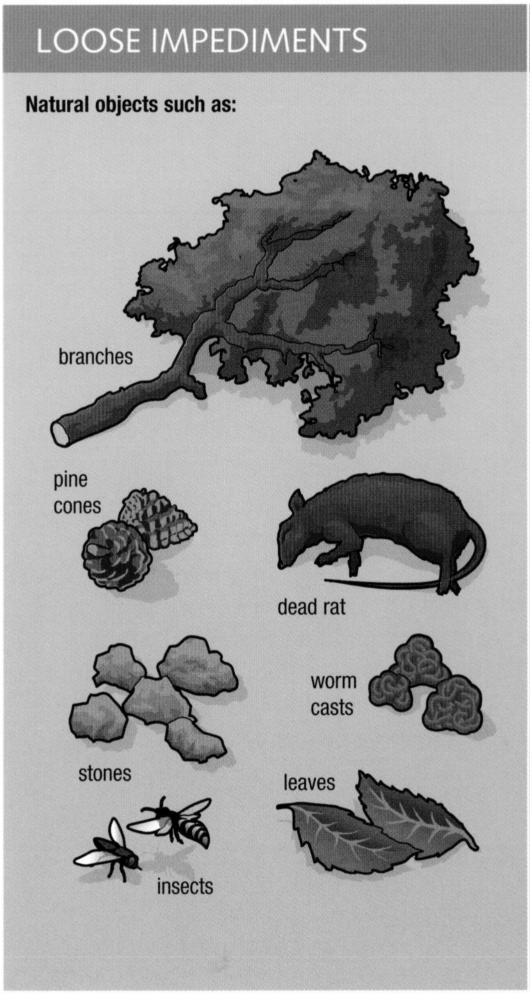

LOOSE IMPEDIMENTS

Natural objects such as:

branches

pine cones

dead rat

worm casts

stones

leaves

insects

MOVABLE OBSTRUCTIONS

Artificial/manufactured objects such as:

litter

bottle

rake

tin can

booklet

score card

tee

at ground level. When both stakes and lines are used to indicate a *lateral water hazard*, the stakes identify the *hazard* and the lines define the *hazard* margin. When the margin of a *lateral water hazard* is defined by a line on the ground, the line itself is in the *lateral water hazard*. The margin of a *lateral water hazard* extends vertically upwards and downwards.

A ball is in a *lateral water hazard* when it lies in or any part of it touches the *lateral water hazard*.

Stakes used to define the margin of or identify a *lateral water hazard* are *obstructions*.

Note 1: That part of a *water hazard* to be played as a *lateral water hazard* must be distinctively marked. Stakes or lines used to define the margin of or identify a *lateral water hazard* must be red.

Note 2: The *Committee* may make a Local Rule prohibiting play from an environmentally-sensitive area defined as a *lateral water hazard*.

Note 3: The *Committee* may define a *lateral water hazard* as a *water hazard*.

Line of Play The *"line of play"* is the direction that the player wishes his ball to take after a *stroke*, plus a reasonable distance on either side of the intended direction. The *line of play* extends vertically upwards from the ground, but does not extend beyond the *hole*.

Line of Putt The *"line of putt"* is the line that the player wishes his ball to take after a *stroke* on the *putting green*. Except with respect to Rule 16-1e, the *line of putt* includes a reasonable distance on either side of the intended line. The *line of putt* does not extend beyond the *hole*.

Loose Impediments *"Loose impediments"* are natural objects including:
- stones, leaves, twigs, branches and the like,
- dung, and
- worms, insects and the like, and the casts and heaps made by them,

provided they are not:
- fixed or growing,
- solidly embedded, or
- adhering to the ball.

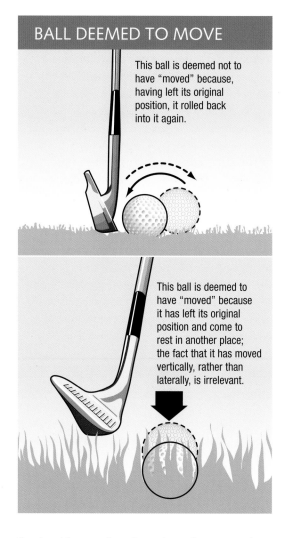

BALL DEEMED TO MOVE

This ball is deemed not to have "moved" because, having left its original position, it rolled back into it again.

This ball is deemed to have "moved" because it has left its original position and come to rest in another place; the fact that it has moved vertically, rather than laterally, is irrelevant.

Sand and loose soil are *loose impediments* on the *putting green*, but not elsewhere.

Snow and natural ice, other than frost, are either *casual water* or *loose impediments*, at the option of the player.

Dew and frost are not *loose impediments*.

Lost Ball A ball is deemed *"lost"* if:
a It is not found, or identified as his by the player, within five minutes after the player's *side* or his or their *caddies* have begun to search for it; or
b The player has made a *stroke* at a *provisional ball* from the place where the original ball is likely to be or from a point nearer the *hole* than that place (see Rule 27-2b); or
c The player has put another ball into play under penalty of stroke and distance (see Rule 27-1a); or

d The player has put another ball into play because it is known or virtually certain that the ball, which has not been found, has been moved by an *outside agency* (see Rule 18-1), is in an *obstruction* (see Rule 24-3), is in an *abnormal ground condition* (see Rule 25-1c) or is in a *water hazard* (see Rule 26-1); or

e The player has made a *stroke* at a *substituted* ball.

Time spent in playing a *wrong ball* is not counted in the five-minute period allowed for search.

Marker A "*marker*" is one who is appointed by the *Committee* to record a *competitor's* score in stroke play. He may be a *fellow-competitor*. He is not a *referee*.

Move or Moved A ball is deemed to have "*moved*" if it leaves its position and comes to rest in any other place.

Nearest Point of Relief The "*nearest point of relief*" is the reference point for taking relief without penalty from interference by an immovable *obstruction* (Rule 24-2), an *abnormal ground condition* (Rule 25-1) or a *wrong putting green* (Rule 25-3).

It is the point on the *course* nearest to where the ball lies:
(i) that is not nearer the *hole*, and
(ii) where, if the ball were so positioned, no interference by the condition from which relief is sought would exist for the *stroke* the player would have made from the original position if the condition were not there.

Note: In order to determine the *nearest point of relief* accurately, the player should use the club with which he would have made his next *stroke* if the condition were not there to simulate the *address* position, direction of play and swing for such a *stroke*.

Observer An "*observer*" is one who is appointed by the *Committee* to assist a *referee* to decide questions of fact and to report to him any breach of a *Rule*. An *observer* should not attend the *flagstick*, stand at or mark the position of the *hole*, or lift the ball or mark its position.

Obstructions An "*obstruction*" is anything artificial, including the artificial surfaces and sides of roads and paths and manufactured ice, except:
a Objects defining *out of bounds*, such as walls, fences, stakes and railings;

NEAREST POINT OF RELIEF

b   Any part of an immovable artificial object that is *out of bounds*; and

c   Any construction declared by the *Committee* to be an integral part of the *course*.

An *obstruction* is a movable *obstruction* if it may be moved without unreasonable effort, without unduly delaying play and without causing damage. Otherwise, it is an immovable *obstruction*.

Note: The *Committee* may make a Local Rule declaring a movable *obstruction* to be an immovable *obstruction*.

Out of Bounds   "*Out of bounds*" is beyond the boundaries of the *course* or any part of the *course* so marked by the *Committee*.

When *out of bounds* is defined by reference to stakes or a fence or as being beyond stakes or a fence, the *out of bounds* line is determined by the nearest inside points at ground level of the stakes or fence posts (excluding angled supports). When both stakes and lines are used to indicate *out of bounds*, the stakes identify *out of bounds* and the lines define *out of bounds*. When *out of bounds* is defined by a line on the ground, the line itself is *out of bounds*. The *out of bounds* line extends vertically upwards and downwards.

A ball is *out of bounds* when all of it lies *out of bounds*. A player may stand *out of bounds* to play a ball lying within bounds.

Objects defining *out of bounds* such as walls, fences, stakes and railings, are not *obstructions* and are deemed to be fixed. Stakes identifying *out of bounds* are not *obstructions* and are deemed to be fixed.

Note 1: Stakes or lines used to define *out of bounds* should be white.

Note 2: A *Committee* may make a Local Rule declaring stakes identifying but not defining *out of bounds* to be movable *obstructions*.

Outside Agency   In match play, an "*outside agency*" is any agency other than either the player's or opponent's *side*, any *caddie* of either *side*, any ball played by either *side* at the hole being played or any *equipment* of either *side*.

In stroke play, an *outside agency* is any agency other than the *competitor's side*, any *caddie* of

the *side*, any ball played by the *side* at the hole being played or any *equipment* of the *side*.

An *outside agency* includes a *referee*, a *marker*, an *observer* and a *forecaddie*. Neither wind nor water is an *outside agency*.

Partner   A "*partner*" is a player associated with another player on the same *side*.

In *threesome*, *foursome*, *best-ball* or *four-ball* play, where the context so admits, the word "player" includes his *partner* or *partners*.

Penalty Stroke   A "*penalty stroke*" is one added to the score of a player or *side* under certain *Rules*. In a *threesome* or *foursome*, *penalty strokes* do not affect the order of play.

Provisional Ball   A "*provisional ball*" is a ball played under Rule 27-2 for a ball that may be *lost* outside a *water hazard* or may be *out of bounds*.

PARTNER

A partner is a player associated with another player on the same side.

Putting Green The *"putting green"* is all ground of the hole being played that is specially prepared for putting or otherwise defined as such by the *Committee*. A ball is on the *putting green* when any part of it touches the *putting green*.

Referee A *"referee"* is one who is appointed by the *Committee* to accompany players to decide questions of fact and apply the *Rules*. He must act on any breach of a *Rule* that he observes or is reported to him.

A *referee* should not attend the *flagstick*, stand at or mark the position of the *hole*, or lift the ball or mark its position.

Rub of the Green A *"rub of the green"* occurs when a ball in motion is accidentally deflected or stopped by any *outside agency* (see Rule 19-1).

Rule or Rules The term *"Rule"* includes:

a   The Rules of Golf and their interpretations as contained in "Decisions on the Rules of Golf";

b   Any Conditions of Competition established by the *Committee* under Rule 33-1 and Appendix I;

c   Any Local Rules established by the *Committee* under Rule 33-8a and Appendix I; and

d   The specifications on clubs and the ball in Appendices II and III and their interpretations as contained in "A Guide to the Rules on Clubs and Balls."

Side A *"side"* is a player, or two or more players who are *partners*.

Single See *"Forms of Match Play"* and *"Forms of Stroke Play."*

Stance Taking the *"stance"* consists in a player placing his feet in position for and preparatory to making a *stroke*.

Stipulated Round The *"stipulated round"* consists of playing the holes of the *course* in their correct sequence, unless otherwise authorized by the *Committee*. The number of holes in a *stipulated round* is 18 unless a smaller number is authorized by the *Committee*. As to extension of *stipulated round* in match play, see Rule 2-3.

DEFINITION OF A STROKE

At this point, as the player has not started his downswing, he has not begun his stroke. It is once the player begins his downswing that he is considered to have made a stroke, unless he checks his downswing voluntarily.

Stroke A *"stroke"* is the forward movement of the club made with the intention of striking at and moving the ball, but if a player checks his downswing voluntarily before the clubhead reaches the ball he has not made a *stroke*.

Substituted Ball A *"substituted ball"* is a ball put into play for the original ball that was either *in play*, *lost*, *out of bounds* or lifted.

Tee A *"tee"* is a device designed to raise the ball off the ground. It must not be longer than 4 inches (101.6 mm) and it must not be designed or manufactured in such a way that it could indicate the *line of play* or influence the movement of the ball.

Teeing Ground The *"teeing ground"* is the starting place for the hole to be played. It is a rectangular area two club-lengths in depth, the front and the sides of which are defined by the outside limits of two tee-markers. A ball is outside the *teeing ground* when all of it lies outside the *teeing ground*.

Three-Ball See *"Forms of Match Play."*

Threesome See *"Forms of Match Play."*

Through the Green *"Through the green"* is the whole area of the *course* except:

a The *teeing ground* and *putting green* of the hole being played; and

b All *hazards* on the *course*.

Water Hazard A *"water hazard"* is any sea, lake, pond, river, ditch, surface drainage ditch or other open water course (whether or not containing water) and anything of a similar nature on the *course*. All ground and water within the margin of a *water hazard* are part of the *water hazard*.

When the margin of a *water hazard* is defined by stakes, the stakes are inside the *water hazard*, and the margin of the *hazard* is defined by the nearest outside points of the stakes at ground level. When both stakes and lines are used to indicate a *water hazard*, the stakes identify the *hazard* and the lines define the *hazard* margin. When the margin of a *water hazard* is defined by a line on the ground, the line itself is in the *water hazard*. The margin of a *water hazard* extends vertically upwards and downwards.

A ball is in a *water hazard* when it lies in or any part of it touches the *water hazard*.

Stakes used to define the margin of or identify a *water hazard* are *obstructions*.

Note 1: Stakes or lines used to define the margin of or identify a *water hazard* must be yellow.

Note 2: The *Committee* may make a Local Rule prohibiting play from an environmentally-sensitive area defined as a *water hazard*.

Wrong Ball A *"wrong ball"* is any ball other than the player's:

• *ball in play*,

• *provisional ball*, or

• second ball played under Rule 3-3 or Rule 20-7c in stroke play;

and includes:

• another player's ball,

• an abandoned ball, and

• the player's original ball when it is no longer *in play*.

Note: *Ball in play* includes a ball *substituted* for the *ball in play* whether or not the substitution is permitted.

Wrong Putting Green A *"wrong putting green"* is any *putting green* other than that of the hole being played. Unless otherwise prescribed by the *Committee*, this term includes a practice *putting green* or pitching green on the *course*.

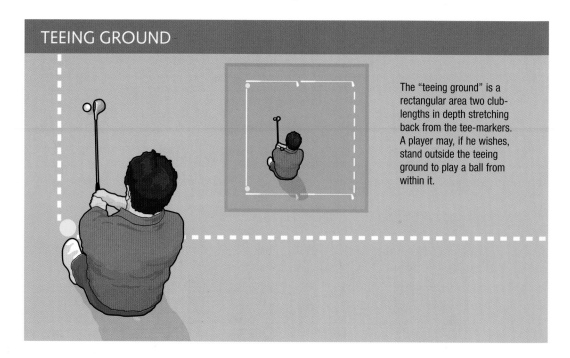

TEEING GROUND

The "teeing ground" is a rectangular area two club-lengths in depth stretching back from the tee-markers. A player may, if he wishes, stand outside the teeing ground to play a ball from within it.

SECTION III
THE RULES OF PLAY

THE GAME

RULE **THE GAME**

DEFINITIONS

All defined terms are in *italics* and are listed alphabetically in the Definitions section – see pages 9–20.

1-1. GENERAL

The Game of Golf consists of playing a ball with a club from the *teeing ground* into the *hole* by a *stroke* or successive *strokes* in accordance with the *Rules*.

1-2. EXERTING INFLUENCE ON BALL

A player or *caddie* must not take any action to influence the position or the movement of a ball except in accordance with the *Rules*.
(Removal of loose impediment – see Rule 23-1.)
(Removal of movable obstruction – see Rule 24-1.)

*PENALTY FOR BREACH OF RULE 1-2:
Match play – Loss of hole; Stroke play – Two strokes.
*In the case of a serious breach of Rule 1-2, the *Committee* may impose a penalty of disqualification.

Note: A player is deemed to have committed a serious breach of Rule 1-2 if the *Committee* considers that his act of influencing the position or movement of the ball has allowed him or another player to gain a significant

MATCH PLAY: AGREEMENT TO CONSIDER HOLE HALVED

How about a half?

Good idea, let's move on to the next hole.

An agreement to halve a hole being played is not an agreement to waive the Rules.

advantage or has placed another player, other than his *partner*, at a significant disadvantage.

1-3. AGREEMENT TO WAIVE RULES

Players must not agree to exclude the operation of any *Rule* or to waive any penalty incurred.

PENALTY FOR BREACH OF RULE 1-3:
Match play – Disqualification of both *sides*;
Stroke play – Disqualification of *competitors* concerned.

(Agreeing to play out of turn in stroke play – see Rule 10-2c.)

1-4. POINTS NOT COVERED BY RULES

If any point in dispute is not covered by the *Rules*, the decision should be made in accordance with equity.

RULE 1 INCIDENT

Anticipation and forward thinking are essential for strategic effectiveness and quickly paced play. With his ball in the Road bunker at the Old Course's 17th hole during the 1990 Dunhill Cup at St. Andrews, Philip Walton walked into the sand in order to ponder his next stroke just as his fellow-competitor, Mark James, was about to play from off the road itself.

Much of what makes the Road Hole the most famous, and arguably the most difficult, par 4 in the world is that the putting surface is flanked on the right by the road and on the left by the Road bunker. Only the hard, elevated, fairly narrow piece of putting green separates the hazard from road. The road is an integral part of the course and, therefore, not an obstruction. No relief is granted for a ball lying on the road.

Walton and James's predicaments were equally precarious. If misplayed, their positions might simply be exchanged. Anticipating such a possibility as he was preparing for his third shot from the road, James asked a Rules official if he could have Walton's footprints in the Road bunker raked. If his shot from the road was overplayed, James argued that he did not want to end up in one of Walton's footprints in the bunker.

The referee ruled, in equity (Rule 1-4), that James could indeed have the bunker restored to the condition it was in after James' ball came to rest on the road and before Walton walked into the sand. A player is entitled to the lie his stroke gave him (Rule 20). By extension of this reasoning, a player is also entitled to the field of play that his stroke gave him should it be subsequently altered by another player. Following this incident, Decision 13-2/29.5 was introduced in the Decisions on the Rules of Golf to address specifically and authorize the ruling in this situation.

EQUITY: SOME EXAMPLES

Distractions are commonplace, but some problems less so.
Wildlife needs to be protected and sometimes so does the golfer.

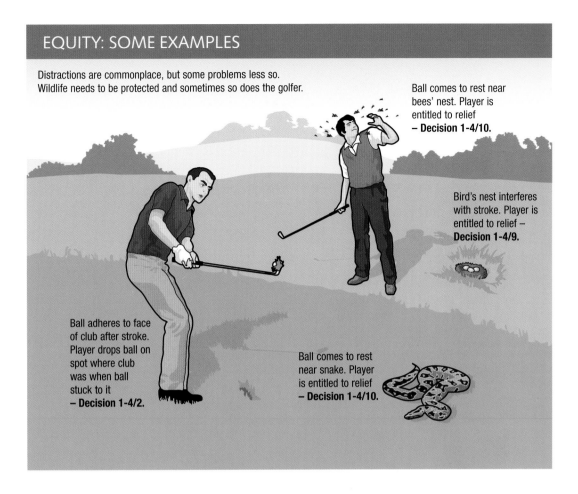

Ball comes to rest near bees' nest. Player is entitled to relief – **Decision 1-4/10.**

Bird's nest interferes with stroke. Player is entitled to relief – **Decision 1-4/9.**

Ball adheres to face of club after stroke. Player drops ball on spot where club was when ball stuck to it – **Decision 1-4/2.**

Ball comes to rest near snake. Player is entitled to relief – **Decision 1-4/10.**

Frequently asked question

Q What does the term "Equity" mean as used in the Rules of Golf?

A Equity means to treat like situations alike. Some situations are not covered by the Rules of Golf, thus the decision must be made according to what is fair under the Rules of Golf. Equity is not a substitute for a Rule.

RULE **2**

MATCH PLAY

DEFINITIONS

All defined terms are in *italics* and are listed alphabetically in the Definitions section – see pages 9–20.

2-1. GENERAL

A match consists of one *side* playing against another over a *stipulated round* unless otherwise decreed by the *Committee*.

In match play the game is played by holes.

Except as otherwise provided in the *Rules*, a hole is won by the *side* that *holes* its ball in the fewer *strokes*. In a handicap match the lower net score wins the hole.

23

The state of the match is expressed by the terms: so many "holes up" or "all square," and so many "to play."

A *side* is "dormie" when it is as many holes up as there are holes remaining to be played.

2-2. HALVED HOLE

A hole is halved if each *side holes* out in the same number of *strokes*.

When a player has *holed* out and his opponent has been left with a *stroke* for the half, if the player subsequently incurs a penalty, the hole is halved.

2-3. WINNER OF MATCH

A match is won when one *side* leads by a number of holes greater than the number remaining to be played.

If there is a tie, the *Committee* may extend the *stipulated round* by as many holes as are required for a match to be won.

See **incident** involving Rule 2-4 on pages 26–27.

2-4. CONCESSION OF MATCH, HOLE OR NEXT STROKE

A player may concede a match at any time prior to the start or conclusion of that match.

A player may concede a hole at any time prior to the start or conclusion of that hole.

A player may concede his opponent's next *stroke* at any time, provided the opponent's ball is at rest. The opponent is considered to have *holed* out with his next *stroke* and the ball may be removed by either *side*.

A concession may not be declined or withdrawn.

(Ball overhanging hole – see Rule 16-2.)

2-5. DOUBT AS TO PROCEDURE; DISPUTES AND CLAIMS

In match play, if a doubt or dispute arises between the players, a player may make a claim. If no duly authorized representative of the *Committee* is available within a reasonable time, the players must continue the match without delay. The *Committee* may consider a claim only if the player making the claim notifies his opponent (i) that he is making a claim, (ii) of the facts of the situation and (iii) that he wants a ruling. The claim must be made before any player in the match plays from the next *teeing ground* or, in the case of the last hole of the match, before all players in the match leave the *putting green*.

A later claim may not be considered by the *Committee* unless it is based on facts previously unknown to the player making the claim and he had been given wrong information (Rules 6-2a and 9) by an opponent.

Once the result of the match has been officially announced, a later claim may not be considered by the *Committee* unless it is satisfied that the opponent knew he was giving wrong information.

2-6. GENERAL PENALTY

The penalty for a breach of a *Rule* in match play is loss of hole except when otherwise provided.

STATUS OF LATE CLAIM

I've just realized that my opponent should have lost the 4th when he grounded his club in the bunker.

I'm afraid such a claim had to be made before you or your opponent played from the 5th tee. The Committee can only consider a later claim if the facts were previously unknown to you.

Tony Jacklin and Jack Nicklaus shake hands on the 18th green during the 1969 Ryder Cup.

RULE 2 INCIDENT

Jack Nicklaus's concession of Tony Jacklin's putt on the final hole during the final match of the 1969 Ryder Cup resulted in this match play event's first tie, and is hailed as one of golf's finest acts of sportsmanship.

In 1969, going into the final day's competition at the Royal Birkdale Golf Club in Southport, England, the United States and Great Britain/Ireland were tied at eight points each. That morning's singles matches resulted in a two-point lead by the British, which was reciprocated by the U.S. in the afternoon. This left the matches tied at 15½ with only the final match of Jack Nicklaus and Tony Jacklin still on the course. Eighteen of the 32 Ryder Cup matches went to the final hole that year, and it was there that the three-day competition would be ultimately decided.

Nicklaus had the upper hand, as Jacklin had fallen behind on the back nine. As the reigning British Open Champion, Jacklin would not relent. Indeed, he eagled the 17th to go all square.

As the defending champions after their victory in 1967 at Champions Golf Club in Houston, the U.S. Team needed only a tie at Birkdale's last hole to tie the overall 1969 competition. Under the conditions of the competition, a tie in the Ryder Cup results in the previously victorious team retaining the cup.

At the 18th, Jacklin missed his putt for birdie leaving him a 20 inch putt for 4. Nicklaus missed his 10 foot birdie and then holed his four-footer for par. If Jacklin holed his short putt, it would be the first time the Ryder Cup ended in a tie. A miss by Jacklin would result in an outright win by the Americans.

Before Jacklin could putt, Nicklaus picked up Jacklin's marker, conceding the Englishman's putt and ensuring the tie. "I don't think you would have missed that, Tony," Nicklaus reportedly said, "but under these circumstances I'd never give you the opportunity."

"The length of the putt has varied after 30 some years," Jacklin has said. "It's been as long as four feet. But my recollection is 20 inches. Of course, I could have missed it; there are no guarantees in golf, especially in the crucible of the Ryder Cup, but I believe I would have made it. But Jack saw the big picture.

"Two months before I had become the first British player in 18 years to win the British Open, so there was very much a pro-British fervor at the Ryder Cup in England that year. Jack saw that the putt on the last hole in 1969 meant a heck of a lot more to the Ryder Cup than who won or lost that particular match. It was a great moment."

Frequently asked question

Q Is there a penalty for putting out on the putting green after the opponent has conceded the next stroke?

A There is no penalty for putting out in this case. Once a concession is made, it may not be withdrawn. The concession stands and it is irrelevant whether the player makes the putt or misses. However, in a four-ball or best-ball match, if the act would assist a partner, the partner is, in equity, disqualified for the hole.

RULE **3**   # STROKE PLAY

DEFINITIONS   All defined terms are in *italics* and are listed alphabetically in the Definitions section – see pages 9–20.

3-1. GENERAL; WINNER

A stroke-play competition consists of *competitors* completing each hole of a *stipulated round* or *rounds* and, for each round, returning a score card on which there is a gross score for each hole. Each *competitor* is playing against every other *competitor* in the competition.

The *competitor* who plays the *stipulated round* or *rounds* in the fewest *strokes* is the winner.

In a handicap competition, the *competitor* with the lowest net score for the *stipulated round* or *rounds* is the winner.

27

3-2. FAILURE TO HOLE OUT

If a *competitor* fails to *hole* out at any hole and does not correct his mistake before he makes a *stroke* on the next *teeing ground* or, in the case of the last hole of the round, before he leaves the *putting green*, **he is disqualified**.

See **incident** involving Rule 3 on pages 29–30.

3-3. DOUBT AS TO PROCEDURE
a. Procedure

In stroke play, if a *competitor* is doubtful of his rights or the correct procedure during the play of a hole, he may, without penalty, complete the hole with two balls.

After the doubtful situation has arisen and before taking further action, the *competitor* must announce to his *marker* or a *fellow-competitor* that he intends to play two balls and which ball he wishes to count if the *Rules* permit.

The *competitor* must report the facts of the situation to the *Committee* before returning his score card. If he fails to do so, **he is disqualified**.

Note: If the *competitor* takes further action before dealing with the doubtful situation, Rule 3-3 is not applicable. The score with the original ball counts or, if the original ball is not one of the balls being played, the first ball put into play counts, even if the *Rules* do not allow the procedure adopted for that ball. However, the *competitor* incurs no penalty for having played a second ball, and any *penalty strokes* incurred solely by playing that ball do not count in his score.

b. Determination of Score for Hole

(i)   If the ball that the *competitor* selected in advance to count has been played in accordance with the *Rules*, the score with that ball is the *competitor's* score for the hole. Otherwise, the score with the other ball counts if the *Rules* allow the procedure adopted for that ball.

(ii) If the *competitor* fails to announce in advance his decision to complete the hole with two balls, or which ball he wishes to count, the score with the original ball counts, provided it has been played in accordance with the *Rules*. If the original ball is not one of the balls being played, the first ball put into play counts, provided it has been played in accordance with the *Rules*. Otherwise, the score with the other ball counts if the *Rules* allow the procedure adopted for that ball.

Note 1: If a *competitor* plays a second ball under Rule 3-3, the *strokes* made after this Rule has been invoked with the ball ruled not to count and *penalty strokes* incurred solely by playing that ball are disregarded.

Note 2: A second ball played under Rule 3-3 is not a *provisional ball* under Rule 27-2.

3-4. REFUSAL TO COMPLY WITH A RULE

If a *competitor* refuses to comply with a *Rule* affecting the rights of another *competitor*, **he is disqualified**.

3-5. GENERAL PENALTY

The penalty for a breach of a *Rule* in stroke play is two strokes except when otherwise provided.

RULE 3 BACKGROUND

Match play came first to golf. One played against another, one hole and one match at a time. Then, sometimes, two might play against two, or maybe two played against one. Whatever the configuration, the match being played was that match's total universe until it was decided. Putts, holes and matches could be conceded. If you lay 2 beside the hole and your opponent lay 9, he could give you the hole and you walked to the next tee. If your opponents were too ill to play, they could give you the match.

By the mid-18th century, when golf clubs were being formed in Scotland, their members desired a different form of competition in which the total number of strokes taken to play a course would be counted. On May 9, 1759 the Society of St. Andrews Golfers resolved "… whoever puts in the Ball at the fewest Strokes Over the Field, being 22 Holes, Shall be Declared and Sustain Victor." The victor was often awarded a medal from which the term "medal play" finds its origin.

During stroke play a few things, which had been decided by loss of hole in match play, needed more precise direction. These Rules remain today. For instance, all balls must be holed out in stroke play. Without such a stipulation, a player's round is incomplete and the score incomparable to those who have holed out. The player now, as then, is disqualified if he does not hole out, because he has not completed the course.

To ensure that everyone plays the same course, tee-markers take on added importance in stroke play. Beginning a hole from outside the markers results in a two-stroke penalty and a ball must be played from within their boundaries. Just as all players must end in the same place, they must also begin in the same place. Failure to correct an error of this type also results in disqualification.

Another important distinction is the method used when doubt arises about how to proceed. Rule 3-3 allows those competing in stroke play to play a second ball. The player must announce ahead of time his intent to play a second ball and which ball he wishes to use should the Rules allow it. In match play, playing a second ball is not permitted. Rather, the player must make a specific claim if he objects to an action taken by his opponent before anyone plays from the next teeing ground.

Because the total number of strokes determines the winner in stroke play, the score card becomes each player's testament to what he has accomplished on the course, and a marker must attest it. Errors in scorekeeping cannot be tolerated when the best score is what determines the winner. Thus, a score for a hole that is recorded higher than actually taken can be included because it would not create an advantage, but a lower score must result in disqualification because it would create one.

The responsibility for violations in both forms of play rests with the players themselves. However, a loss of hole penalty in match play can be assessed and the match continued. While there are 15 one-stroke penalties that apply to both forms of play, the general penalty in stroke play is two strokes and play continues. However, a stroke play violation that results in a serious inequity between a player's procedure and that of the entire field must logically result in disqualification.

Frequently asked question

Q What is the maximum score a player may have for a hole?

A The Rules of Golf do not set a maximum score for a hole; the ball must be holed (see Rules 1-1, 2-1, and 3-2). In match play only, an opponent may concede a stroke. The USGA Handicapping System specifies that players must adjust their scores under Equitable Stroke Control prior to posting those scores for Handicapping purposes. Any adjustments for ESC are made after the round is completed.

CLUBS AND THE BALL

The USGA reserves the right, at any time, to change the Rules relating to clubs and balls (see Appendices II and III) and make or change the interpretations relating to these Rules.

RULE # CLUBS

A player in doubt as to the conformity of a club should consult the United States Golf Association.

A manufacturer should submit to the USGA a sample of a club to be manufactured for a ruling as to whether the club conforms with the *Rules*. The sample becomes the property of the USGA for reference purposes. If a manufacturer fails to submit a sample or, having submitted a sample, fails to await a ruling before manufacturing and/or marketing the club, the manufacturer assumes the risk of a ruling that the club does not conform with the *Rules*.

DEFINITIONS   All defined terms are in *italics* and are listed alphabetically in the Definitions section – see pages 9–20.

4-1. FORM AND MAKE OF CLUBS
a. General
The player's clubs must conform with this Rule and the provisions, specifications and interpretations set forth in Appendix II.

31

Note: The *Committee* may require, in the conditions of a competition (Rule 33-1), that any driver the player carries must have a clubhead, identified by model and loft, that is named on the current List of Conforming Driver Heads issued by the USGA.

b. Wear and Alteration

A club that conforms with the *Rules* when new is deemed to conform after wear through normal use. Any part of a club that has been purposely altered is regarded as new and must, in its altered state, conform with the *Rules*.

4-2. PLAYING CHARACTERISTICS CHANGED AND FOREIGN MATERIAL
a. Playing Characteristics Changed

During a *stipulated round*, the playing characteristics of a club must not be purposely changed by adjustment or by any other means.

b. Foreign Material

Foreign material must not be applied to the club face for the purpose of influencing the movement of the ball.

*PENALTY FOR CARRYING, BUT NOT MAKING STROKE WITH, CLUB OR CLUBS IN BREACH OF RULE 4-1 or 4-2:
Match play – At the conclusion of the hole at which the breach is discovered, the state of the match is adjusted by deducting one hole for each hole at which a breach occurred; maximum deduction per round – Two holes.
Stroke play – Two strokes for each hole at which any breach occurred; maximum penalty per round – Four strokes.
Match or stroke play – In the event of a breach between the play of two holes, the penalty applies to the next hole.
Bogey and par competitions – See Note 1 to Rule 32-1a.
Stableford competitions – See Note 1 to Rule 32-1b.
*Any club or clubs carried in breach of Rule 4-1 or 4-2 must be declared out of play by the player to his opponent in match play or his *marker* or a *fellow-competitor* in stroke play immediately upon discovery that a breach has occurred. If the player fails to do so, he is disqualified.

PENALTY FOR MAKING STROKE WITH CLUB IN BREACH OF RULE 4-1 or 4-2: Disqualification.

4-3. DAMAGED CLUBS: REPAIR AND REPLACEMENT
a. Damage in Normal Course of Play

If, during a *stipulated round*, a player's club is damaged in the normal course of play, he may:
(i)   use the club in its damaged state for the remainder of the *stipulated round*; or
(ii) without unduly delaying play, repair it or have it repaired; or
(iii) as an additional option available only if the club is unfit for play, replace the damaged club with any club. The replacement of a

club must not unduly delay play and must not be made by borrowing any club selected for play by any other person playing on the *course*.

PENALTY FOR BREACH OF RULE 4-3a:
See Penalty Statements for Rule 4-4a or b, and Rule 4-4c.

Note: A club is unfit for play if it is substantially damaged, e.g., the shaft is dented, significantly bent or broken into pieces; the clubhead becomes loose, detached or significantly deformed; or the grip becomes loose. A club is not unfit for play solely because the club's lie or loft has been altered, or the clubhead is scratched.

See **incident** involving Rule 4-3b on pages 34–35.

b. Damage Other Than in Normal Course of Play
If, during a *stipulated round*, a player's club is damaged other than in the normal course of play rendering it non-conforming or changing its playing characteristics, the club must not subsequently be used or replaced during the round.

c. Damage Prior to Round
A player may use a club damaged prior to a round provided the club, in its damaged state, conforms with the *Rules*.
  Damage to a club that occurred prior to a round may be repaired during the round, provided the playing characteristics are not changed and play is not unduly delayed.

PENALTY FOR BREACH OF RULE 4-3b or c: Disqualification.
(Undue delay – see Rule 6-7.)

See **incident** involving Rule 4-4 on page 35.

4-4. MAXIMUM OF 14 CLUBS
a. Selection and Addition of Clubs
The player must not start a *stipulated round* with more than 14 clubs. He is limited to the clubs thus selected for that round, except that if he started with fewer than 14 clubs, he may add any number, provided his total number does not exceed 14.
  The addition of a club or clubs must not unduly delay play (Rule 6-7) and the player must not add or borrow any club selected for play by any other person playing on the *course*.

b. Partners May Share Clubs
Partners may share clubs, provided that the total number of clubs carried by the *partners* so sharing does not exceed 14.

PENALTY FOR BREACH OF RULE 4-4a or b,
REGARDLESS OF NUMBER OF EXCESS CLUBS CARRIED:
Match play – At the conclusion of the hole at which the breach is discovered, the state of the match is adjusted by deducting one hole for each hole at which a breach occurred. Maximum deduction per round: Two holes.

33

BREACH OF 14-CLUB RULE IN MATCH PLAY

Stroke play – Two strokes for each hole at which any breach occurred;
maximum penalty per round: Four strokes.
Bogey and par competitions – See Note 1 to Rule 32-1a.
Stableford competitions – See Note 1 to Rule 32-1b.

c. Excess Club Declared Out of Play

Any club or clubs carried or used in breach of Rule 4-3a(iii) or Rule 4-4 must
be declared out of play by the player to his opponent in match play or his
marker or a *fellow-competitor* in stroke play immediately upon discovery
that a breach has occurred. The player must not use the club or clubs for the
remainder of the *stipulated round*.

PENALTY FOR BREACH OF RULE 4-4c: Disqualification.

RULE 4 INCIDENT

Fourteen clubs is the maximum number allowed under the Rules.
During a stipulated round, a player may use, replace or repair a club that
is damaged in the normal course of play. A club damaged prior to the
round may be used if it conforms to the Rules.

Losing a club must be endured as simply bad luck. A lost club cannot be replaced as Tiger Woods and his caddie, Steve Williams, learned during the 2006 Ryder Cup. At the K Club's seventh green, Williams went to a greenside lake to soak a towel. He was also holding Woods's 9-iron at the time, and lost his grip on the club. The club disappeared into the depth of the lake, where it was not retrievable. Woods was required to continue his singles match against Robert Karlsson with 13 clubs.

Just as Williams could not believe he had dropped his boss's 9-iron into a water hazard, neither could Ian Woosnam's caddie believe he had left an extra driver in his boss's bag during the final round of the 2001 British Open at Royal Lytham & St. Annes.

On the practice tee before the final round began, Woosnam was trying to decide which of two drivers to use that day. His testing apparently went a little longer than expected. His caddie hurried to the practice chipping and putting greens before moving to the first tee for their 2:15 starting time.

A championship anomaly, Royal Lytham begins with a par-3. Woosnam struck a glorious 6-iron to within inches of the hole. However, in their haste to get underway and with their focus toward the job at hand, both Woosnam and his caddie failed to count their clubs before

Tiger Woods looks on in dismay as his 9-iron slips out of the grasp of his caddie and into the water at the 7th hole at the K Club. He then had to play the rest of the round with only 13 clubs.

starting. Both drivers that had been tested on the practice ground were in the bag, 15 clubs in all, when Woosnam struck his first shot from the first tee. The fact that the first hole is a par-3 may have added to the distraction. Had a driver been required at the first, the extra driver may have been discovered before the round started. Woosnam's caddie discovered the violation on the first green and revealed it to his boss on the second tee.

Instead of being tied for the lead in the British Open, Woosnam, following the ensuing two-stroke penalty (Rule 4-4), was reeling in disbelief. He threw his hat to the ground and the extra club into the rough. "You've only got one job to think about and that's taking care of the bloody clubs," Woosnam was overheard to say to his caddie.

Although bogeying two of the next three holes, the Welshman's tenacity in the face of adversity was admirable. He eagled the sixth and played the last 13 in three under par, finishing tied for third place, four shots behind David Duval.

In the press tent following the round, Woosnam was more forgiving of his caddie's mistake. "It is the biggest he will make in his life. He won't do it again. He's a good caddie…" When asked if he has a system for counting his clubs, Woosnam replied, "Yeah. You start counting at one and stop when you get to 14."

When a club is damaged is germane under the Rules because in order for the damage to be ignored, repaired or the club to be replaced, the damage must have occurred during the round. A club damaged prior to the round must be conforming before the round begins. Kevin Stadler suffered under this provision of the Rules during the 2005 Michelin Championship in Las Vegas.

During the first hole of the fourth round, Stadler discovered that the shaft of one of his clubs was bent. He had not yet used that club during the fourth round. Additionally, nothing extraneous had taken place to damage the club during the round. Therefore, it was determined that Stadler had begun the round with the club in its bent condition.

The Rules (Appendix II, 2a) state that, "the shaft must be straight from the top of the grip to a point not more than 5 inches (127 mm) above the sole …" Because the club in question did not meet this requirement, it was non-conforming. In 2005, the penalty for beginning a round with a non-conforming club was disqualification whether or not a stroke was ever played with the club. Therefore, Stadler was disqualified.

For 2008, the rule was changed: The penalty for carrying a non-conforming club with which a stroke has not been made is the same as carrying more than 14 clubs. In stroke play, two penalty strokes are added for each hole at which any breach occurred; maximum penalty per round is four strokes. In match play, at the conclusion of the hole at which the breach is discovered, the state of the match is adjusted by deducting one hole for each hole at which a breach occurred. Maximum deduction per round is two holes.

Frequently asked questions

Q Can a "chipper" have two striking faces?

A No. A "chipper" is an iron club designed primarily for use off the putting green, generally with a loft greater than ten degrees. As most players adopt a "putting stroke" when using a chipper, there can be a tendency to design the club as if it were a putter. To eliminate confusion, the Rules that apply to "chippers" include:

(1) the club must not be designed to be adjustable except for weight;

(2) the shaft must be attached to the clubhead at the heel;

(3) the grip must be circular in cross-section, and only one grip is permitted;

(4) the clubhead must be generally plain in shape and have only one striking face; and

(5) the face of the club must conform to specifications with regard to hardness, surface roughness, material and markings in the impact area.

Q Is it permissible to add tape or gauze to any part of the club?

A During the round, the playing characteristics of the club may not be changed – see Rule 4-2a. Prior to the player's stipulated round, tape or gauze may be applied to the grip of the club provided the application of such materials does not create a waist or bulge – see Appendix II; Part 3.

Tape applied to the club head or shaft is an external attachment, which renders the club non-conforming (see Appendix II; Part 1a). The following are exceptions to the prohibition against external attachments provided such applications are made prior to the player's stipulated round:

• Lead tape may be applied to the head or shaft of the club for the purpose of adding weight (see Decisions 4-1/4 and 4-2/0.5)

• Tape may be applied to the shaft of the club to protect it.

• Decals may be applied to the shaft for identification purposes. These decals may also be covered by clear tape.

RULE **THE BALL**

DEFINITIONS

All defined terms are in *italics* and are listed alphabetically in the Definitions section – see pages 9–20.

5-1. GENERAL

The ball the player plays must conform to requirements specified in Appendix III.

Note: The *Committee* may require, in the conditions of a competition (Rule 33-1), that the ball the player plays must be named on the current List of Conforming Golf Balls issued by the United States Golf Association.

THE BALL

Can I use a crossed-out ball in today's club competition?

Yes. The only time you may not use such a ball is in events when there is a condition requiring use of a ball on the "List of Conforming Golf Balls".

Note:
A Committee should not introduce such a Rule in a club event.

5-2. FOREIGN MATERIAL

Foreign material must not be applied to a ball for the purpose of changing its playing characteristics.

PENALTY FOR BREACH OF RULE 5-1 OR 5-2: Disqualification.

See **incident** involving Rule 5-3 on page 40.

5-3. BALL UNFIT FOR PLAY

A ball is unfit for play if it is visibly cut, cracked or out of shape. A ball is not unfit for play solely because mud or other materials adhere to it, its surface is scratched or scraped or its paint is damaged or discolored.

If a player has reason to believe his ball has become unfit for play during play of the hole being played, he may lift the ball, without penalty, to determine whether it is unfit.

Before lifting the ball, the player must announce his intention to his opponent in match play or his *marker* or a *fellow-competitor* in stroke play and mark the position of the ball. He may then lift and examine it, provided that he gives his opponent, *marker* or *fellow-competitor* an opportunity to examine the ball and observe the lifting and replacement. The ball must not be cleaned when lifted under Rule 5-3.

If the player fails to comply with all or any part of this procedure, or if he lifts the ball without having reason to believe that it has become unfit for play during play of the hole being played, **he incurs a penalty of one stroke**.

If it is determined that the ball has become unfit for play during play of the hole being played, the player may *substitute* another ball, placing it on the spot where the original ball lay. Otherwise, the original ball must be replaced. If a player *substitutes* a ball when not permitted and he makes a *stroke* at the wrongly *substituted ball*, **he incurs the general penalty for a breach of Rule 5-3**, but there is no additional penalty under this Rule or Rule 15-2.

If a ball breaks into pieces as a result of a *stroke*, the *stroke* is canceled and the player must play a ball, without penalty, as nearly as possible at the spot from which the original ball was played (see Rule 20-5).

*PENALTY FOR BREACH OF RULE 5-3:
Match play – Loss of hole; Stroke play – Two strokes.
*If a player incurs the general penalty for breach of Rule 5-3, there is no additional penalty under this Rule.

Note 1: If the opponent, *marker* or *fellow-competitor* wishes to dispute a claim of unfitness, he must do so before the player plays another ball.

Note 2: If the original lie of a ball to be placed or replaced has been altered, see Rule 20-3b.
(Cleaning ball lifted from putting green or under any other Rule – see Rule 21.)

BALL UNFIT FOR PLAY

RULE 5 INCIDENT

During the final match of the 1994 U.S. Amateur Championship, Tiger Woods learned that one of the very specific instances in the Rules when a referee is not to be involved, except as a last resort, is in determining whether or not a ball is unfit for play during the play of a hole.

One down to Trip Kuehne with five holes left in the 36-hole match, Woods' drive from the 14th tee of the TPC at Sawgrass struck a cart path and a media vehicle before finally coming to rest. The lie and angle to the green were good enough for him to reach the green with his second shot, which he did.

Once on the putting green, Woods marked and lifted his ball. It was then that he questioned whether or not his ball had been rendered unfit for play by virtue of its striking the path and the vehicle. Woods' inquiry was directed to the referee who was walking with the match. The referee responded that Woods would have to make that determination after giving his opponent an opportunity to examine the ball.

After inspecting Woods' ball, Kuehne said he was unsure whether or not it was unfit. This sent Woods back to the referee for an opinion. While Decision 5-3/7 permits a referee to make such a call, it also states that every effort should be made to have the opponent, marker or fellow-competitor fulfill his responsibilities under Rule 5-3. In this situation, Woods' opponent was not able to fulfill his responsibilities because he did not know if a ball was unfit simply because it was scarred from bouncing off of a cart path.

With Kuehne unsure and Woods entitled to a ruling, the referee determined that a new ball could not be substituted. Rule 5-3 is specific in stating that a ball is not unfit when its surface is scratched or scraped or its paint is damaged or discolored.

Woods halved the hole with the scraped ball. After birdies at the 16th and 17th, Woods was 1 up. Woods' par, conceded by Kuehne at the 18th, gave Woods a 2 up victory and the first of his three consecutive U.S. Amateur titles.

Frequently asked questions

Q What is the maximum number of balls I can have in my bag or use during the stipulated round?

A The Rules of Golf do not place a limit on the number of balls that can be carried or used during the round.

Q If a player runs out of golf balls during a round, may he borrow a ball from another player?

A Yes. There is nothing in the Rules of Golf that prohibits a player from borrowing a golf ball from an opponent or fellow-competitor. A player who runs out of balls may get a new supply from any source, provided he does not unduly delay play (Rule 6-7) in the process. Although golf balls are part of a player's equipment, the only type of equipment that the Rules limit the borrowing of is clubs.

Q Must a player announce to his opponent(s) or fellow-competitor(s) that he intends to use a different ball between the play of two holes?

A Although such an announcement would be courteous and is good practice, a player is not required under the Rules to inform an opponent or fellow-competitor that he intends to play a different ball between the play of two holes.

PLAYER'S RESPONSIBILITIES

RULE  **6**

THE PLAYER

DEFINITIONS
All defined terms are in *italics* and are listed alphabetically in the Definitions section – see pages 9–20.

6-1. RULES
The player and his *caddie* are responsible for knowing the *Rules*. During a *stipulated round*, for any breach of a *Rule* by his *caddie*, the player incurs the applicable penalty.

6-2. HANDICAP
a. Match Play
Before starting a match in a handicap competition, the players should determine from one another their respective handicaps. If a player begins a match having declared a handicap higher than that to which he is entitled and this affects the number of strokes given or received, **he is disqualified**; otherwise, the player must play off the declared handicap.

b. Stroke Play
In any round of a handicap competition, the *competitor* must ensure that his handicap is recorded on his score card before it is returned to the *Committee*. If no handicap is recorded on his score card before it is returned (Rule 6-6b), or if the recorded handicap is higher than that to which he is entitled and this affects the number of strokes received, **he is disqualified** from the handicap competition; otherwise, the score stands.

Note: It is the player's responsibility to know the holes at which handicap strokes are to be given or received.

6-3. TIME OF STARTING AND GROUPS
a. Time of Starting
The player must start at the time established by the *Committee*.

b. Groups
In stroke play, the *competitor* must remain throughout the round in the group arranged by the *Committee*, unless the *Committee* authorizes or ratifies a change.

PLAYING THE PROPER BALL

The responsibility for playing the proper ball rests with the player. PGA Tour player Duffy Waldorf has his wife and children assist him in putting identification marks on his golf balls.

PENALTY FOR BREACH OF RULE 6-3: Disqualification.
(Best-ball and four-ball play – see Rules 30-3a and 31-2.)

Note: The *Committee* may provide, in the conditions of a competition (Rule 33-1), that, if the player arrives at his starting point, ready to play, within five minutes after his starting time, in the absence of circumstances that warrant waiving the penalty of disqualification as provided in Rule 33-7, the penalty for failure to start on time is **loss of the first hole in match play or two strokes at the first hole in stroke play** instead of disqualification.

6-4. CADDIE
The player may be assisted by a *caddie*, but he is limited to only one *caddie* at any one time.

PENALTY FOR BREACH OF RULE 6-4:
Match play – At the conclusion of the hole at which the breach is discovered, the state of the match is adjusted by deducting one hole for each hole at which a breach occurred; maximum deduction per round – Two holes.
Stroke play – Two strokes for each hole at which any breach occurred; maximum penalty per round – Four strokes.
Match or stroke play – In the event of a breach between the play of two holes, the penalty applies to the next hole.
A player having more than one *caddie* in breach of this Rule must immediately upon the discovery that a breach has occurred ensure that he has no more than one *caddie* at any one time during the remainder of the *stipulated round*. Otherwise, the player is disqualified.
Bogey and par competitions – See Note 1 to Rule 32-1a.
Stableford competitions – See Note 1 to Rule 32-1b.

Note: The *Committee* may, in the conditions of a competition (Rule 33-1), prohibit the use of *caddies* or restrict a player in his choice of *caddie*.

6-5. BALL

The responsibility for playing the proper ball rests with the player. Each player should put an identification mark on his ball.

See **incident** involving Rule 6-6b on pages 48–49.

6-6. SCORING IN STROKE PLAY

a. Recording Scores

After each hole the *marker* should check the score with the *competitor* and record it. On completion of the round the *marker* must sign the score card and hand it to the *competitor*. If more than one *marker* records the scores, each must sign for the part for which he is responsible.

b. Signing and Returning Score Card

After completion of the round, the *competitor* should check his score for each hole and settle any doubtful points with the *Committee*. He must ensure that the *marker* or *markers* have signed the score card, sign the score card himself and return it to the *Committee* as soon as possible.

PENALTY FOR BREACH OF RULE 6-6b: Disqualification.

c. Alteration of Score Card

No alteration may be made on a score card after the *competitor* has returned it to the *Committee*.

See **incident** involving Rule 6-6d on pages 48–49.

d. Wrong Score for Hole

The *competitor* is responsible for the correctness of the score recorded for each hole on his score card. If he returns a score for any hole lower than actually taken, **he is disqualified**. If he returns a score for any hole higher than actually taken, the score as returned stands.

Note 1: The *Committee* is responsible for the addition of scores and application of the handicap recorded on the score card – see Rule 33-5.

Note 2: In *four-ball* stroke play, see also Rules 31-3 and 31-7a.

CORRECTNESS OF SCORE CARD

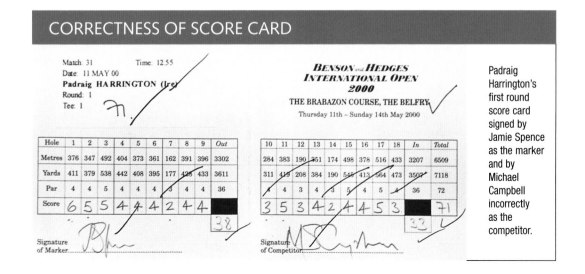

Padraig Harrington's first round score card signed by Jamie Spence as the marker and by Michael Campbell incorrectly as the competitor.

SCORING IN STROKE PLAY

COMPETITION **SPRING STROKE PLAY**   DATE **14 · 6 · 95**

PLAYER **D. BROWN**   HANDICAP **10**   Game No **21**

Hole	Yards	Par	Stroke Index	Score	W=+ L=- H=0 POINTS	Mar Score	Hole	Yards	Par	Stroke Index	Score	W=+ L=- H=0 POINTS	Mar Score
1	312	4	17	5		6	10	369	4	12	6̶5 (c)	
2	446	4	1	4		4	11	433	4	2	3	
3	310	4	13	4		3	12	361	4	14	4	
4	370	4	9	5	(b)	5	13	415	4	6	5	
5	478	5	3	6			14	155	3	16	6	
8̶7	429	4	11	4			15	338	4	8	5	
7̶6	385	4	5	3			16	316	4	10	4	
8	178	3	7	4			17	191	3	4	5	
9	354	4	15	6			18	508	5	18	7	
OUT	3262			41			IN	3086	35		44	
							OUT	3262	36		41	
							TOTAL	6348	71		85	

(a)

Markers Signature **D.B.** (e) & (f)

Players Signature **Bill White**

HANDICAP **10** (d)

NETT **75**

Competitor's Responsibilities:
1. To record the correct handicap somewhere on the score card before it is returned to the Committee.
2. To check the gross score recorded for each hole is correct.
3. To ensure that the marker has signed the card and to countersign the card himself before it is returned to the Committee.

Committee Responsibilities:
1. Issue to each competitor a score card containing the date and the competitor's name.
2. To add the scores for each hole and apply the handicap recorded on the card.

(a) Hole numbers may be altered if hole scores have been recorded in the wrong boxes.

(b) A marker need not keep a record of his own score, however it is recommended.

(c) There is nothing in the Rules that requires an alteration to be initialled.

(d) The competitor is responsible only for the correctness of the score recorded for each hole. If the competitor records a wrong total score or net score, the Committee must correct the error, without penalty to the competitor. In this instance, the Committee have added the scores for each hole and applied the handicap.

(e) There is no penalty if a marker signs the competitor's score card in the space provided for the competitor's signature, and the competitor then signs in the space provided for the marker's signature.

(f) The initialing of the score card by the competitor is sufficient for the purpose of countersignature.

UNDUE DELAY: ENTERING CLUBHOUSE

I must go into the clubhouse for a moment on our way past. I will catch up with you on the 10th tee.

OK. No doubt we will have to wait on the tee anyway, but you must not unduly delay play.

10th Tee

6-7. UNDUE DELAY; SLOW PLAY

The player must play without undue delay and in accordance with any pace of play guidelines that the *Committee* may establish. Between completion of a hole and playing from the next *teeing ground*, the player must not unduly delay play.

PENALTY FOR BREACH OF RULE 6-7:
Match play – Loss of hole; Stroke play – Two strokes.
Bogey and par competitions – See Note 2 to Rule 32-1a.
Stableford competitions – See Note 2 to Rule 32-1b.
For subsequent offense – Disqualification.

Note 1: If the player unduly delays play between holes, he is delaying the play of the next hole and, except for bogey, par and Stableford competitions (Rule 32), the penalty applies to that hole.

Note 2: For the purpose of preventing slow play, the *Committee* may, in the conditions of a competition (Rule 33-1), establish pace of play guidelines including maximum periods of time allowed to complete a *stipulated round*, a hole or a *stroke*.

In stroke play only, the *Committee* may, in such a condition, modify the penalty for a breach of this Rule as follows:
First offense – One stroke;
Second offense – Two strokes.
For subsequent offense – Disqualification.

6-8. DISCONTINUANCE OF PLAY; RESUMPTION OF PLAY

a. When Permitted

The player must not discontinue play unless:

(i)   the *Committee* has suspended play;

(ii) he believes there is danger from lightning;

(iii) he is seeking a decision from the *Committee* on a doubtful or disputed point (see Rules 2-5 and 34-3); or

(iv) there is some other good reason such as sudden illness.

Bad weather is not of itself a good reason for discontinuing play.

  If the player discontinues play without specific permission from the *Committee*, he must report to the *Committee* as soon as practicable. If he does so and the *Committee* considers his reason satisfactory, there is no penalty. Otherwise, **the player is disqualified**.

Exception in match play: Players discontinuing match play by agreement are not subject to disqualification, unless by so doing the competition is delayed.

Note: Leaving the *course* does not of itself constitute discontinuance of play.

b. Procedure When Play Suspended by Committee

When play is suspended by the *Committee*, if the players in a match or group are between the play of two holes, they must not resume play until the *Committee* has ordered a resumption of play. If they have started play of a hole, they may discontinue play immediately or continue play of the hole,

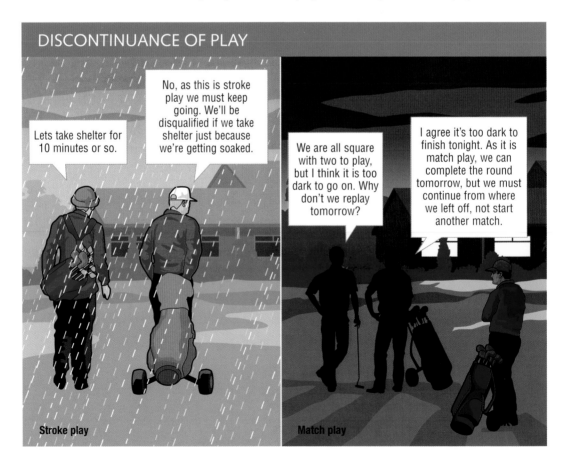

DISCONTINUANCE OF PLAY

Lets take shelter for 10 minutes or so.

No, as this is stroke play we must keep going. We'll be disqualified if we take shelter just because we're getting soaked.

We are all square with two to play, but I think it is too dark to go on. Why don't we replay tomorrow?

I agree it's too dark to finish tonight. As it is match play, we can complete the round tomorrow, but we must continue from where we left off, not start another match.

Stroke play

Match play

provided they do so without delay. If the players choose to continue play of the hole, they are permitted to discontinue play before completing it. In any case, play must be discontinued after the hole is completed.

The players must resume play when the *Committee* has ordered a resumption of play.

PENALTY FOR BREACH OF RULE 6-8b: Disqualification.

Note: The *Committee* may provide, in the conditions of a competition (Rule 33-1), that in potentially dangerous situations play must be discontinued immediately following a suspension of play by the *Committee*. If a player fails to discontinue play immediately, **he is disqualified**, unless circumstances warrant waiving the penalty as provided in Rule 33-7.

c. Lifting Ball When Play Discontinued

When a player discontinues play of a hole under Rule 6-8a, he may lift his ball, without penalty, only if the *Committee* has suspended play or there is a good reason to lift it. Before lifting the ball the player must mark its position. If the player discontinues play and lifts his ball without specific permission from the *Committee*, he must, when reporting to the *Committee* (Rule 6-8a), report the lifting of the ball.

If the player lifts the ball without a good reason to do so, fails to mark the position of the ball before lifting it or fails to report the lifting of the ball, **he incurs a penalty of one stroke.**

d. Procedure When Play Resumed

Play must be resumed from where it was discontinued, even if resumption occurs on a subsequent day. The player must, either before or when play is resumed, proceed as follows:

(i)   if the player has lifted the ball, he must, provided he was entitled to lift it under Rule 6-8c, place the original ball or a *substituted ball* on the spot from which the original ball was lifted. Otherwise, the original ball must be replaced;

(ii) if the player has not lifted his ball, he may, provided he was entitled to lift it under Rule 6-8c, lift, clean and replace the ball, or *substitute* a ball, on the spot from which the original ball was lifted. Before lifting the ball he must mark its position; or

(iii) if the player's ball or ball-marker is moved (including by wind or water) while play is discontinued, a ball or ball-marker must be placed on the spot from which the original ball or ball-marker was moved.

Note: If the spot where the ball is to be placed is impossible to determine, it must be estimated and the ball placed on the estimated spot. The provisions of Rule 20-3c do not apply.

*PENALTY FOR BREACH OF RULE 6-8d:
Match play – Loss of hole; Stroke play – Two strokes.
*If a player incurs the general penalty for a breach of Rule 6-8d, there is no additional penalty under Rule 6-8c.

A befuddled Padraig Harrington following his final day disqualification from the 2000 Benson & Hedges International for failing to sign his first round score card.

RULE 6 INCIDENTS

Although the score card has no status in match play, in stroke play it is the ultimate testament to a player's performance. The score card must not contain a score lower than actually taken, it must be signed by the competitor, attested by the competitor's marker, and returned as soon as possible to the Committee. Failure to meet any of these criteria results in disqualification.

Failure to sign his first round score card arguably cost Padraig Harrington the 2000 Benson and Hedges International Open at the Belfry. As he prepared to begin the final round with a five-shot lead, the 28-year-old Irishman was informed by officials that there was a problem.

Anticipating the ultimate victory, members of the Club had begun to collect Harrington's three previous score cards for souvenir purposes when it was noticed that he had not signed his first round card. Jamie Spence, Harrington's first round marker, had signed the card as required, but Michael Campbell, the third player in the group had mistakenly signed Harrington's card instead of Harrington. The resulting penalty under Rule 6-6b was disqualification.

Roberto De Vicenzo signed for a score higher than he actually made in the final round of the 1968 Masters Tournament. The higher score did not disqualify him but it did keep the Argentinean from forcing a play-off with Bob Goalby.

Playing in front of Goalby on Sunday, De Vincenzo, the reigning British Open Champion, sank a five-foot birdie putt on the 17th hole for a 3. He followed that with a bogey at the 18th giving him 66 for the day and 277 for the tournament. Goalby managed a five-footer for par at the 18th that also gave him 66 for the day and a total of 277.

However, De Vincenzo's fellow-competitor and marker, Tommy Aaron, had mistakenly recorded a 4 for De Vincenzo at the 17th rather than the 3. De Vincenzo did not notice the mistake, signed and returned the score card, and was rushed away from the scorer's table to talk to the press. A little later, Aaron noticed the mistake and brought it to the attention of tournament officials.

Augusta National founder Bob Jones searched for a way around the ensuing ruling but none could be found. Once the score card was signed and returned, the decision under the Rules was unavoidable: The higher score must stand (Rule 6-6d). Goalby was the Masters Champion.

An hour later, De Vincenzo told the media, "It's my fault. Tommy feels like I feel, very bad. I think the Rule is hard." The day's drama was compounded by the fact that it was De Vincenzo's 45th birthday.

Frequently asked questions

Q A player starts a round with a caddie from the course as his normal caddie is late. May the player switch caddies once he arrives at the golf course?

A Yes. Rule 6-4 requires that the player have only one caddie at a time. There is no limit on the number of caddies a player may have during the round.

Q It is recommended for the player to place an identification mark on his golf ball. May a line or an arrow that will also help in aligning the club face be used?

A Rules 6-5 and 12-2 state that each player should put an identification mark on his ball. Thus, the Rules do not limit the type of markings a player may put on the ball (i.e. arrows, lines, words, etc). Additionally, there is no penalty for using such lines to "line up" prior to a stroke on the putting green or any other place on the course.

Q Can a player be disqualified for not initialling any alterations made on his score card?

A A Committee cannot require that alterations made on score cards be initialled. Consequently, a player should not be disqualified for failure to do so.

RULE **7** **PRACTICE**

DEFINITIONS

All defined terms are in *italics* and are listed alphabetically in the Definitions section – see pages 9–20.

7-1. BEFORE OR BETWEEN ROUNDS
a. Match Play
On any day of a match-play competition, a player may practice on the competition *course* before a round.

b. Stroke Play
Before a round or play-off on any day of a stroke-play competition, a *competitor* must not practice on the competition *course* or test the surface of any *putting green* on the *course* by rolling a ball or roughening or scraping the surface.

When two or more rounds of a stroke-play competition are to be played over consecutive days, a *competitor* must not practice between those rounds on any competition *course* remaining to be played, or test the surface of any *putting green* on such *course* by rolling a ball or roughening or scraping the surface.

Exception: Practice putting or chipping on or near the first *teeing ground* before starting a round or play-off is permitted.

PENALTY FOR BREACH OF RULE 7-1b: Disqualification.

Note: The *Committee* may, in the conditions of a competition (Rule 33-1), prohibit practice on the competition *course* on any day of a match-play competition or permit practice on the competition *course* or part of the *course* (Rule 33-2c) on any day of or between rounds of a stroke-play competition.

See **incident** involving Rule 7-2 on pages 51–52.

7-2. DURING ROUND
A player must not make a practice *stroke* during play of a hole.

Between the play of two holes, a player must not make a practice *stroke*, except that he may practice putting or chipping on or near:
(a) the *putting green* of the hole last played,
(b) any practice *putting green*, or
(c) the *teeing ground* of the next hole to be played in the round,
provided a practice *stroke* is not made from a *hazard* and does not unduly delay play (Rule 6-7).

Strokes made in continuing the play of a hole, the result of which has been decided, are not practice *strokes*.

Exception: When play has been suspended by the *Committee*, a player may, prior to resumption of play, practice (a) as provided in this Rule, (b) anywhere other than on the competition *course* and (c) as otherwise permitted by the *Committee*.

PRACTICE DURING A ROUND

Practice putting and chipping on or near the teeing ground of the next hole to be played is permitted as long as play is not delayed.

PENALTY FOR BREACH OF RULE 7-2:
Match play – Loss of hole; Stroke play – Two strokes.
In the event of a breach between the play of two holes, the penalty applies to the next hole.

Note 1: A practice swing is not a practice *stroke* and may be taken at any place, provided the player does not breach the *Rules*.

Note 2: The *Committee* may, in the conditions of a competition (Rule 33-1), prohibit:
(a) practice on or near the *putting green* of the hole last played, and
(b) rolling a ball on the *putting green* of the hole last played.

RULE 7 INCIDENTS

After a suspension of play during the final round of the 2001 Players Championship at Sawgrass, both the penultimate group and the final group were required to resume play from the 10th tee. Tiger Woods, playing in the final group, was aware that the group in front would resume play first, and his group would have an additional wait on the tee before their resumption.

Concerned that Woods might continue to hit practice shots on the practice range after the signal for resumption of play had been sounded, officials advised Woods and his fellow-competitor that such action would be in breach of Rule 7-2, which prohibits practice during the round. Play was resumed without incident, and Woods went on to win The Players Championship by one stroke over Vijay Singh.

Also under Rule 7-2, players may practice, with certain restrictions, on the course while play is suspended and prior to resumption. During the first round of the 2000 U.S. Open at Pebble Beach, thick fog forced a suspension of play and the players were advised to remain in position on the course in hope that the fog would lift and play could be resumed.

Therefore those players who were between holes were permitted to practice under the provisions of Rule 7-2. Walking officials confirmed this point with the players in their group.

When it became evident that the fog would not clear quickly, the players were evacuated from the course and returned to the clubhouse. The following morning, when play was resumed, practice under Rule 7-2 was again applicable before the siren signaled the resumption of play.

Frequently asked questions

Q May a player practice on the competition course before the stipulated round?

A Before a match play competition, a player may practice on the competition course unless prohibited by the Committee – see the Note to Rule 7-1. However, in stroke play, a competitor is not permitted to practice on the competition course before the competition or test the surface of any putting green unless specifically permitted by the Committee.

Q Is practice putting permitted between the play of two holes?

A In both match play and stroke play, a player may practice putting or chipping on or near the putting green of the hole last played, any practice putting green or the teeing ground of the next hole to be played, provided such a practice stroke is not played from a hazard and does not unduly delay play. If the Committee has adopted Note 2 to Rule 7-2, then such practice between holes is prohibited.

RULE **8**

ADVICE; INDICATING LINE OF PLAY

DEFINITIONS

All defined terms are in *italics* and are listed alphabetically in the Definitions section – see pages 9–20.

See **incident** involving Rule 8-1 on page 54.

8-1. ADVICE

During a *stipulated round*, a player must not:

(a) give *advice* to anyone in the competition playing on the *course* other than his *partner*, or

(b) ask for *advice* from anyone other than his *partner* or either of their *caddies*.

8-2. INDICATING LINE OF PLAY
a. Other Than on Putting Green

Except on the *putting green*, a player may have the *line of play* indicated to him by anyone, but no one may be positioned by the player on or close

ADVICE

to the line or an extension of the line beyond the *hole* while the *stroke* is being made. Any mark placed by the player or with his knowledge to indicate the line must be removed before the *stroke* is made.

Exception: *Flagstick* attended or held up – see Rule 17-1.

See **incident** involving Rule 8-2b on page 54.

b. On the Putting Green

When the player's ball is on the *putting green*, the player, his *partner* or either of their *caddies* may, before but not during the *stroke*, point out a line for putting, but in so doing the *putting green* must not be touched. A mark must not be placed anywhere to indicate a line for putting.

INDICATING LINE OF PLAY

PENALTY FOR BREACH OF RULE:
Match play – Loss of hole;
Stroke play – Two strokes.

Note: The *Committee* may, in the conditions of a team competition (Rule 33-1), permit each team to appoint one person who may give *advice* (including pointing out a line for putting) to members of that team. The *Committee* may establish conditions relating to the appointment and permitted conduct of that person, who must be identified to the *Committee* before giving *advice*.

RULE 8 INCIDENTS

It may be that no good deed goes unpunished, but that does not mean it goes unrewarded. Mark Wilson was contending for the 2007 Honda Classic at PGA National when it became incumbent upon him to penalize himself.

Wilson was playing the 217-yard, par-3 5th hole when his caddie, Chris Jones, reflexively offered advice to Camilo Villegas, who was playing with Wilson. Following Wilson's tee shot with an 18-degree hybrid club, Villegas took his place on the tee and contemplated his club selection. Villegas asked his own caddie what club he thought Wilson had hit. Villegas' caddie speculated that a 2- or 3-iron had been used.

"Oh, it's an 18-degree," Jones injected reflexively.

Wilson was fully aware of the violation under Rule 8-1 that prohibits a player or his caddie from giving advice to a fellow-competitor in stroke play or an opponent in match play.

"I played out that hole," Wilson said later, "and immediately called an official over to see what he thought. He wasn't sure at first if that was necessarily advice, but within 60 seconds, he made the decision."

Jones said he was shaken when his boss pointed out the violation. "I heard Camilo and his caddie talking, and I just blurted it out. I was getting too comfortable and too friendly." Wilson forgave his caddie and told him to shake it off.

"I've called penalties on myself before," Wilson said following a tournament-winning play-off three days later that included Villegas and Boo Weekly (see incident for Rule 17), "and I've never won. It didn't work out those times. … It was the right thing to do. I don't think I'd be here [in the winner's circle] if I hadn't called it on myself. And, if I would be sitting here and hadn't called it on myself, every time I looked at that trophy, it would be tarnished."

When the giving of advice is penalized in golf, it is usually due to a light-hearted friendly moment. Tom Watson and Lee Trevino were playing together in the 1980 Tournament of Champions when Watson casually told Trevino about a little flaw he noticed in his fellow-competitor's swing. Overheard by the television audience, Watson was asked about it following the round. Watson agreed that he had indeed given Trevino a swing tip. Fortunately, the penalty was assessed before Watson returned his score card. Equally fortunate was that he had a three stroke lead at the time and still won the tournament. As he had not asked for advice, Trevino incurred no penalty.

Also addressed under Rule 8 are the regulations regarding indicating line of play. During the third round of the 1991 PGA Championship, there was intense concern that John Daly's caddie, Jeff "Squeeky" Medlen, had violated one of them.

As the ninth alternate, Daly had been included in the championship field when Nick Price withdrew to be present at the birth of his child, and three alternates ahead of Daly declined for various reasons. The, until then, unknown Arkansan took the outright lead for the major championship after posting 69 and 67 for the first and second rounds respectively. Playing with Bruce Lietzke in Saturday's third round, Daly was on his way to posting another 69.

At the 11th, Medlen used his hand to point out the line of Daly's first putt. In his other hand, Medlen held the flagstick and inadvertently allowed it to touch the green. The potential breach of Rule 8 was broadcast to millions and, fortunately, videotaped so it could be reviewed.

Alerted almost immediately as to the question at hand – had Medlen touched the green in pointing out a line for putting? – Rules officials met with Daly at the end of the round to discuss the matter and make a decision before Daly returned his score card.

Daly, Medlen, Lietzke and Rules officials reviewed the videotape. It showed Medlen holding the removed flagstick and allowing it to touch the putting green about three feet to the right of the hole while indicating the line of putt with his other hand. He was not using the flagstick to indicate the line for putting.

Officials were satisfied that no penalty was incurred. Daly returned his third round score card with a score of 69. The following day he won the PGA Championship by three strokes.

Frequently asked question

Q A player asks his opponent or fellow-competitor the distance from one object (e.g. his ball or the teeing ground) to another object (e.g. the putting green, a water hazard, or a bunker). Is he considered to be asking for advice and in breach of Rule 8-1?

A The distance between any objects is considered to be a matter of public information and therefore not advice. As this information is not advice, it may be exchanged without restriction.

RULE **9** INFORMATION AS TO STROKES TAKEN

DEFINITIONS

All defined terms are in *italics* and are listed alphabetically in the Definitions section – see pages 9–20.

9-1. GENERAL

The number of *strokes* a player has taken includes any *penalty strokes* incurred.

See **incident** involving Rule 9-2 on pages 57–58.

9-2. MATCH PLAY
a. Information as to Strokes Taken

An opponent is entitled to ascertain from the player, during the play of a hole, the number of *strokes* he has taken and, after play of a hole, the number of *strokes* taken on the hole just completed.

b. Wrong Information

A player must not give wrong information to his opponent. If a player gives wrong information, **he loses the hole**.

A player is deemed to have given wrong information if he:

(i)   fails to inform his opponent as soon as practicable that he has incurred a penalty, unless (a) he was obviously proceeding under a *Rule* involving a penalty and this was observed by his opponent, or (b) he corrects the mistake before his opponent makes his next *stroke*; or

(ii) gives incorrect information during play of a hole regarding the number of *strokes* taken and does not correct the mistake before his opponent makes his next *stroke*; or

(iii) gives incorrect information regarding the number of *strokes* taken to complete a hole and this affects the opponent's understanding of the result of the hole, unless he corrects the mistake before any player makes a *stroke* from the next *teeing ground* or, in the case of the last hole of the match, before all players leave the *putting green*.

A player has given wrong information even if it is due to the failure to include a penalty that he did not know he had incurred. It is the player's responsibility to know the *Rules*.

9-3. STROKE PLAY

A *competitor* who has incurred a penalty should inform his *marker* as soon as practicable.

RULE 9 INCIDENT

The One Ball Condition from Appendix I in the Rules of Golf is straightforward enough when adopted for individual competition. It becomes a little less obvious in team play, or so it seemed at the 1991 Ryder Cup Matches.

On the 7th tee of Kiawah Island's Ocean Course during the first morning's foursomes, Chip Beck and Paul Azinger were overheard by their European opponents discussing which type of ball they would select to optimize their performance on that hole.

The Americans mistakenly believed that the One Ball Condition applied to them individually – not as a team – and, since they each played different types of balls, they were entitled to a choice between them. As they were about to learn, that is not the case. Appendix I, Part C, 1c clearly states that, "if it is desired to prohibit changing brands and types of golf balls during a stipulated round, the [one ball] condition is recommended.

Each player must use the same brand and type of ball for the entire round. Therefore, whichever player's turn it was to drive at the 7th, that player was required to use the same type of ball with which he began the round.

With one player driving the odd-numbered holes and the other driving the even-numbered holes, as required in foursome competition, the Americans erred when the driving player selected the ball type used by his partner. The European side of Seve Ballesteros and Jose Maria Olazabal suspected this was a breach of the Rules. Nothing was said to Beck and Azinger. Sam Torrance, a fellow European Team member who was not playing in the morning foursomes, was in the gallery following the match. He was called over by Ballesteros, told of the situation, and sent to fetch the European Captain Bernard Gallacher.

While Gallacher was being located, play of the 7th hole, 8th and 9th holes was completed. On the way to the 10th tee, the Europeans made a claim concerning what had taken place on the 7th hole. The chief referee was called for a ruling.

In match play, Rule 9-2 requires a player who has incurred a penalty to notify his opponents as soon as practicable. If he does not, even when he doesn't know his has incurred a penalty, he is considered to have given wrong information. In this case, the Americans gave wrong information as a penalty was associated with their playing of the wrong type of ball from the 7th tee. However, since the European side was aware of the error and did not make a claim (Rule 2-5) before anyone played from the 8th tee, their belated claim could not be considered. It was as if the statute of limitations ran out for that particular violation.

The match continued from the 10th tee without Beck and Azinger being penalized for their infraction at the 7th.

ORDER OF PLAY

RULE **10**

ORDER OF PLAY

DEFINITIONS

All defined terms are in *italics* and are listed alphabetically in the Definitions section – see pages 9–20.

10-1. MATCH PLAY
a. When Starting Play of Hole
The *side* that has the *honor* at the first *teeing ground* is determined by the order of the draw. In the absence of a draw, the *honor* should be decided by lot.

The *side* that wins a hole takes the *honor* at the next *teeing ground*. If a hole has been halved, the *side* that had the *honor* at the previous *teeing ground* retains it.

See **incident** involving Rule 10-1b on pages 60–61.

b. During Play of Hole
After both players have started play of the hole, the ball farther from the *hole* is played first. If the balls are equidistant from the *hole* or their positions relative to the *hole* are not determinable, the ball to be played first should be decided by lot.

Exception: Rule 30-3c (*best-ball* and *four-ball* match play).

Note: When it becomes known that the original ball is not to be played as it lies and the player is required to play a ball as nearly as possible at the spot from which the original ball was last played (see Rule 20-5), the order of play is determined by the spot from which the previous *stroke* was made. When a ball may be played from a spot other than where the previous *stroke* was made, the order of play is determined by the position where the original ball came to rest.

c. Playing Out of Turn

If a player plays when his opponent should have played, there is no penalty, but the opponent may immediately require the player to cancel the *stroke* so made and, in correct order, play a ball as nearly as possible at the spot from which the original ball was last played (see Rule 20-5).

10-2. STROKE PLAY
a. When Starting Play of Hole

The *competitor* who has the *honor* at the first *teeing ground* is determined by the order of the draw. In the absence of a draw, the *honor* should be decided by lot.

The *competitor* with the lowest score at a hole takes the *honor* at the next *teeing ground*. The *competitor* with the second lowest score plays next and so on. If two or more *competitors* have the same score at a hole, they play from the next *teeing ground* in the same order as at the previous *teeing ground*.

Exception: Rule 32-1 (handcap bogey, par and Stableford competitions).

See **incident** involving Rule 10-2b on page 60.

b. During Play of Hole

After the *competitors* have started play of the hole, the ball farthest from the *hole* is played first. If two or more balls are equidistant from the *hole* or their positions relative to the *hole* are not determinable, the ball to be played first should be decided by lot.

Exceptions: Rules 22 (ball assisting or interfering with play) and 31-4 (*four-ball* stroke play).

Note: When it becomes known that the original ball is not to be played as it lies and the *competitor* is required to play a ball as nearly as possible at the spot from which the original ball was last played (see Rule 20-5), the order of play is determined by the spot from which the previous *stroke* was made. When a ball may be played from a spot other than where the previous *stroke* was made, the order of play is determined by the position where the original ball came to rest.

c. Playing Out of Turn

If a *competitor* plays out of turn, there is no penalty and the ball is played as it lies. If, however, the *Committee* determines that *competitors* have agreed to play out of turn to give one of them an advantage, **they are disqualified**.
(Making stroke while another ball in motion after stroke from putting green – see Rule 16-1f.)
(Incorrect order of play in threesomes and foursomes stroke play – see Rule 29-3.)

10-3. PROVISIONAL BALL OR ANOTHER BALL FROM TEEING GROUND

If a player plays a *provisional ball* or another ball from the *teeing ground*, he must do so after his opponent or *fellow-competitor* has made his first *stroke*. If more than one player elects to play a *provisional ball* or is required to play another ball from the *teeing ground*, the original order of play must be retained. If a player plays a *provisional ball* or another ball out of turn, Rule 10-1c or -2c applies.

RULE 10 INCIDENTS

While there is no penalty for playing out of turn, the strategic consequences of doing so can have impressively different weight in stroke play and match play.

There are many speculative reasons why Sam Snead came so close but never won the U.S. Open Championship. In a play-off with Lew Worsham in 1947, Snead came as close as it is possible to come without success.

Of the 1,356 entries that year, it had come down to Worsham and Snead who played the regulation 72 holes in two-under-par (282). An 18-hole play-off ensued. Coming to the last tee of the play-off round, the two men were still tied. After playing to the final green, both were left with putts for par from about the same distance.

Rule 10 is unequivocal: In stroke play "after the competitors have started play of the hole, the ball farthest from the hole is played first." It also states that no penalty is incurred if a competitor plays out of turn, as long as it has not been agreed upon in order to create an advantage.

Snead and Worsham were each less than three feet from the hole. Worsham voiced no objection when Snead began his procedure for putting first. This would indicate that it must have been apparent to both men that Snead was away.

Snead recalled not only addressing his putt, but actually taking the club back before Worsham objected. "In the middle of my backswing, Lew said, 'Sam, I think I'm away,'" Snead recalled later. At that point, Snead interrupted his stroke.

Isaac Grainger was the Rules official with the group. "When Ike came over," Snead remembered, "I said, 'I know I can continue putting and, besides, I am away as well.'"

Grainger, an authority on the Rules who would serve as president of the U.S.G.A. from 1954-1955, was renowned for being fastidious.

"Ike never replied," Snead said, "but he did have a ruler."

The players backed slightly away and watched intently as Grainger measured from the flagstick to each ball. Snead recalled that his ball was 30½ inches from the flagstick. The distance to Worsham's ball was 30 inches. It was, indeed, Snead's turn to play.

The interruption proved distracting. In the film, Snead appears to have lost his focus before he could simply bang the ball into the hole.

Snead missed. Worsham holed and, with a score of 69, became the 1947 U.S. Open Champion.

In match play, playing out of turn has more severe ramifications, as Annika Sorenstam discovered at the 2000 Solheim Cup.

After a suspension of play due to unplayable conditions at Loch Lomond, Sorenstam and Janice Moodie of the European Team returned to the 13th hole to resume their four-ball match against Kelly Robbins and Pat Hurst of the U.S. Team.

Hurst was the first to play from the fairway, as the other three balls were either on or close to the putting green. Sorenstam played next and holed her chip from just off the green for a birdie 4.

Robbins, who had been talking to Hurst, walked back to where her ball-marker was to replace her ball on the putting green. She then realized that she was farther from the hole than Sorenstam had been and she had been entitled to play before Sorenstam. In match play, Rule 10-1 provides that the ball farther from the hole shall be played first, and if a player plays when her opponent should have played the opponent may require the player to cancel and replay the stroke in the correct order.

As Sorenstam had holed her chip, it was clearly advantageous for the Americans to have the stroke cancelled and replayed. Uncertain of whether to exercise this right under the Rule, the Americans consulted with Pat Bradley, their captain. The decision was made that Sorenstam would be required to replay in the correct order, and the match's referee was so informed. On her second attempt, Sorenstam failed to hole her chip. Hurst made birdie, and the hole was won by the Americans who went on to win the match 2 and 1.

Frequently asked question

Q Player A's ball lies 15 feet from the hole, but in a bunker. Player B's ball lies 20 feet from the hole on the putting green. Who must play first?

A The ball farther from the hole must be played first, regardless of the location of the ball. Player B must play first from the putting green before A plays from the bunker.

RULE **11**

TEEING GROUND

DEFINITIONS

All defined terms are in *italics* and are listed alphabetically in the Definitions section – see pages 9–20.

11-1. TEEING

When a player is putting a ball into play from the *teeing ground*, it must be played from within the *teeing ground* and from the surface of the ground or from a conforming *tee* in or on the surface of the ground.

For the purposes of this Rule, the surface of the ground includes an irregularity of surface (whether or not created by the player) and sand or other natural substance (whether or not placed by the player).

If a player makes a *stroke* at a ball on a non-conforming *tee*, or at a ball teed in a manner not permitted by this Rule, **he is disqualified**.

A player may stand outside the *teeing ground* to play a ball within it.

11-2. TEE-MARKERS

Before a player makes his first *stroke* with any ball on the *teeing ground* of the hole being played, the tee-markers are deemed to be fixed. In these circumstances, if the player moves or allows to be moved a tee-marker for the purpose of avoiding interference with his *stance*, the area of his intended swing or his *line of play*, **he incurs the penalty for a breach of Rule 13-2**.

11-3. BALL FALLING OFF TEE

If a ball, when not *in play*, falls off a *tee* or is knocked off a *tee* by the player in *addressing* it, it may be re-teed, without penalty. However, if a *stroke* is made at the ball in these circumstances, whether the ball is moving or not, the *stroke* counts, but there is no penalty.

See **incident** involving Rule 11-4 on pages 63–64.

11-4. PLAYING FROM OUTSIDE TEEING GROUND
a. Match Play

If a player, when starting a hole, plays a ball from outside the *teeing ground* there is no penalty, but the opponent may immediately require the player to cancel the *stroke* and play a ball from within the *teeing ground*.

b. Stroke Play

If a *competitor*, when starting a hole, plays a ball from outside the *teeing ground*, **he incurs a penalty of two strokes** and must then play a ball from within the *teeing ground*.

If the *competitor* plays a *stroke* from the next *teeing ground* without first correcting his mistake or, in the case of the last hole of the round, leaves the *putting green* without first declaring his intention to correct his mistake, **he is disqualified**.

The *stroke* from outside the *teeing ground* and any subsequent *strokes* by the *competitor* on the hole prior to his correction of the mistake do not count in his score.

PLAYING FROM THE WRONG TEEING GROUND IN STROKE PLAY

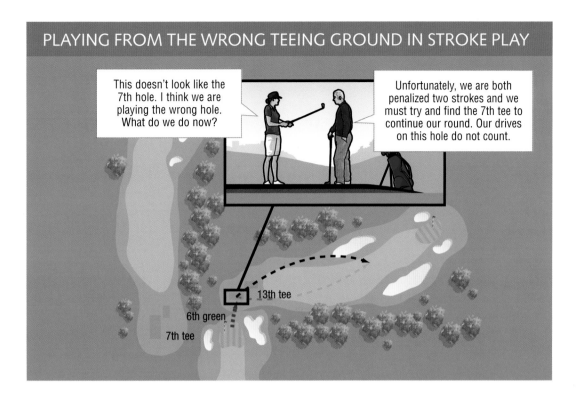

11-5. PLAYING FROM WRONG TEEING GROUND

The provisions of Rule 11-4 apply.

RULE 11 INCIDENT

"**Most of the time** nothing happens," reflects C.Grant Spaeth recalling the 1990 U.S. Open Championship play-off, "but when it does you better be ready."

The final result of the championship lent substantiation to the USGA's 18-hole play-off policy. At eight-under-par, 280, Mike Donald and Hale Irwin were tied after 72 holes of regulation play at Medinah C.C.

The competitive tension had been intense all week, as is usually the case at the Open. Irwin summoned a surge of talent reflective of his 33 professional victories that included two previous U.S. Open victories (1974 and 1979). Indeed, he holed a 45-foot birdie putt on the 72nd hole to force an 18-hole play-off the following day with Donald, whose sole PGA Tour victory had come the previous year in Williamsburg, Virginia.

A momentary lapse of concentration regarding the Rules might have determined the winner had it not been for Spaeth's diligence as the attending referee.

"After a long week, I was tired," Spaeth recalled. "Walking off the 17th green (of the play-off round) I was tempted not to go down a hill to the 18th tee, which sits out on a peninsula that stretches into the lake. I thought I might cut over to the 18th fairway, contrary to the strictures in the book [that suggest walking officials be present at each teeing ground]. Thank God I resisted and trudged back to the tee."

After days of athletic and psychological competition, the players walked off the 17th green with Donald leading by a stroke and with the honor. On the 18th tee, Donald mistakenly teed his ball in front of the tee markers. Spaeth noticed the error and, as a dutiful referee, brought it to the attention of Donald, who re-teed appropriately within the teeing ground.

Rule 11, as it applies to stroke play, is exact. If a competitor plays from outside the teeing ground, he incurs a penalty of two strokes and must then play a ball from within the teeing ground. Had Donald's mistake been observed a few moments after his ball was played, the resulting two-stroke penalty would have reversed the state of the play-off and given Irwin a one-stroke lead.

Spaeth's intervention prevented the breach. Donald's bogey and Irwin's par at the 90th hole resulted in both men scoring 74 in the play-off round. By the conditions outlined in the entry form, and for the first time in U.S. Open history, the championship then moved to hole-by-hole play-off to determine the champion.

On the first hole-by-hole play-off hole, the 91st of the championship, Irwin holed an eight-foot birdie putt to become the U.S. Open's oldest winner.

Frequently asked question

Q May a player use a tee that he has found or is this a breach sharing equipment?

A A player may use a conforming tee (see Definition of "Tee") that he has found (including a broken tee). There is no general Rule that prohibits the sharing of equipment. Please refer to Rule 4-4 that discusses the sharing of clubs and to Decision 5-1/5 that discusses the sharing of balls and other equipment such as towels, tees etc.

PLAYING THE BALL

RULE **12**

SEARCHING FOR AND IDENTIFYING BALL

DEFINITIONS

All defined terms are in *italics* and are listed alphabetically in the Definitions section – see pages 9–20.

See **incident** involving Rule 12-1 on page 67.

12-1. SEARCHING FOR BALL; SEEING BALL

In searching for his ball anywhere on the *course*, the player may touch or bend long grass, rushes, bushes, whins, heather or the like, but only to the extent necessary to find and identify it, provided that this does not improve the lie of the ball, the area of his intended *stance* or swing or his *line of play*.

SEARCHING FOR A BALL IN BUNKER

If a player's ball is buried in a bunker, he may search for it by probing the sand with his fingers or he may use a rake or a club. If the ball is moved, there is no penalty but it must be replaced and, if necessary, re-covered so that only part of it is visible.

A player is not necessarily entitled to see his ball when making a *stroke*.

In a *hazard*, if a ball is believed to be covered by *loose impediments* or sand, the player may remove by probing or raking with a club or otherwise, as many *loose impediments* or as much sand as will enable him to see a part of the ball. If an excess is removed, there is no penalty and the ball must be re-covered so that only a part of the ball is visible. If the ball is *moved* during the removal, there is no penalty; the ball must be replaced and, if necessary, re-covered. As to removal of *loose impediments* outside a *hazard*, see Rule 23-1.

If a ball lying in or on an *obstruction* or in an *abnormal ground condition* is accidentally *moved* during search, there is no penalty; the ball must be replaced, unless the player elects to proceed under Rule 24-1b, 24-2b or 25-1b as applicable. If the player replaces the ball, he may still proceed under Rule 24-1b, 24-2b or 25-1b if applicable.

If a ball is believed to be lying in water in a *water hazard*, the player may probe for it with a club or otherwise. If the ball is *moved* in probing, it must be replaced, unless the player elects to proceed under Rule 26-1. There is no penalty for causing the ball to *move*, provided the movement of the ball was directly attributable to the specific act of probing. Otherwise, **the player incurs a *penalty stroke* under Rule 18-2a.**

PENALTY FOR BREACH OF RULE 12-1:
Match play – Loss of hole; Stroke play – Two strokes.

12-2. IDENTIFYING BALL

The responsibility for playing the proper ball rests with the player. Each player should put an identification mark on his ball.

If a player has reason to believe a ball at rest is his and it is necessary to lift the ball in order to identify it, he may lift the ball, without penalty, in order to do so.

IDENTIFYING A BALL IN A BUNKER

A player may lift a ball in order to identify it, even if the ball lies in a bunker or water hazard. The position of the ball must be marked before it is lifted and the player must tell his opponent, fellow-competitor or marker what of his intentions before he lifts the ball. The ball must not be cleaned beyond what is necessary to identify it.

Before lifting the ball, the player must announce his intention to his opponent in match play or his *marker* or a *fellow-competitor* in stroke play and mark the position of the ball. He may then lift the ball and identify it, provided that he gives his opponent, *marker* or *fellow-competitor* an opportunity to observe the lifting and replacement. The ball must not be cleaned beyond the extent necessary for identification when lifted under Rule 12-2.

If the ball is the player's ball and he fails to comply with all or any part of this procedure or he lifts his ball in order to identify it when not necessary to do so, **he incurs a penalty of one stroke**. If the lifted ball is the player's ball he must replace it. If he fails to do so, **he incurs the general penalty for a breach of Rule 12-2**, but there is no additional penalty under this Rule.

Note: If the original lie of a ball to be placed or replaced has been altered, see Rule 20-3b.

*PENALTY FOR BREACH OF RULE 12-2:
 Match play – Loss of hole; Stroke play – Two strokes.
*If a player incurs the general penalty for a breach of Rule 12-2, there is no additional penalty under this Rule.

Golf balls can come to rest in some odd places. At the 1992 U.S. Open Nick Faldo scaled a tree in search of his ball that had apparently come to rest there. See the story below.

RULE 12 INCIDENT

Nick Faldo discovered that within the Rules of Golf there are protective nuances that can come in handy even while you are up a tree at the U.S. Open.

In the second round of the 1992 championship at Pebble Beach, Faldo's second shot at the par-5 14th finished dangerously close to the out of bounds that runs along the right rough. For his third, the Englishman chose a short iron in order to play over the singular tree that protects the green. As the ball climbed in elevation, it struck the trunk of the tree and no one saw it fall to the ground.

Faldo asked the walking Rules Official if a provisional ball could be played under the circumstances. Because the official did not see the ball come down from the tree, he replied that Faldo was entitled to play a provisional ball as the original might be lost.

After playing the provisional ball and as the group walked toward the tree to look for the original ball, the two-time British Open and two-time Masters Champion asked the Rules Official if it was permissible to climb the tree in order to search for his ball. The official affirmed that it was, but cautioned Faldo that if the ball moved as a result of his being in the tree, there would be a penalty stroke assessed and the ball would have to be replaced (Decision 18-2a/26).

That provision not withstanding, the Rules Official further advised Faldo that if, before climbing or shaking the tree, he stated his intention to deem his ball unplayable should he find it, there would be no penalty for moving the ball during search. With such prior notification, one penalty stroke would be assessed for a ball unplayable (Rule 28) but no additional penalty would be incurred for moving a ball at rest (Rule 18).

Faldo took the official's advice. Before climbing the tree, he declared that should he find the ball he intended to proceed under Rule 28. He then climbed to search. Having no luck, he shook the tree in hope of dislodging the ball.

"Where's Jane?," he quipped while standing on a high limb.

Unable to find his original ball, Faldo's provisional ball became the ball in play under penalty of stroke and distance (Rule 27).

RULE **13**   BALL PLAYED AS IT LIES

DEFINITIONS   All defined terms are in *italics* and are listed alphabetically in the Definitions section – see pages 9–20.

13-1. GENERAL
The ball must be played as it lies, except as otherwise provided in the *Rules*.
(Ball at rest moved – see Rule 18.)

13-2. IMPROVING LIE, AREA OF INTENDED STANCE OR SWING, OR LINE OF PLAY
A player must not improve or allow to be improved:
  • the position or lie of his ball,
  • the area of his intended *stance* or swing,
  • his *line of play* or a reasonable extension of that line beyond the *hole*, or
  • the area in which he is to drop or place a ball,
by any of the following actions:
  • pressing a club on the ground,
  • moving, bending or breaking anything growing or fixed (including immovable *obstructions* and objects defining *out of bounds*),
  • creating or eliminating irregularities of surface,
  • removing or pressing down sand, loose soil, replaced divots or other cut turf placed in position, or
  • removing dew, frost or water.
However, the player incurs no penalty if the action occurs:
  • in grounding the club lightly when *addressing the ball*,
  • in fairly taking his *stance*,

IMPROVING AREA OF INTENDED SWING OR LINE OF PLAY

A player must not break an interfering branch or remove sand or loose soil which is off the putting green but on the line of play.

CREATING OR ELIMINATING IRREGULARITIES OF SURFACE

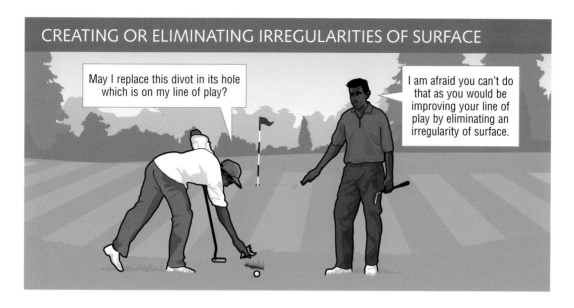

- in making a *stroke* or the backward movement of his club for a *stroke* and the *stroke* is made,
- in creating or eliminating irregularities of surface within the *teeing ground* (Rule 11-1) or in removing dew, frost or water from the *teeing ground*, or
- on the *putting green* in removing sand and loose soil or in repairing damage (Rule 16-1).

Exception: Ball in *hazard* – see Rule 13-4.

See **incident** involving Rule 13-3 on page 72.

13-3. BUILDING STANCE

A player is entitled to place his feet firmly in taking his *stance*, but he must not build a *stance*.

IMPROVING AREA OF INTENDED STANCE

BALL IN A BUNKER

Before making a stroke at a ball which is in a bunker the player shall not:

... touch the ground with his club.

... touch a loose impediment with his club at address or on his backswing.

... remove loose impediments.

... or smooth sand.

See **incident** involving Rule 13-4 on pages 71–72.

13-4. BALL IN HAZARD; PROHIBITED ACTIONS

Except as provided in the *Rules*, before making a *stroke* at a ball that is in a *hazard* (whether a *bunker* or a *water hazard*) or that, having been lifted from a *hazard*, may be dropped or placed in the *hazard*, the player must not:

a. Test the condition of the *hazard* or any similar *hazard*;

b. Touch the ground in the *hazard* or water in the *water hazard* with his hand or a club; or

c. Touch or move a *loose impediment* lying in or touching the *hazard*.

Exceptions:

1. Provided nothing is done that constitutes testing the condition of the *hazard* or improves the lie of the ball, there is no penalty if the player (a) touches the ground or *loose impediments* in any *hazard* or water in a *water hazard* as a result of or to prevent falling, in removing an *obstruction*, in measuring or in marking the position of, retrieving, lifting, placing or replacing a ball under any *Rule* or (b) places his clubs in a *hazard*.

2. After making the *stroke*, if the ball is still in the *hazard* or has been lifted from the *hazard* and may be dropped or placed in the *hazard*, the player may smooth sand or soil in the *hazard*, provided nothing is done to breach Rule 13-2 with respect to his next *stroke*. If the ball lies outside the *hazard* after the *stroke*, the player may smooth sand or soil in the *hazard* without restriction.

3. If the player makes a *stroke* from a *hazard* and the ball comes to rest in another *hazard*, Rule 13-4a does not apply to any subsequent actions taken in the *hazard* from which the *stroke* was made.

Note: At any time, including at *address* or in the backward movement for the *stroke*, the player may touch, with a club or otherwise, any *obstruction*, any construction declared by the *Committee* to be an integral part of the *course* or any grass, bush, tree or other growing thing.

PENALTY FOR BREACH OF RULE:
Match play – Loss of hole; Stroke play – Two strokes.

(Searching for ball – see Rule 12-1.)
(Relief for ball in water hazard – see Rule 26.)

Richie Ramsay is informed of his Rule 13 infraction during the semifinals of the 2006 U.S. Amateur. He unknowingly grounded his club in a hazard. Although he lost the hole, Ramsay ultimately prevailed in this match and the championship.

RULE 13 INCIDENTS

The tenet of playing the ball as it lies is protected under Rule 13 in the most obvious instances, as well as seemingly minor ones. Principles embedded in the Rules are the same regardless of the magnitude of circumstances under which they are brought to bear.

In 2006, Richie Ramsay became the first Scotsman to win the U.S. Amateur since 1898, but not before encountering a penalty during the semifinals for grounding his club in a hazard.

Hazeltine National G.C.'s 16th hole is a beautiful par-4 that runs beside Lake Hazeltine from tee to green. Although Ramsay was unaware of having grounded his club in a hazard at the 16th, the violation was witnessed by two officials who were walking with the match, as well as a television commentator and an official assisting the commentator in the broadcast booth. All confirmed that Ramsay had grounded his club while addressing his ball in the hazard.

Ramsay, 1 up after the Rule 13 loss-of-hole infraction, remained stoic for the last two holes and won 1 up over Webb Simpson.

Although it is an infraction to touch the ground, water, or loose impediments in a hazard while your ball is in that hazard, the Rules do permit touching obstructions, integral parts of the golf course, and growing plants or trees. Lee Westwood caused some unnecessary concern among television commentators when he played from a bridge in a water hazard during the final of the 2004 HSBC World Match Play Championship.

John Paramor, the referee with the match, in which Westwood was playing Ernie Els, was aware that Westwood's ball had come to rest on the bridge at 7th hole of Wentworth's West Course. Walking to the ball, Paramor and Westwood discussed what was permitted and what was not.

With Paramor standing a few yards away, the television commentators were taken aback when Westwood took a practice swing and hit the bridge with his club, just as they were when he grounded his club on the bridge at address prior to making his stroke. The Note under Rule 13-4 permits such actions, at any time.

However, the authority to touch the bridge, did not remove the prohibition against Westwood removing loose impediments on the bridge, and Paramor was careful to be certain that Westwood understood that distinction.

Stephen Ames demonstrated his alacrity under the Rules, after playing an unsuccessful bunker shot at The Player's Championship. As a result of his first bunker shot, Ames' ball came to rest in the same bunker. Before playing again from the bunker, he smoothed his footprints in the area from where he had played his first stroke.

While the Rules prohibit touching the ground in a bunker before playing a shot, they do permit the smoothing of sand or soil in a hazard provided that, if the ball is still in the hazard, nothing is done that improves the lie of the ball or assists the player in the subsequent play of the hole. Exception 2 under Rule 13-4 gives the player the right to do so.

Rule 13 very simply states that a player must play his ball as it lies. The building of a stance, no matter how great or insignificant, is prohibited because it may improve the situation with which the player must deal. There is no difference under the Rule between knocking down the side of bunker to level your stance or placing a towel on the ground to keep from soiling your trousers, as Craig Stadler discovered in 1987.

In the third round of an event at Torrey Pines, Stadler's ball came to rest beneath some branches of a tree where it would be necessary for him to play his next shot from a kneeling position. To keep his trousers dry, Stadler spread a towel on the ground and then knelt on it to play his shot.

The following day, a television viewer brought the infraction to the attention of tournament officials. Unfortunately, because Stadler had returned his score card for the third round containing a lower score for a hole than actually taken – he had not included the two-stroke penalty for building a stance – he was disqualified (Rule 6-6d).

Frequently asked questions

Q Is it permissible to place the rake or clubs in a bunker or water hazard while I play my stroke from the same hazard?

A Yes, provided the lie of the ball is not improved, or the player does not test the condition of the hazard.

Q A player's ball is in a bunker that runs approximately 20 yards along the left side of the fairway. He plays a stroke and the ball advances about 10 yards and remains in the bunker. May he rake the bunker from where he last played as he walks to the new position of the ball?

A Yes, provided he does not improve the lie of the ball or assist his subsequent play of the hole. If the ball were to subsequently come to rest in the smoothed area, he would incur a penalty of loss of hole in match play or two strokes in stroke play. (Exception 2 to Rule 13-4 and Decision 13-4/36)

STRIKING THE BALL

DEFINITIONS

All defined terms are in *italics* and are listed alphabetically in the Definitions section – see pages 9–20.

14-1. BALL TO BE FAIRLY STRUCK AT

The ball must be fairly struck at with the head of the club and must not be pushed, scraped or spooned.

BALL TO BE FAIRLY STRUCK AT WITH CLUBHEAD

A player may strike the ball with the back or toe of the clubhead.

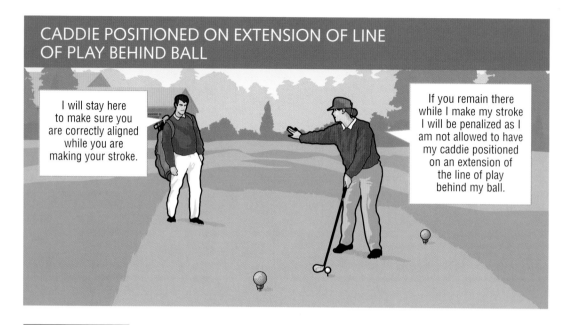

CADDIE POSITIONED ON EXTENSION OF LINE
OF PLAY BEHIND BALL

See **incident**
involving Rule 14-2
on pages 76–77.

14-2. ASSISTANCE

In making a *stroke*, a player must not:

a.   Accept physical assistance or protection from the elements; or

b.   Allow his *caddie*, his *partner* or his *partner's caddie* to position himself on or close to an extension of the *line of play* or the *line of putt* behind the ball.

PENALTY FOR BREACH OF RULE 14-1 or 14-2:
Match play – Loss of hole; Stroke play – Two strokes.

14-3. ARTIFICIAL DEVICES, UNUSUAL EQUIPMENT AND UNUSUAL USE OF EQUIPMENT

The United States Golf Association (USGA) reserves the right, at any time, to change the Rules relating to artificial devices, unusual *equipment* and the unusual use of *equipment*, and make or change the interpretations relating to these Rules.

A player in doubt as to whether use of an item would constitute a breach of Rule 14-3 should consult the USGA.

A manufacturer should submit to the USGA a sample of an item to be manufactured for a ruling as to whether its use during a *stipulated round* would cause a player to be in breach of Rule 14-3. The sample becomes the property of the USGA for reference purposes. If a manufacturer fails to submit a sample or, having submitted a sample, fails to await a ruling before manufacturing and/or marketing the item, the manufacturer assumes the risk of a ruling that use of the item would be contrary to the *Rules*.

Except as provided in the *Rules*, during a *stipulated round* the player must not use any artificial device or unusual *equipment*, or use any *equipment* in an unusual manner:

a.   That might assist him in making a *stroke* or in his play; or

b.   For the purpose of gauging or measuring distance or conditions that might affect his play; or

c. That might assist him in gripping the club, except that:
(i) plain gloves may be worn;
(ii) resin, powder and drying or moisturizing agents may be used; and
(iii) a towel or handkerchief may be wrapped around the grip.

Exceptions:

1. A player is not in breach of this Rule if (a) the *equipment* or device is designed for or has the effect of alleviating a medical condition, (b) the player has a legitimate medical reason to use the *equipment* or device, and (c) the *Committee* is satisfied that its use does not give the player any undue advantage over other players.

2. A player is not in breach of this Rule if he uses *equipment* in a traditionally accepted manner.

PENALTY FOR BREACH OF RULE 14-3: Disqualification.

Note: The *Committee* may make a Local Rule allowing players to use devices that measure or gauge distance only.

14-4. STRIKING THE BALL MORE THAN ONCE
If a player's club strikes the ball more than once in the course of a *stroke*, the player must count the *stroke* and **add a *penalty stroke***, making two *strokes* in all.

14-5. PLAYING MOVING BALL
A player must not make a *stroke* at his ball while it is moving.

Exceptions:
• Ball falling off *tee* – Rule 11-3.
• Striking the ball more than once – Rule 14-4.
• Ball moving in water – Rule 14-6.

When the ball begins to *move* only after the player has begun the *stroke* or the backward movement of his club for the *stroke*, he incurs no penalty under this Rule for playing a moving ball, but he is not exempt from any penalty under the following Rules:
• Ball at rest *moved* by player – Rule 18-2a.
• Ball at rest moving after *address* – Rule 18-2b.
(Ball purposely deflected or stopped by player, partner or caddie – see Rule 1-2.)

14-6. BALL MOVING IN WATER
When a ball is moving in water in a *water hazard*, the player may, without penalty, make a *stroke*, but he must not delay making his *stroke* in order to allow the wind or current to improve the position of the ball. A ball moving in water in a *water hazard* may be lifted if the player elects to invoke Rule 26.

PENALTY FOR BREACH OF RULE 14-5 or 14-6:
Match play – Loss of hole; Stroke play – Two strokes.

75

One of golf's most infamous Rules situations involved T.C. Chen at the 1985 U.S. Open. This incident, which had a dramatic effect on the final results of the championship, is retold below.

RULE 14 INCIDENTS

No matter how insignificant the effect, a player must never accept physical assistance or protection from the elements. On a rainy day at the 1995 British Masters, Domingo Hospital's first putt on the 11th hole came to rest just a few inches from the hole. His caddie held an umbrella over Hospital's head as the two men walked to the hole for the tap-in.

The caddie did not, unfortunately, remove the umbrella before the slight stroke completing the hole was made. Consequently, Hospital was penalized two strokes under Rule 14. Had Hospital held the umbrella himself there would have been no penalty, as a player is always entitled to protect himself.

Rule 14 is also crystal clear in stating that there is a one-stroke penalty for striking a ball more than once in the course of a stroke. In nearly all cases, a player is completely aware when such misfortune finds him.

For the thick rough, short and right of Oakland Hills' 5th green during the 1985 U.S. Open, T.C. Chen encountered that unfortunate fluke in golf when one swing of the club strikes the ball more than once.

Chen's third shot left his ball about 10 feet off the right front of the green with an additional 10 feet of putting green to the hole. He was faced with a delicate pitch that needed enough clubhead speed to get the lofted club through the grass but not so much that the force imparted to the ball would cause it to run past the hole.

Practice swings left the necessary feeling in Chen's hands for gauging the grabbing effect of the grass. He addressed the ball and swung slowly but firmly. On the downswing, as the club approached the ball, the tall grass slowed the club. Chen firmly but gently pulled the club into the ball. It rebounded slowly off the decelerating clubface rising ahead of the clubface and into the air. As the club finished its path through the grass, the resistance it was encountering became less and the club was released.

However, the firm pulling action still left in Chen's swing gave the club added momentum as it left the grass. In a spurt of speed, the clubhead caught up with the slow-moving ball and collided with it a second time. As the ball ricocheted off the clubface, a spectator rose from his kneeling position, directly behind Chen, raising two fingers as an indication of what he had just witnessed.

As the lofted clubface was going up at the moment of the second impact, the ball was pushed a little higher in the air and slightly to Chen's left. It came to rest on the apron of the putting green about 10 feet from the hole.

Prior to the infraction, Chen led the championship by four strokes with 14 holes to play. Visibly shaken, he took three more to finish the par-4 hole with an eight. His hopes of winning the U.S. Open were dashed. He tied for second with Denis Watson and Dave Barr, just one shot behind Andy North.

Frequently asked questions

Q Am I permitted to use the following during a stipulated round?
   (a) a distance measuring device, for example, a range-finder or GPS;
   (b) a compass; or
   (c) a pair of binoculars?

A (a) No. Rule 14-3 provides that "during a stipulated round the player shall not use any artificial device or unusual equipment ... for the purpose of gauging or measuring distance or conditions which might affect his play". However, the Committee may, by Local Rule, permit the use of devices that measure distance only (i.e., the device may not be used to measure other conditions such as wind-speed or the slope of the ground).
   (b) No. Using a compass would be contrary to Rule 14-3.
   (c) Yes. Binoculars that have no range-finder attachments or markings are not artificial devices in terms of Rule 14-3.

Q Is the use of a golf ball warmer permitted during a round?

A No. Use of such a device would be a breach of Rule 14-3, the penalty for which is disqualification.

RULE **15** SUBSTITUTED BALL; WRONG BALL

DEFINITIONS

All defined terms are in *italics* and are listed alphabetically in the Definitions section – see pages 9–20.

15-1. GENERAL

A player must *hole* out with the ball played from the *teeing ground* unless the ball is *lost* or *out of bounds* or the player *substitutes* another ball, whether or not substitution is permitted (see Rule 15-2). If a player plays a *wrong ball*, see Rule 15-3.

See **incident** involving Rule 15-2 on page 80.

15-2. SUBSTITUTED BALL

A player may *substitute* a ball when proceeding under a *Rule* that permits the player to play, drop or place another ball in completing the play of a hole. The *substituted ball* becomes the *ball in play*.

If a player *substitutes* a ball when not permitted to do so under the *Rules*, that *substituted ball* is not a *wrong ball*; it becomes the *ball in play*. If the mistake is not corrected as provided in Rule 20-6 and the player makes a *stroke* at a wrongly *substituted ball*, **he loses the hole in match play or incurs a penalty of two strokes in stroke play under the applicable *Rule*** and, in stroke play, must play out the hole with the *substituted ball*.

Exception: If a player incurs a penalty for making a *stroke* from a wrong place, there is no additional penalty for substituting a ball when not permitted.

(Playing from wrong place – see Rule 20-7.)

PLAYING A SUBSTITUTED BALL

I lifted my ball from the putting green to clean it, but I have just noticed that I have played the other ball I had in my pocket.

Unfortunately, you have substituted a ball when not permitted to do so. It is now the ball in play and you incur a two-stroke penalty. If we had been playing a match you would have lost the hole.

PLAYING WRONG BALL IN STROKE PLAY

15-3. WRONG BALL
a. Match Play
If a player makes a *stroke* at a *wrong ball*, **he loses the hole**.

If the *wrong ball* belongs to another player, its owner must place a ball on the spot from which the *wrong ball* was first played.

If the player and opponent exchange balls during the play of a hole, the first to make a *stroke* at a *wrong ball*, **loses the hole**; when this cannot be determined, the hole must be played out with the balls exchanged.

Exception: There is no penalty if a player makes a *stroke* at a *wrong ball* that is moving in water in a *water hazard*. Any strokes made at a *wrong ball* moving in water in a *water hazard* do not count in the player's score. The player must correct his mistake by playing the correct ball or by proceeding under the *Rules*.

See **incident** involving Rule 15-3b on page 80.

b. Stroke Play
If a *competitor* makes a *stroke* or *strokes* at a *wrong ball*, **he incurs a penalty of two strokes**.

The *competitor* must correct his mistake by playing the correct ball or by proceeding under the *Rules*. If he fails to correct his mistake before making a *stroke* on the next *teeing ground*, or in the case of the last hole of the round, fails to declare his intention to correct his mistake before leaving the *putting green*, **he is disqualified**.

Strokes made by a *competitor* with a *wrong ball* do not count in his score. If the *wrong ball* belongs to another *competitor*, its owner must place a ball on the spot from which the *wrong ball* was first played.

Exception: There is no penalty if a *competitor* makes a *stroke* at a *wrong ball* that is moving in water in a *water hazard*. Any *strokes* made at a *wrong ball* moving in water in a *water hazard* do not count in the *competitor's* score.
(Lie of ball to be placed or replaced altered – see Rule 20-3b.)
(Spot not determinable – see Rule 20-3c.)

RULE 15 INCIDENTS

Nick Faldo managed to snatch disaster out of the jaws of failure after playing a wrong ball during the first round of the 1994 British Open at Turnberry's Ailsa Course.

Facing driving rain and strong winds as he came to the 17th tee two-over-par, Faldo pushed his drive to the right and did not see where the ball finished. Jim McGovern, playing with Faldo, did the same, although his appeared to go a bit farther and less far afield. Indeed, Faldo found a ball short of where McGovern was looking for his ball. Assuming it was his and failing to take the time to identify it as his, Faldo played what turned out to be a wrong ball.

After Faldo played, McGovern was notified that the other ball, presumably McGovern's, was in deep rough. This was confusing because McGovern believed his drive to have finished less off-line than Faldo's. When McGovern reached the "other ball", he saw that it was Faldo's

The mistake cost Faldo a two-stroke penalty and, as required under Rule 15-3b, he was required to play his own ball. His resulting score was 8 for the hole and 75 for the round. Three days later, he finished the championship tied for eighth.

Ian Poulter learned the hard way that once you have marked the position of and lifted your ball in play it is necessary to keep a firm grip on it.

At the 4th green during the final round of The Players Championship in 2004, Poulter lifted his ball, lost his grip on it, and then watched as it sank to the bottom of the adjacent lake. Facing a two-stroke penalty for having to substitute a ball when not permitted to do so under the Rules (Rule 15-2), Poulter looked for a way to retrieve his ball. Kam Bhambra, Poulter's fitness coach, was following the group and saw what had taken place. Bhambra stripped down to his boxer shorts, jumped into the water, and retrieved the ball.

"It was the first ball I found," Bhambra said. "I was a bit worried about alligators, but duty called." Poulter replaced the ball and completed the hole with a par. The two-stroke penalty that he did not incur would have dropped him 20 places on the leader board and cost him $20,000 in prize money.

Frequently asked question

Q May a player change golf balls during the play of a hole or a stipulated round? When the player is permitted to substitute another golf ball may he change to a ball of a different brand or type?

A Rules 15-1 and 15-2 explain that the player must complete play of the hole with the ball with which he began the hole unless he is proceeding under a Rule that permits him to substitute a ball. The player may change balls between the play of two holes as well.

Rules 26-1 (Water Hazard Rule), 27-1 (Ball Lost or Out of Bounds) and 28 (Ball Unplayable) are examples of Rules that permit the player to substitute another ball. Rule 5-3 permits a player to substitute another ball during the play of a hole when his original ball has become unfit for play during the play of that hole. Other Rules (e.g. Rule 18, Rule 24, and Rule 25-1) permit the player to substitute another ball only if the original ball is not immediately recoverable.

Note that Rule 16-1b, the Rule that allows the player to lift his ball from the putting green, does not permit the player to substitute another ball; this precludes the player from substituting a "putting ball."

When changing balls, the player is permitted to substitute a ball of another brand or type unless the Committee has adopted the One Ball Condition (see Appendix I; Part C; Section 1c). This optional condition (usually referred to as "The One Ball Rule") is generally adopted only in events that are limited to professional golfers or highly-skilled amateur golfers. Generally, this condition of competition is not adopted in club-level competitions.

THE PUTTING GREEN

 RULE **16**

THE PUTTING GREEN

DEFINITIONS

All defined terms are in *italics* and are listed alphabetically in the Definitions section – see pages 9–20.

16-1. GENERAL
a. Touching Line of Putt

The *line of putt* must not be touched except:

(i) the player may remove *loose impediments*, provided he does not press anything down;

(ii) the player may place the club in front of the ball when *addressing* it, provided he does not press anything down;

(iii) in measuring – Rule 18-6;

(iv) in lifting or replacing the ball – Rule 16-1b;

(v) in pressing down a ball-marker;

(vi) in repairing old *hole* plugs or ball marks on the *putting green* – Rule 16-1c; and

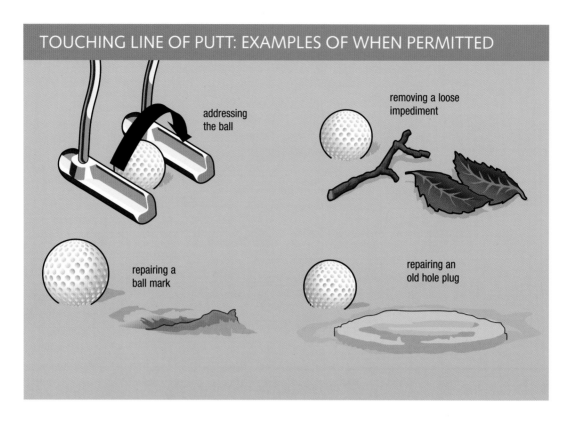

TOUCHING LINE OF PUTT: EXAMPLES OF WHEN PERMITTED

addressing the ball

removing a loose impediment

repairing a ball mark

repairing an old hole plug

(vii) in removing movable *obstructions* – Rule 24-1.
(Indicating line for putting on putting green – see Rule 8-2b.)

b. Lifting and Cleaning Ball

A ball on the *putting green* may be lifted and, if desired, cleaned. The position of the ball must be marked before it is lifted and the ball must be replaced (See Rule 20-1).

c. Repair of Hole Plugs, Ball Marks and Other Damage

The player may repair an old *hole* plug or damage to the *putting green* caused by the impact of a ball, whether or not the player's ball lies on the *putting green*. If a ball or ball-marker is accidentally *moved* in the process of the repair, the ball or ball-marker must be replaced. There is no penalty, provided the movement of the ball or ball-marker is directly attributable to the specific act of repairing an old *hole* plug or damage to the *putting green* caused by the impact of a ball. Otherwise, Rule 18 applies.

Any other damage to the *putting green* must not be repaired if it might assist the player in his subsequent play of the hole.

d. Testing Surface

During the *stipulated round*, a player must not test the surface of any *putting green* by rolling a ball or roughening or scraping the surface.

Exception: Between the play of two holes, a player may test the surface of any practice *putting green* and the *putting green* of the hole last played, unless the *Committee* has prohibited such action (see Note 2 to Rule 7-2).

CLEANING BALL AND REPAIRING DAMAGE

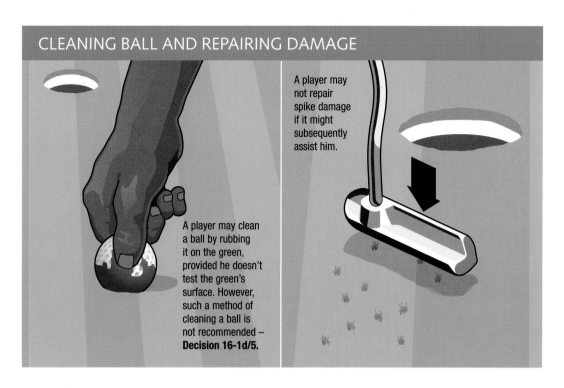

A player may clean a ball by rubbing it on the green, provided he doesn't test the green's surface. However, such a method of cleaning a ball is not recommended – **Decision 16-1d/5.**

A player may not repair spike damage if it might subsequently assist him.

STANDING ON THE LINE OF PUTT

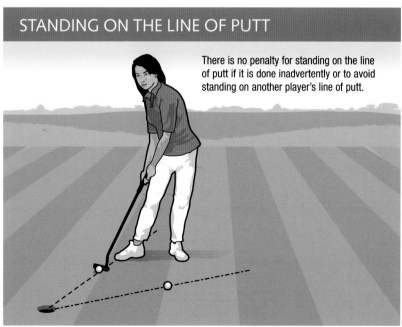

There is no penalty for standing on the line of putt if it is done inadvertently or to avoid standing on another player's line of putt.

e. Standing Astride or on Line of Putt

The player must not make a *stroke* on the *putting green* from a *stance* astride, or with either foot touching, the *line of putt* or an extension of that line behind the ball.

Exception: There is no penalty if the *stance* is taken inadvertently on or astride the *line of putt* (or an extension of that line behind the ball) or is taken to avoid standing on another player's *line of putt* or prospective *line of putt*.

83

f. Making Stroke While Another Ball in Motion

The player must not make a *stroke* while another ball is in motion after a *stroke* from the *putting green*, except that if a player does so, there is no penalty if it was his turn to play.

(Lifting ball assisting or interfering with play while another ball in motion – see Rule 22.)

PENALTY FOR BREACH OF RULE 16-1:
Match play – Loss of hole; Stroke play – Two strokes.

(Position of caddie or partner – see Rule 14-2.)
(Wrong putting green – see Rule 25-3.)

See **incident** involving Rule 16-2 on page 85.

16-2. BALL OVERHANGING HOLE

When any part of the ball overhangs the lip of the *hole*, the player is allowed enough time to reach the *hole* without unreasonable delay and an additional ten seconds to determine whether the ball is at rest. If by then the ball has not fallen into the *hole*, it is deemed to be at rest. If the ball subsequently falls into the *hole*, the player is deemed to have *holed* out with his last *stroke*, and **must add a *penalty stroke*** to his score for the hole; otherwise, there is no penalty under this Rule.

(Undue delay – see Rule 6-7.)

REMOVING LOOSE IMPEDIMENTS FROM LINE OF PUTT

BALL OVERHANGING HOLE

How long may I wait to see if my ball will fall into the hole?

There's no point in waiting more than 10 seconds. After that time the ball is deemed to be at rest and if it then falls in you have holed out with your last stroke, but you add a penalty stroke.

RULE 16 INCIDENTS

Television giveth, and television taketh away.

When a ball overhangs a hole, the player is permitted enough time to reach the hole without unreasonable delay and an additional ten seconds to determine whether the ball is at rest. Estimating those ten seconds is imprecise; videotape of such an event is exact, both of which Soren Hansen discovered at the 2000 Qatar Masters.

Hansen's ten-foot putt hung on the edge of the hole before ultimately dropping into it. Mathias Gronberg, a fellow-competitor in the same group, stated that he had been counting and 11 seconds had passed before the ball dropped. Therefore, it was reasoned, Hansen should add a penalty stroke to his score and the ball would be considered holed with his last stroke. However, Hansen was not so sure, and a Rules Official was summoned to make a ruling.

After the official listened to the accounts of various witnesses, he ruled that a penalty stroke was in order under Rule 16-2. After leaving the scene and returning to the tournament office, it occurred to the official that there might be television videotape of the incident. There was and, fortunately, it showed that only eight seconds elapsed before the ball fell into the hole. Hansen was exonerated and the penalty rescinded.

Meg Mallon, on the other hand, tarried in circumstances similar to Hansen's. While leading during the second round of the 1996 Jami Farr Classic, Mallon's birdie putt on the 17th hole stopped just short of going in.

Video of the incident shows Mallon taking perhaps a bit too long to reach her putt and then waiting more than 20 seconds before watching it fall into the hole. Believing that her ball was properly holed, Mallon did not include the penalty stroke she had incurred and then returned a score for the hole that was lower than she had actually taken. She was subsequently disqualified under Rule 6-6d.

Frequently asked questions

Q A player reaches across the hole to tap in a short putt (the hole is between the player and the ball). Is this a breach of Rule 16-1e, Standing Astride or on the Line of Putt?

A No. The line of putt does not extend beyond the hole. There is no penalty for making a stroke in this manner, provided the ball is fairly struck at and not raked into the hole. (Definition of "Line of Putt" and Rule 16-1e).

Q Our group reaches the putting green, and we noticed the hole is damaged. What should we do?

A If the damage is a ball mark, you may repair it. (Rule 16-1c). However, if the damage is something other than the ball mark, the answer depends on the extent of the damage. A hole that is damaged, but the dimensions of the hole have not been materially changed, must not be touched, and you must continue play of the hole. If the hole is damaged materially, a member of the Committee should be requested to repair the damage. In this case, you may only repair the hole if a Committee member is not readily available. Repairing the hole when not permitted will result in a breach of Rule 16-1a for touching the line of putt.

RULE **17**

THE FLAGSTICK

DEFINITIONS

All defined terms are in *italics* and are listed alphabetically in the Definitions section – see pages 9–20.

17-1. FLAGSTICK ATTENDED, REMOVED OR HELD UP

Before making a *stroke* from anywhere on the *course*, the player may have the *flagstick* attended, removed or held up to indicate the position of the *hole*.

If the *flagstick* is not attended, removed or held up before the player makes a *stroke*, it must not be attended, removed or held up during the *stroke* or while the player's ball is in motion if doing so might influence the movement of the ball.

Note 1: If the *flagstick* is in the *hole* and anyone stands near it while a *stroke* is being made, he is deemed to be attending the *flagstick*.

Note 2: If, prior to the *stroke*, the *flagstick* is attended, removed or held up by anyone with the player's knowledge and he makes no objection, the player is deemed to have authorized it.

Note 3: If anyone attends or holds up the *flagstick* while a *stroke* is being made, he is deemed to be attending the *flagstick* until the ball comes to rest.

See **incident** involving Rule 17-2 on pages 89–90.

17-2. UNAUTHORIZED ATTENDANCE
If an opponent or his *caddie* in match play or a *fellow-competitor* or his *caddie* in stroke play, without the player's authority or prior knowledge, attends, removes or holds up the *flagstick* during the *stroke* or while the ball is in motion, and the act might influence the movement of the ball, the opponent or *fellow-competitor* incurs the applicable penalty.

*PENALTY FOR BREACH OF RULE 17-1 or 17-2:
Match play – Loss of hole; Stroke play – Two strokes.
*In stroke play, if a breach of Rule 17-2 occurs and the *competitor's* ball subsequently strikes the *flagstick*, the person attending or holding it or anything carried by him, the *competitor* incurs no penalty. The ball is played as it lies, except that if the *stroke* was made on the *putting green*, the *stroke* is canceled and the ball must be replaced and replayed.

17-3. BALL STRIKING FLAGSTICK OR ATTENDANT

The player's ball must not strike:

a. The *flagstick* when it is attended, removed or held up;

b. The person attending or holding up the *flagstick* or anything carried by him;

c. The *flagstick* in the *hole*, unattended, when the *stroke* has been made on the *putting green*.

Exception: When the *flagstick* is attended, removed or held up without the player's authority – see Rule 17-2.

> **PENALTY FOR BREACH OF RULE 17-3:**
> **Match play – Loss of hole;**
> **Stroke play – Two strokes and the ball must be played as it lies.**

17-4. BALL RESTING AGAINST FLAGSTICK

When a player's ball rests against the *flagstick* in the *hole* and the ball is not *holed*, the player or another person authorized by him may move or remove the *flagstick*, and if the ball falls into the *hole*, the player is deemed to have *holed* out with his last *stroke*; otherwise, the ball, if *moved*, must be placed on the lip of the *hole*, without penalty.

See **incident** involving Rule 17-3a on pages 90–91.

BALL STRIKES FLAGSTICK LYING ON GREEN IN MATCH PLAY

No. I'm afraid I've just lost the hole for hitting the flagstick.

That's a lucky break. Otherwise, your putt for a half would have been much longer.

RULE 17 INCIDENTS

No good deed goes unpunished, or at least no deed intended to be good. Philanthropy has no status under Rule 1-2, even when the flagstick is involved.

At the 2007 Arnold Palmer Invitational, Boo Weekly hoped to come to the aid of his fellow-competitor and it cost him a two-stroke penalty.

Weekly and Tom Johnson were playing the par-3 second hole at Bay Hill. Johnson's ball was on the right-hand side of the putting green about 85 feet from the back, left hole location. Because of the steep slope of the green, he chose to chip his ball from the putting surface to the fringe in hope of it being slowed by the longer grass and then trickling down toward the hole.

Although playing from the putting green, he did not, however, ask that the flagstick be attended. Perhaps because he was chipping to a point off the green, he forgot that he would incur a two-stroke penalty if his ball subsequently struck the unattended flagstick in the hole after he made his stroke from the putting green.

Johnson's chip was well played and, as it made its way to the hole, Weekly came to the realization that if the ball struck the flagstick Johnson would be penalized. Wishing to come to the aid of his fellow-competitor, Weekly raced to the hole and removed the flagstick.

In his heart, Weekly's action had been taken to prevent a possible violation by Johnson. However, under the Rules, Weekly's action was an attempt to influence the position or movement of the ball, which was not in accordance with the Rules (Rules 1-2 and 17-2).

Once Johnson played his ball, the resulting situation and any of its ramifications were his reward and his responsibility, and his alone. Weekly's attempt to change that situation violated that basic premise of the game.

Before Johnson played, he could have asked that the flagstick be attended; or Weekly could have asked if Johnson wanted him to attend it. But once Johnson's stroke was played, the die was cast.

The Rules Official who made the ruling, Mark Russell, commented, "I've never heard of that [happening] in my 27 years in golf."

Boo Weekly said, "I learned another Rule in the game of golf."

There are fourteen double putting greens at St. Andrews' Old Course that often result in situations where a player is playing a pitch shot from one side of the green to a hole location some distance away but on the same green. An awareness of Rule 17 is particularly important in such circumstances.

During the 1995 British Open, Peter Fowler of Australia found himself on the front edge of the 2nd green with the hole having been cut in the back left corner beyond the huge humps and swales that are a feature of that green. He asked the Rules Official if he was permitted to play his stroke from the green with a wedge which, of course, the Rules permit. He pitched to within three feet of the hole.

Corey Pavin, who was playing the 16th hole, which shares a putting surface with the 2nd, congratulated Fowler on his inspired pitch but warned, "Next time have the flag attended. It's a two-stroke penalty if you hit the stick."

As these incidents illustrate, golf sometimes requires imagination in formulating how best to get to the hole. At Pebble Beach's par-3 17th hole, Miguel Angel Jimenez found himself in such a situation during the 100th U.S. Open.

When H. Chandler Egan made design changes to the course prior to the 1929 U.S. Amateur Championship, one of those changes included redesigning the 17th green into the shape of an hourglass divided by a diagonal ridge. The effect was to create a double green. Hence when the hole is cut at point B [see illustration], it is difficult for a ball played from point A to get close to the hole. This was Jimenez's dilemma in 2000.

The pinched, hourglass shape brought the rough into the line of putt necessary for him to get close to the hole. Like Tom Johnson and Peter Fowler in the incidents above, Jimenez chose to play a pitch shot from

The shape and contours of the 17th green at Pebble Beach Golf Links resulted in an unusual sight at the 2000 U.S. Open. For the details of this incident involving eventual runner-up Michael Angel Jimenez, see incident on pages 90–91.

the green, over the rough and the ridge, to the hole on the other side of the same green.

Jimenez was, however, aware of the Rule regarding the flagstick and wisely sought confirmation from the Rule Official walking with his group. In order to avoid an infraction that could be caused by his ball striking the flagstick, he directed his caddie to attend the flagstick.

Rule 17-3a also states that an infraction occurs if a ball strikes an attended flagstick regardless of from where the shot is played. The penalty in stroke play is two strokes. Therefore, Jimenez's caddie was further directed to remove the flagstick if it looked as though the ball might strike it or go into the hole.

Playing a delicate pitch, Jimenez took a small divot. His ball landed on the down slope of the ridge and ran to about 10 feet from the hole. Two putts were taken for bogey.

Frequently asked questions

Q May the player have the flagstick attended even if his ball is not on the putting green?

A Yes. Rule 17-1 states that, before making a stroke from anywhere on the course, the player may have the flagstick attended, removed or held up.

Q May a player putt with one hand while holding the flagstick with the other?

A Yes, provided the flagstick has been removed from the hole and the ball therefore does not strike it. If the ball were to strike the flagstick, a breach of Rule 17-3a would occur. The player must not lean on the flagstick in order to steady himself while he putts, as that would be contrary to Rule 14-3, resulting in a penalty of disqualification.

BALL MOVED, DEFLECTED OR STOPPED

RULE

BALL AT REST MOVED

DEFINITIONS

All defined terms are in *italics* and are listed alphabetically in the Definitions section – see pages 9–20.

See **incident** involving Rule 18-1 on page 95.

18-1. BY OUTSIDE AGENCY

If a ball at rest is *moved* by an *outside agency*, there is no penalty and the ball must be replaced.

Note: It is a question of fact whether a ball has been *moved* by an *outside agency*. In order to apply this Rule, it must be known or virtually certain that an *outside agency* has *moved* the ball. In the absence of such knowledge or certainty, the player must play the ball as it lies or, if the ball is not found, proceed under Rule 27-1.
(Player's ball at rest moved by another ball – see Rule 18-5.)

See **incident** involving Rule 18-2 on page 95.

18-2. BY PLAYER, PARTNER, CADDIE OR EQUIPMENT
a. General

When a player's ball is *in play*, if:
(i) the player, his *partner* or either of their *caddies* lifts or *moves* it, touches it purposely (except with a club in the act of *addressing* it) or causes it to *move* except as permitted by a *Rule*, or
(ii) *equipment* of the player or his *partner* causes the ball to *move*,
the player incurs a penalty of one stroke. If the ball is moved, it must be replaced, unless the movement of the ball occurs after the player has begun the *stroke* or the backward movement of the club for the *stroke* and the *stroke* is made.
Under the *Rules* there is no penalty if a player accidentally causes his ball to *move* in the following circumstances:
• In searching for a ball in a *hazard* covered by *loose impediments* or sand, for a ball in an *obstruction* or *abnormal ground condition* or for a ball believed to be in water in a *water hazard* – Rule 12-1
• In repairing a *hole* plug or ball mark – Rule 16-1c
• In measuring – Rule 18-6
• In lifting a ball under a *Rule* – Rule 20-1
• In placing or replacing a ball under a *Rule* – Rule 20-3a
• In removing a *loose impediment* on the *putting green* – Rule 23-1
• In removing movable *obstructions* – Rule 24-1.

b. Ball Moving After Address

If a player's *ball in play moves* after he has *addressed* it (other than as a result of a *stroke*), the player is deemed to have *moved* the ball and **incurs a penalty of one stroke**. The ball must be replaced, unless the movement of the ball occurs after the player has begun the *stroke* or the backward movement of the club for the *stroke* and the *stroke* is made.

BALL AT REST MOVED

By Outside Agency – no penalty and replace ball (Rule 18-1).

By Player, Partner, Caddie or Equipment – one stroke penalty and replace ball (Rule 18-2a).

After Address – one stroke penalty and replace ball (Rule 18-2b).

By Opponent, Caddie or Equipment Not During Search – opponent incurs one stroke penalty and replace ball (Rule 18-3b).

By Opponent, Caddie or Equipment During Search – no penalty and replace ball (Rule 18-3a).

By Another Ball – replace moved ball (Rule 18-5).

By Fellow-Competitor, Caddie or Equipment – no penalty and replace ball (Rule18-4).

In Measuring – no penalty and replace ball (Rule 18-6).

93

18-3. BY OPPONENT, CADDIE OR EQUIPMENT IN MATCH PLAY

a. During Search

If, during search for a player's ball, an opponent, his *caddie* or his *equipment moves* the ball, touches it or causes it to *move*, there is no penalty. If the ball is *moved*, it must be replaced.

b. Other Than During Search

If, other than during search for a player's ball, an opponent, his *caddie* or his *equipment moves* the ball, touches it purposely or causes it to *move*, except as otherwise provided in the *Rules*, **the opponent incurs a penalty of one stroke**. If the ball is *moved*, it must be replaced.

(Playing a wrong ball – see Rule 15-3.)

(Ball moved in measuring – see Rule 18-6.)

18-4. BY FELLOW-COMPETITOR, CADDIE OR EQUIPMENT IN STROKE PLAY

If a *fellow-competitor*, his *caddie* or his *equipment moves* the player's ball, touches it or causes it to *move*, there is no penalty. If the ball is *moved*, it must be replaced.

(Playing a wrong ball – see Rule 15-3.)

18-5. BY ANOTHER BALL

If a *ball in play* and at rest is *moved* by another ball in motion after a *stroke*, the *moved* ball must be replaced.

18-6. BALL MOVED IN MEASURING

If a ball or ball-marker is *moved* in measuring while proceeding under or in determining the application of a *Rule*, the ball or ball-marker must be replaced. There is no penalty, provided the movement of the ball or ball-marker is directly attributable to the specific act of measuring. Otherwise, the provisions of Rules 18-2a, 18-3b or 18-4 apply.

> *PENALTY FOR BREACH OF RULE:
> Match play – Loss of hole; Stroke play – Two strokes.
> *If a player who is required to replace a ball fails to do so, or if he makes a *stroke* at a ball *substituted* under Rule 18 when such *substitution* is not permitted, he incurs the general penalty for breach of Rule 18, but there is no additional penalty under this Rule.

Note 1: If a ball to be replaced under this Rule is not immediately recoverable, another ball may be *substituted*.

Note 2: If the original lie of a ball to be placed or replaced has been altered, see Rule 20-3b.

Note 3: If it is impossible to determine the spot on which a ball is to be placed, see Rule 20-3c.

RULE 18 INCIDENTS

Widely regarded as one of the most famous examples of sportsmanship in golf, a first round Rule 18 infraction, called on himself, ultimately cost Bob Jones the 1925 U.S. Open Championship

At Worcester C.C. in Massachusetts, Jones saw his ball move after he addressed it on a steep bank at the 11th hole. He added a penalty stroke to his score for the hole and carried on.

Later, praised for his honesty, Jones replied, "You just might as well praise me for not breaking into banks. There is only one way to play this game."

Jones began the final round in a tie for fourth place and, by the end of the day, was able to force a 36-hole play-off with Willie Macfarlane. The following day, Jones (75-73) lost to Macfarlane (75-72) by one stroke.

A ball moved by an outside agency is another matter. At the 1998 Players Championship, a seagull flew off with Steve Lowery's ball that was at rest on the putting green of the 17th hole. Lowery had safely played his tee shot onto the island green of the par-3 hole. As Lowery's group walked to the green, a seagull landed on the green and began pushing Lowery's ball toward the water hazard with its beak. Upon reaching the edge of the water hazard, the bird was able to lift the ball with its beak and fly off over the water. The ball proved too heavy for the bird and was ultimately dropped from about 30 feet in the air into the water below.

Under Rule 18-1, Lowery was entitled, without penalty, to replace his ball on the spot from which the seagull had moved it. Because his original ball was at the bottom of the lake, Lowery was entitled to substitute another ball.

If a player's ball at rest is moved by another ball in motion after a stroke, the ball that was moved must be replaced. An approach played by Mhairi McKay during the third round of the 2003 U.S. Women's Open flew into a greenside bunker where it struck and moved the ball of her fellow-competitor, Hilary Lunke.

The two balls' tracks in the sand were clearly discernible and were used to determine the spot on which Lunke's ball was to be replaced. Failure to replace the ball would have resulted in a two-stroke penalty. Under the Rule, the ball in motion, McKay's ball in this incident, must be played from where it finishes.

Frequently asked question

Q While making a practice swing, the ball in play is accidentally moved by the club. What is the ruling?

A The player incurs a one stroke penalty, and must replace the ball to its original position. If she fails to replace the ball, she will incur a total penalty of loss of hole in match play or two strokes in stroke play. Please refer to the Penalty Statement under Rule 18. (Rule 18-2a and Decision 18-2a/20)

RULE **19** BALL IN MOTION DEFLECTED OR STOPPED

DEFINITIONS

All defined terms are in *italics* and are listed alphabetically in the Definitions section – see pages 9–20.

See **incident** involving Rule 19-1 on pages 98–99.

19-1. BY OUTSIDE AGENCY

If a player's ball in motion is accidentally deflected or stopped by any *outside agency*, it is a *rub of the green*, there is no penalty and the ball must be played as it lies, except:

a. If a player's ball in motion after a *stroke* other than on the *putting green* comes to rest in or on any moving or animate *outside agency*, the ball must, *through the green* or in a *hazard*, be dropped, or on the *putting green* be placed, as near as possible to the spot directly under the place where the ball came to rest in or on the *outside agency*, but not nearer the *hole*, and

b. If a player's ball in motion after a *stroke* on the *putting green* is deflected or stopped by, or comes to rest in or on, any moving or animate *outside agency*, except a worm, insect or the like, the *stroke* is canceled. The ball must be replaced and replayed.

If the ball is not immediately recoverable, another ball may be *substituted*.

Exception: Ball striking person attending or holding up *flagstick* or anything carried by him – see Rule 17-3b.

Note: If the *referee* or the *Committee* determines that a player's ball has been purposely deflected or stopped by an *outside agency*, Rule 1-4 applies to the player. If the *outside agency* is a *fellow-competitor* or his *caddie*, Rule 1-2 applies to the *fellow-competitor*.
(Player's ball deflected or stopped by another ball – see Rule 19-5.)

See **incident** involving Rule 19-2 on pages 99–100.

19-2. BY PLAYER, PARTNER, CADDIE OR EQUIPMENT

If a player's ball is accidentally deflected or stopped by himself, his *partner* or either of their *caddies* or *equipment*, **the player incurs a penalty of one stroke.** The ball must be played as it lies, except when it comes to rest in or on the player's, his *partner's* or either of their *caddies'* clothes or *equipment*, in which case the ball must *through the green* or in a *hazard* be dropped, or on the *putting green* be placed, as near as possible to the spot directly under the place where the ball came to rest in or on the article, but not nearer the *hole*.

Exception 1: Ball striking person attending or holding up a *flagstick* or anything carried by him – see Rule 17-3b.

Exception 2: Dropped ball – see Rule 20-2a.
(Ball purposely deflected or stopped by player, partner or caddie – see Rule 1-2.)

BALL IN MOTION DEFLECTED OR STOPPED

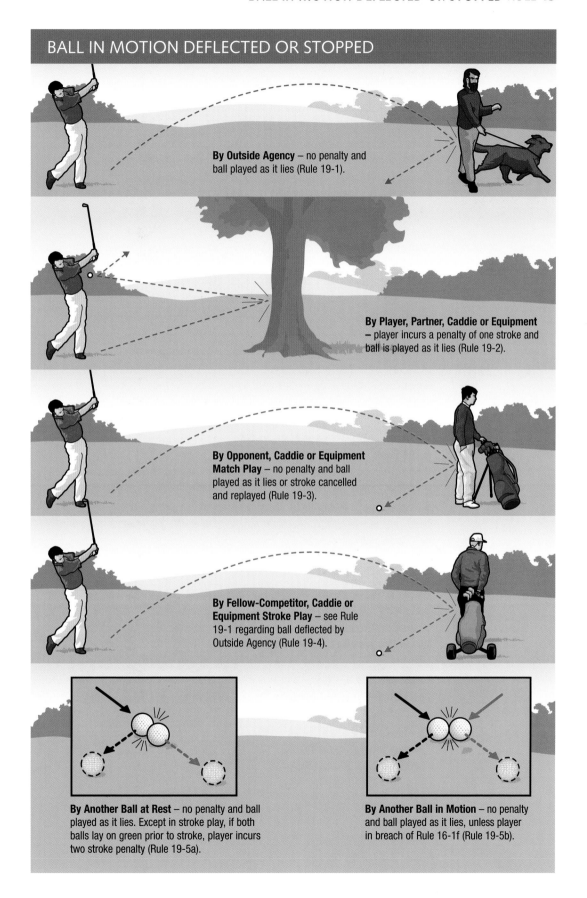

By Outside Agency – no penalty and ball played as it lies (Rule 19-1).

By Player, Partner, Caddie or Equipment – player incurs a penalty of one stroke and ball is played as it lies (Rule 19-2).

By Opponent, Caddie or Equipment Match Play – no penalty and ball played as it lies or stroke cancelled and replayed (Rule 19-3).

By Fellow-Competitor, Caddie or Equipment Stroke Play – see Rule 19-1 regarding ball deflected by Outside Agency (Rule 19-4).

By Another Ball at Rest – no penalty and ball played as it lies. Except in stroke play, if both balls lay on green prior to stroke, player incurs two stroke penalty (Rule 19-5a).

By Another Ball in Motion – no penalty and ball played as it lies, unless player in breach of Rule 16-1f (Rule 19-5b).

19-3. BY OPPONENT, CADDIE OR EQUIPMENT IN MATCH PLAY

If a player's ball is accidentally deflected or stopped by an opponent, his *caddie* or his *equipment*, there is no penalty. The player may, before another *stroke* is made by either *side*, cancel the *stroke* and play a ball, without penalty, as nearly as possible at the spot from which the original ball was last played (see Rule 20-5) or he may play the ball as it lies. However, if the player elects not to cancel the *stroke* and the ball has come to rest in or on the opponent's or his *caddie's* clothes or *equipment*, the ball must *through the green* or in a *hazard* be dropped, or on the *putting green* be placed, as near as possible to the spot directly under the place where the ball came to rest in or on the article, but not nearer the *hole*.

Exception: Ball striking person attending or holding up *flagstick* or anything carried by him – see Rule 17-3b.
(Ball purposely deflected or stopped by opponent or caddie – see Rule 1-2.)

19-4. BY FELLOW-COMPETITOR, CADDIE OR EQUIPMENT IN STROKE PLAY

See Rule 19-1 regarding ball deflected by *outside agency*.

Exception: Ball striking person attending or holding up *flagstick* or anything carried by him – see Rule 17-3b.

19-5. BY ANOTHER BALL
a. At Rest

If a player's ball in motion after a *stroke* is deflected or stopped by a *ball in play* and at rest, the player must play his ball as it lies. In match play, there is no penalty. In stroke play, there is no penalty, unless both balls lay on the *putting green* prior to the *stroke*, in which case **the player incurs a penalty of two strokes**.

b. In Motion

If a player's ball in motion after a *stroke* is deflected or stopped by another ball in motion after a *stroke*, the player must play his ball as it lies. There is no penalty, unless the player was in breach of Rule 16-1f, in which case **he incurs the penalty for breach of that Rule**.

Exception: If the player's ball is in motion after a *stroke* on the *putting green* and the other ball in motion is an *outside agency* – see Rule 19-1b.

PENALTY FOR BREACH OF RULE:
Match play – Loss of hole;
Stroke play – Two strokes.

RULE 19 INCIDENTS

When a **ball** in motion is deflected or stopped, the consequences under the Rules vary depending on who or what interfered. Sometimes it is a

If a player accidentally deflects his own ball, as Jeff Maggert did at the 2003 Masters, the player incurs a one-stroke penalty.

rub of the green, sometimes a penalty is involved, and sometimes it must be estimated where the ball would have ended up, had it not been deflected or stopped, so it can be put into play at that spot.

Sergio Garcia's drive at Pebble Beach's 4th hole struck and killed a seagull during the second round of the 100th U.S. Open in 2000.

The bird swooped down into the ball's path just 20 yards from the teeing ground. Moving at such a high velocity, the ball killed the bird and somehow continued on its decelerated way until it struck the top of the out of bounds fence that shelters the beach club car park to the right of the hole. One bounce atop the picket fence and the ball rebounded back onto the course, where it settled in the rough.

Garcia was distraught at the bird's misfortune as well as the bizarre rub of the green. In such a situation, no penalty is incurred, and the ball must be played as it lies. At first, many of the assembled spectators thought the ruling was unfair and that Garcia would be justified in replaying his drive. Their concerns were assuaged when it was pointed out that had Garcia's ball been deflected into the hole, the result would have been a hole in one.

At the 2003 Masters Tournament, Jeff Maggert accidentally deflected his own ball in an attempt to play from the fairway bunker at the 3rd hole.

Maggert was playing in the final group on the final day when his drive at the par-4 finished in one of four bunkers at the left of the landing zone. The ball was far enough behind the forward lip of the bunker so that he judged that he could play a full approach to the putting green. However, once struck, the ball smashed into the lip, ricocheted backwards, and hit him. The Rules Official stationed on that hole informed Maggert that a two-stroke penalty had been incurred and the ball had to be played as it lies (Rule 19-2b).

For 2008, a change to Rule 19 reduces the penalty to one stroke in such an instance.

Brett Ogle suffered a similar but more painful fate when he was both injured and penalized by deflecting his ball during the 1990 Australian Open.

Two shots off the lead with two holes left to play, Ogle attempted to play his second shot at the 17th around a tree that was immediately in front of where his ball lay. After leaving the face of his 2-iron, the ball struck the tree, rebounded backwards and struck Ogle on the knee. A two-stroke penalty was levied under Rule 19-2b, and Ogle lay on the ground as ice was applied to his injured leg. After being allowed time to recover, as permitted under Decision 6-8a/3, Ogle limped down the two closing holes using his driver as a walking stick and followed by a team of helpers carrying bandages and ice packs behind him.

He finished the 17th hole with a score of nine, including the two penalty strokes, the ricochet having cost him the chance of becoming the Australian Open Champion. Beginning in 2008, the penalty for Ogle's deflection is one stroke.

When an outside agency purposefully deflects or stops a player's ball, equity (Rule 1-4) authorizes the Committee to make a judgment as to where the ball would have come to rest had it not been deflected or stopped, giving the player the benefit of the doubt. The player is then required to drop the ball on that spot.

Before such a procedure is authorized, however, it must be determined if the ball was purposefully deflected or stopped, or if the action was accidental.

Tiger woods found himself in such a situation during second round play of the 1st hole at the 2006 PGA Championship. Wood's drive went left towards the gallery lining the fairway. It bounced near a fairway bunker, was deflected by spectator, and came to rest near the rope line restricting the gallery.

A Rules Official in the area immediately asked for information from spectators and marshals who were present, including whether the ball was purposefully or accidentally deflected. No one was of the opinion that the ball had been purposefully deflected and, therefore, it was played as it lies.

Frequently asked question

Q What is the ruling when a ball in motion is deflected or stopped by a golf cart that is shared by two players?

A Under the Definition of "Equipment," equipment includes a golf cart, whether or not motorized. If two players share a golf cart, the cart and everything in it are deemed to be the equipment of the player whose ball is involved; except that, when the cart is being moved by one of the players, the cart and everything in it are deemed to be that player's equipment.

Thus, for example, in a singles match, if A and B are sharing a cart and A's ball in motion is deflected or stopped by the cart, A incurs a penalty of one stroke (Rule 19-2) unless the cart is being driven or pulled by B when the incident occurs. If B is driving or pulling the cart, there is no penalty, and A would have the option of playing his ball as it lies or replaying the stroke (Rule 19-3).

RULE **20** LIFTING, DROPPING AND PLACING; PLAYING FROM WRONG PLACE

DEFINITIONS

All defined terms are in *italics* and are listed alphabetically in the Definitions section – see pages 9–20.

See **incident** involving Rule 20-1 on pages 109–110.

20-1. LIFTING AND MARKING

A ball to be lifted under the *Rules* may be lifted by the player, his *partner* or another person authorized by the player. In any such case, the player is responsible for any breach of the *Rules*.

The position of the ball must be marked before it is lifted under a *Rule* that requires it to be replaced. If it is not marked, **the player incurs a penalty of one stroke** and the ball must be replaced. If it is not replaced, **the player incurs the general penalty for breach of this Rule**, but there is no additional penalty under Rule 20-1.

If a ball or ball-marker is accidentally *moved* in the process of lifting the ball under a *Rule* or marking its position, the ball or ball-marker must be replaced. There is no penalty, provided the movement of the ball or ball-marker is directly attributable to the specific act of marking the position of or lifting the ball. Otherwise, **the player incurs a penalty of one stroke under this Rule or Rule 18-2a**.

PROCEDURE FOR LIFTING BALL

Although I want your ball lifted because it is interfering with my play, why are you marking it?

Because when a ball is lifted anywhere on the course and has to be replaced, its position must be marked.

Exception: If a player incurs a penalty for failing to act in accordance with Rule 5-3 or 12-2, there is no additional penalty under Rule 20-1.

Note: The position of a ball to be lifted should be marked by placing a ball-marker, a small coin or other similar object immediately behind the ball. If the ball-marker interferes with the play, *stance* or *stroke* of another player, it should be placed one or more clubhead-lengths to one side.

20-2. DROPPING AND RE-DROPPING
a. By Whom and How
A ball to be dropped under the *Rules* must be dropped by the player himself. He must stand erect, hold the ball at shoulder height and arm's length and drop it. If a ball is dropped by any other person or in any other manner and the error is not corrected as provided in Rule 20-6, **the player incurs a penalty of one stroke**.

If the ball, when dropped, touches any person or the *equipment* of any player before or after it strikes a part of the *course* and before it comes to rest, the ball must be re-dropped, without penalty. There is no limit to the number of times a ball must be re-dropped in these circumstances.
(Taking action to influence position or movement of ball – see Rule 1-2.)

See **incident** involving Rule 20-2b on pages 108–09.

b. Where to Drop
When a ball is to be dropped as near as possible to a specific spot, it must be dropped not nearer the *hole* than the specific spot which, if it is not precisely known to the player, must be estimated.

A ball when dropped must first strike a part of the *course* where the applicable *Rule* requires it to be dropped. If it is not so dropped, Rules 20-6 and 20-7 apply.

c. When to Re-Drop
A dropped ball must be re-dropped, without penalty, if it:
(i)   rolls into and comes to rest in a *hazard*;
(ii) rolls out of and comes to rest outside a *hazard*;
(iii) rolls onto and comes to rest on a *putting green*;
(iv) rolls and comes to rest *out of bounds*;
(v)   rolls to and comes to rest in a position where there is interference by the condition from which relief was taken under Rule 24-2b (immovable obstruction), Rule 25-1 (abnormal ground conditions), Rule 25-3 (wrong putting green) or a Local Rule (Rule 33-8a), or rolls back into the pitch-mark from which it was lifted under Rule 25-2 (embedded ball);
(vi) rolls and comes to rest more than two club-lengths from where it first struck a part of the *course*; or
(vii) rolls and comes to rest nearer the *hole* than:
    (a) its original position or estimated position (see Rule 20-2b) unless otherwise permitted by the *Rules*; or
    (b) the *nearest point of relief* or maximum available relief (Rule 24-2, 25-1 or 25-3); or
    (c) the point where the original ball last crossed the margin of the *water hazard* or *lateral water hazard* (Rule 26-1).

WHEN TO RE-DROP BALL

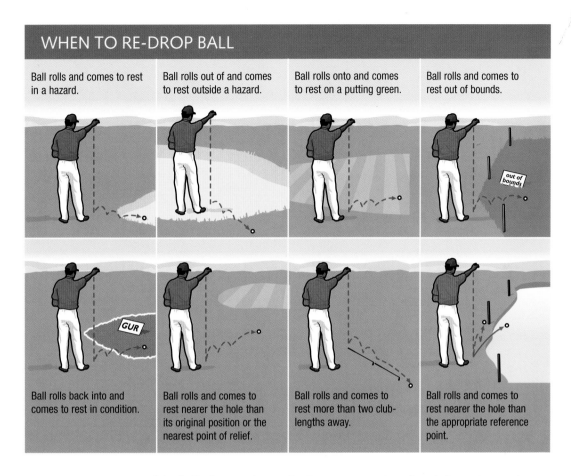

Ball rolls and comes to rest in a hazard.

Ball rolls out of and comes to rest outside a hazard.

Ball rolls onto and comes to rest on a putting green.

Ball rolls and comes to rest out of bounds.

Ball rolls back into and comes to rest in condition.

Ball rolls and comes to rest nearer the hole than its original position or the nearest point of relief.

Ball rolls and comes to rest more than two club-lengths away.

Ball rolls and comes to rest nearer the hole than the appropriate reference point.

If the ball when re-dropped rolls into any position listed above, it must be placed as near as possible to the spot where it first struck a part of the *course* when re-dropped.

Note 1: If a ball when dropped or re-dropped comes to rest and subsequently *moves*, the ball must be played as it lies, unless the provisions of any other *Rule* apply.

Note 2: If a ball to be re-dropped or placed under this Rule is not immediately recoverable, another ball may be *substituted*.
(Use of Dropping Zone – see Appendix I; Part B; Section 8.)

20-3. PLACING AND REPLACING
a. By Whom and Where
A ball to be placed under the *Rules* must be placed by the player or his *partner*. If a ball is to be replaced, the player, his *partner* or the person who lifted or *moved* it must place it on the spot from which it was lifted or *moved*. If the ball is placed or replaced by any other person and the error is not corrected as provided in Rule 20-6, **the player incurs a penalty of one stroke**. In any such case, the player is responsible for any breach of the *Rules* that occurs as a result of the placing or replacing of the ball.

If a ball or ball-marker is accidentally *moved* in the process of placing or replacing the ball, the ball or ball-marker must be replaced. There is no

penalty provided the movement of the ball or ball-marker is directly attributable to the specific act of placing or replacing the ball or removing the ball-marker. Otherwise, **the player incurs a penalty of one stroke under Rule 18-2a or 20-1.**

If a ball to be replaced is placed other than on the spot from which it was lifted or *moved* and the error is not corrected as provided in Rule 20-6, **the player incurs the general penalty, loss of hole in match play or two strokes in stroke play, for a breach of the applicable *Rule*.**

b. Lie of Ball to Be Placed or Replaced Altered

If the original lie of a ball to be placed or replaced has been altered:

(i)   except in a *hazard*, the ball must be placed in the nearest lie most similar to the original lie that is not more than one club-length from the original lie, not nearer the *hole* and not in a *hazard*;

(ii) in a *water hazard*, the ball must be placed in accordance with Clause (i) above, except that the ball must be placed in the *water hazard*;

(iii) in a *bunker*, the original lie must be re-created as nearly as possible and the ball must be placed in that lie.

c. Spot Not Determinable

If it is impossible to determine the spot where the ball is to be placed or replaced:

(i)   *through the green*, the ball must be dropped as near as possible to the place where it lay but not in a *hazard* or on a *putting green*;

(ii) in a *hazard*, the ball must be dropped in the *hazard* as near as possible to the place where it lay;

(iii) on the *putting green*, the ball must be placed as near as possible to the place where it lay but not in a *hazard*.

Exception: When resuming play (Rule 6-8d), if the spot where the ball is to be placed is impossible to determine, it must be estimated and the ball placed on the estimated spot.

d. Ball Fails to Come to Rest on Spot

If a ball when placed fails to come to rest on the spot on which it was placed, there is no penalty and the ball must be replaced. If it still fails to come to rest on that spot:

(i)   except in a *hazard*, it must be placed at the nearest spot where it can be placed at rest that is not nearer the *hole* and not in a *hazard*;

(ii) in a *hazard*, it must be placed in the *hazard* at the nearest spot where it can be placed at rest that is not nearer the *hole*.

If a ball when placed comes to rest on the spot on which it is placed, and it subsequently *moves*, there is no penalty and the ball must be played as it lies, unless the provisions of any other *Rule* apply.

> **PENALTY FOR BREACH OF RULE 20-1, 20-2 or 20-3:**
> **Match play – Loss of hole; Stroke play – Two strokes.**

20-4. WHEN BALL DROPPED OR PLACED IS IN PLAY

If the player's *ball in play* has been lifted, it is again in play when dropped or placed.

A *substituted ball* becomes the *ball in play* when it has been dropped or placed.

(Ball incorrectly substituted – see Rule 15-2.)

(Lifting ball incorrectly substituted, dropped or placed – see Rule 20-6.)

LIE OF BALL ALTERED IN WATER HAZARD

> I am going to play my ball from the water hazard and your ball is in my way. Would you mind marking and lifting it?

> Not at all, but let's note just what kind of lie I have. If, as a result of your shot, my lie is altered I must place my ball in the hazard in the nearest lie most similar, not more than one club-length away and not nearer the hole.

PLAYING FROM THE WRONG PLACE

If a player moves his ball-marker a putter head length to one side, he must remember to put it back before he putts. Otherwise, the player will be penalized for playing from a wrong place.

20-5. MAKING NEXT STROKE FROM WHERE PREVIOUS STROKE MADE

When a player elects or is required to make his next *stroke* from where a previous *stroke* was made, he must proceed as follows:

a. On the Teeing Ground: The ball to be played must be played from within the *teeing ground*. It may be played from anywhere within the *teeing ground* and may be teed.

b. Through the Green: The ball to be played must be dropped and when dropped must first strike a part of the *course through the green*.

c. In a Hazard: The ball to be played must be dropped and when dropped must first strike a part of the *course* in the *hazard*.

d. On the Putting Green: The ball to be played must be placed on the *putting green*.

PENALTY FOR BREACH OF RULE 20-5:
Match play – Loss of hole; Stroke play – Two strokes.

20-6. LIFTING BALL INCORRECTLY SUBSTITUTED, DROPPED OR PLACED

A ball incorrectly *substituted*, dropped or placed in a wrong place or otherwise not in accordance with the *Rules* but not played may be lifted, without penalty, and the player must then proceed correctly.

20-7. PLAYING FROM WRONG PLACE
a. General
A player has played from a wrong place if he makes a stroke at his *ball in play*:
(i)   on a part of the *course* where the *Rules* do not permit a *stroke* to be played or a ball to be dropped or placed; or
(ii) when the *Rules* require a dropped ball to be re-dropped or a *moved* ball to be replaced.

Note: For a ball played from outside the *teeing ground* or from a wrong *teeing ground* – see Rule 11-4.

b. Match Play
If a player makes a *stroke* from a wrong place, **he loses the hole**.

c. Stroke Play
If a *competitor* makes a *stroke* from a wrong place, **he incurs a penalty of two strokes under the applicable *Rule***. He must play out the hole with the ball played from the wrong place, without correcting his error, provided he has not committed a serious breach (see Note 1).

If a *competitor* becomes aware that he has played from a wrong place and believes that he may have committed a serious breach, he must, before making a *stroke* on the next *teeing ground*, play out the hole with a second ball played in accordance with the *Rules*. If the hole being played is the last hole of the round, he must declare, before leaving the *putting green*, that he will play out the hole with a second ball played in accordance with the *Rules*.

If the *competitor* has played a second ball, he must report the facts to the *Committee* before returning his score card; if he fails to do so, **he is disqualified**. The *Committee* must determine whether the *competitor* has committed a serious breach of the applicable *Rule*. If he has, the score with the second ball counts and **the *competitor* must add two *penalty strokes*** to his score with that ball. If the *competitor* has committed a serious breach and has failed to correct it as outlined above, **he is disqualified**.

Note 1: A *competitor* is deemed to have committed a serious breach of the applicable *Rule* if the *Committee* considers he has gained a significant advantage as a result of playing from a wrong place.

Note 2: If a *competitor* plays a second ball under Rule 20-7c and it is ruled not to count, *strokes* made with that ball and *penalty strokes* incurred solely by playing that ball are disregarded. If the second ball is ruled to count, the *stroke* made from the wrong place and any *strokes* subsequently taken with the original ball including *penalty strokes* incurred solely by playing that ball are disregarded.

Note 3: If a player incurs a penalty for making a *stroke* from a wrong place, there is no additional penalty for *substituting* a ball when not permitted.

RULE 20 INCIDENTS

The Rules must be taken literally. Rule 20-2b states: A ball when dropped must first strike a part of the course where the applicable Rule requires it to be dropped.

The words a *part of the course* may lead to our assuming that the ground is the logical part of the course being referred to, but that is not what the Rule states, as Billy Ray Brown discovered at the 1993 Masters Tournament.

On Good Friday, he hooked his second shot on the par-5 13th into some azalea bushes that are planted to the left and slightly above the putting green. The ball embedded beneath one of the bushes. By Local Rule, Brown was entitled to relief for a ball embedded in its own pitch mark through the green.

It was obvious to officials stationed in the area that Brown would be entitled to relief but that dropping the ball would be complicated by the presence of the bush that lay between the ground and the extension Brown's arm would make in using the proper dropping procedure.

Decision 20-2b/1 specifies that a properly dropped ball that lodges in a bush without striking the ground, and does not roll into a position requiring it to be redropped, is in play even though it has never touched the ground

When first dropped, Brown's ball was deflected by the azalea bush, fell to the ground, and moved closer to the hole, requiring a re-drop. The same thing happened after the second drop. Therefore, under Rule 20, he was required to place his ball as near as possible to the spot where it first struck a part of the course when re-dropped. In this case, that spot was on some azalea leaves that would not support the weight of the ball.

Brown was, therefore, required to place his ball at the nearest spot, not closer to the hole, where it could be placed at rest. This was a fork in a branch at the top of the bush. Apparently realizing the potentially unplayable predicament he might be in if required to place his ball on the ground under the bush, and the requisite penalty stroke for an unplayable ball, Brown was pleased when told he would be required to place his ball on the branch near the top of the bush and play from there without penalty.

With the ball having been placed at rest atop the bush, Brown then risked a penalty stroke if he caused it to move before playing it from its precarious perch.

Of equal concern, had the ball moved without any action on Brown's part, he would have been required to play from its new position. To his disadvantage, such a position may have been an unplayable spot within the bush or; to his advantage, the ball could have rolled down the slope into the open and closer to the hole.

Not wishing to test his fate, Brown quickly selected his putter, played a left-handed stroke from the branch of the bush to the edge of the green, two putted for par and moved to the 14th tee.

After taking relief from a water hazard at the EMC World Cup, Thomas Levet's ball came to rest and then subsequently rolled back into the same hazard. Levet was forced to take a second drop and a second penalty stroke. Details of the incident follow below.

Once the criteria for relief under the Rules have been applied, the figurative Rules clock is reset and play continues.

On the 18th hole of the EMC World Cup at Vista Vallarta in Mexico, Thomas Levet could not have realized how quickly his water hazard penalty would repeat itself. With his partner, Rafael Jacquelin, out of the hole and the French team leading by one, Levet played his approach from the fairway into a lateral water hazard at the front and left of the putting green.

He took relief, and the resulting penalty, under Rule 26-1, dropped a ball on the steep, closely mown grass bank beside the hazard where it came to rest. The ball was in play.

Gathering his wits, Levet walked onto the green in order to assess what would be needed from his pitch toward the hole. On his way back to his ball, the ball began to move and rolled back into the lateral water hazard from which he had just taken relief.

Because the ball had been at rest after his taking relief from the hazard, and because Levet had not addressed the ball or done anything to cause it to move, the ball was back in the hazard and could only be removed by playing it or under penalty of an additional stroke. So, he was two in the hazard the first time, three out with the first penalty, and four out with the second penalty. A new point of reference for where the ball last crossed the margin of the hazard had to be determined for the second drop. Levet played his fifth shot expeditiously.

At the 1995 Senior Tour Championship, Hale Irwin learned that being motivated to do what seems to be right can sometimes compound an infraction and add to the resulting penalty.

At the Dunes Club in Myrtle Beach, Irwin erroneously replaced his ball on the 16th putting green in front of his fellow-competitor's marker.

After putting, but not holing, his ball, Irwin realized his mistake and, apparently believing that he should correct the error, lifted his ball, placed it in front of his marker, and completed the hole from that spot.

His penalty was four strokes: When he placed his ball in front of his fellow-competitor's marker and putted, Irwin played from a wrong place incurring a two-stroke penalty (Rule 16-1b). When he subsequently lifted his ball, in order to correct his mistake, from where it was, without marking its position and did not replace it, he also incurred another penalty of two strokes (Rule 20-1).

When a ball has been lifted, the ball-marker takes on the status of the ball under the Rules. If a ball-marker is moved there is no penalty if that movement is directly attributable to the specific act of marking, lifting, placing or replacing the ball. If that is not the case, a penalty will ensue.

Jesper Parnevik marked his ball on the putting green of the 11th hole during the first round of the Doral Genuity Championship and handed it to his caddie for cleaning. The caddie tossed the ball back to Parnevik after having cleaned it, but Parnevik fumbled his catch, and the ball fell onto and moved his ball-marker.

Accidental movement of a ball-marker that occurs before or after the specific acts of marking, lifting, placing, or replacing is not considered to be directly attributable. Parnevik's dropping his ball on his marker was not directly attributable to the specific act of replacing his ball (Decision 20-1/15). He was penalized one stroke, and the ball-marker had to be replaced.

Frequently asked questions

Q Must a player use a small coin or similar object to mark the position of his ball before lifting it?

A The Note to Rule 20-1 states in part that the position of the ball should be marked by placing a ball-marker, small coin or other small object immediately behind the ball. When the word "should" is used in the Rules of Golf it is a recommendation only and failure to comply does not result in a penalty. The intention is to emphasize that use of a ball-marker or other small object (such as a coin) is considered to be the best way to mark a ball.

Q Is the person who lifted the player's ball the only person who may replace it?

A No. Up to a maximum of three different people may replace a ball, depending on the circumstances. The player, his partner or the person who lifted or moved it may replace the ball. For example, in a Four-Ball match, if a player were to authorize his caddie to lift his ball, the caddie, the player or the player's partner could replace it. However, if the player lifts the ball himself, only the player or his partner may replace it – see Rule 20-3a.

RULE **21** CLEANING BALL

DEFINITIONS

All defined terms are in *italics* and are listed alphabetically in the Definitions section – see pages 9–20.

See **incident** involving Rule 21 below.

A ball on the *putting green* may be cleaned when lifted under Rule 16-1b. Elsewhere, a ball may be cleaned when lifted, except when it has been lifted:

a. To determine if it is unfit for play (Rule 5-3);

b. For identification (Rule 12-2), in which case it may be cleaned only to the extent necessary for identification; or

c. Because it is assisting or interfering with play (Rule 22).

If a player cleans his ball during play of a hole except as provided in this Rule, **he incurs a penalty of one stroke** and the ball, if lifted, must be replaced.

If a player who is required to replace a ball fails to do so, **he incurs the general penalty under the applicable *Rule***, but there is no additional penalty under Rule 21.

Exception: If a player incurs a penalty for failing to act in accordance with Rule 5-3, 12-2 or 22, there is no additional penalty under Rule 21.

RULE 21 INCIDENT

During the 1999 U.S. Open played at Pinehurst No.2, Scott Hoch holed his bunker shot at the par-4 12th. During the ensuing clamor, the Rules official walking with the group looked up to see two senior Rules officials motioning him to come over.

The senior officials reported that a spectator was alleging that Hoch's ball was mistakenly cleaned when lifted for interference at the 6th hole (see Rule 22 incident). Rule 22 permits the lifting of a ball that interferes with or assists the play of another player. Under such circumstances, except on a putting green, the ball may not be cleaned when lifted.

The senior officials asked the official with Hoch's group if he could shed any light on the situation. The official stated that his attention had been primarily focused on the lifting and replacing procedures, and he was unaware of any cleaning violation.

It was decided that Hoch should be asked after he finished the round but before he returned his score card. When the inquiry was made, Hoch replied that he did not recall since the incident had occurred two hours before. Hoch's caddie said he also did not recall. Jesper Parenik and Steve Jones, Hoch's fellow-competitors in the same group, said they were not watching and could not confirm or deny the cleaning.

Because there was not compelling evidence, Hoch was found to have acted properly and he began the second round just as he had ended the first, four shots out of the lead.

Frequently asked question

Q Can you list the situations when a player is permitted to clean the ball?

A A player may clean his ball at any time when it has been lifted, except for when it has been lifted under Rule 5-3 (Ball Unfit for Play), Rule 12-2 (Identifying Ball), and Rule 22 (Ball Interfering with or Assisting Play). However, please note that under the following Decisions, a ball may not be cleaned when lifted: Decision 25/21 (Lifting Ball to Determine Whether it Lies in Burrowing Animal Hole) and Decision 25-2/7 (Lifting Ball to Determine Whether it is Embedded).

RULE **22** BALL ASSISTING OR INTERFERING WITH PLAY

DEFINITIONS
All defined terms are in *italics* and are listed alphabetically in the Definitions section – see pages 9–20.

22-1. BALL ASSISTING PLAY

Except when a ball is in motion, if a player considers that a ball might assist any other player, he may:

a.   Lift the ball if it is his ball, or

b.   Have any other ball lifted.

A ball lifted under this Rule must be replaced (see Rule 20-3). The ball must not be cleaned, unless it lies on the *putting green* (see Rule 21).

   In stroke play, a player required to lift his ball may play first rather than lift the ball.

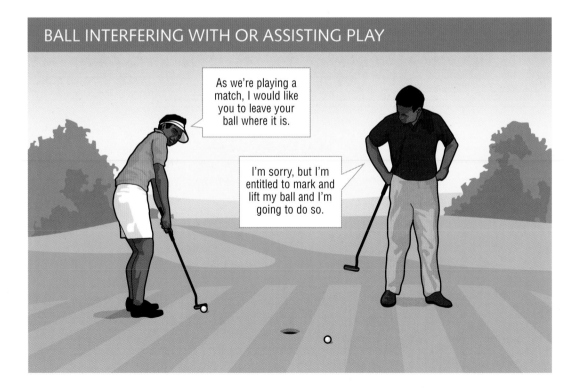

BALL INTERFERING WITH OR ASSISTING PLAY

As we're playing a match, I would like you to leave your ball where it is.

I'm sorry, but I'm entitled to mark and lift my ball and I'm going to do so.

In stroke play, if the *Committee* determines that *competitors* have agreed not to lift a ball that might assist any *competitor*, **they are disqualified**.

See **incident** involving Rule 22-2 below.

22-2. BALL INTERFERING WITH PLAY

Except when a ball is in motion, if a player considers that another ball might interfere with his play, he may have it lifted.

A ball lifted under this Rule must be replaced (see Rule 20-3). The ball must not be cleaned, unless it lies on the *putting green* (see Rule 21).

In stroke play, a player required to lift his ball may play first rather than lift the ball.

Note: Except on the *putting green*, a player may not lift his ball solely because he considers that it might interfere with the play of another player. If a player lifts his ball without being asked to do so, **he incurs a penalty of one stroke for a breach of Rule 18-2a**, but there is no additional penalty under Rule 22.

PENALTY FOR BREACH OF RULE:
Match play – Loss of hole; Stroke play – Two strokes.

RULE 22 INCIDENT

Golf's playing field is the largest of any sport. For this reason, it is rare when one ball comes into contact with or interferes with another. It is even more bizarre when there is such an occurrence at the major championship level.

And yet, Jesper Parnevik and Scott Hoch found themselves in just such a predicament near the 6th green at Pinehurst No.2 during the 1999 U.S. Open.

Rule 22 allows any player to lift his ball if he believes it will assist another player, or have any ball lifted that might interfere with his play or assist any other player. Except on the putting green, a ball lifted under Rule 22 may not be cleaned.

Hoch and Parnevik both played just to the left side of the par-3, 222-yard hole. From the tee, it was difficult to discern whether the balls were on the fringe of the green or in the rough. Their fellow-competitor's ball, belonging to Steve Jones, was visible on the green. Arriving greenside, Hoch and Parnevik found that their balls lay about three inches off the fringe in the Bermuda grass rough and actually touching. Both balls were held slightly off the ground by the stiff consistency of the grass. Because Hoch's ball was closer to the hole, it was necessary that it be lifted in order for Parnevik to play his shot.

Before Hoch lifted his ball, the walking Rules official with the group closely inspected the lie of both balls to be certain 1) that Hoch, upon replacing his ball after Parnevik's stroke, would be afforded the same lie or if that were not possible, the most similar lie and 2) that Parnevik's ball could be accurately replaced should it move when Hoch lifted his ball.

As anticipated, when Hoch lifted his ball, Parnevik's moved an inch closer to the hole. Under the official's watchful eye, Parnevik attempted to replace his ball at its original location. However, the supporting nature of the Bermuda grass could not be reintroduced and Parnevik's ball sunk a little deeper into the rough than its original position. Under the Rules, it doesn't matter if the movement is vertical or horizontal. The ball could not be replaced in its original position so that it would remain at rest.

Rule 20-3d covers such a situation by stating that if a ball, when placed or replaced, fails to come to rest on that spot, it shall be replaced. If it again fails to remain at rest, it must be placed at the nearest spot where it can be placed at rest that is not nearer the hole and not in a hazard.

Parnevik found such a spot and chipped onto the green. In so doing, he altered Hoch's lie. Hoch was entitled to the lie that his tee shot had afforded him, which is one of the Rules' cardinal principles. Since his lie had been altered, Hoch found the nearest lie most similar to his original lie, within one club-length, and placed his ball on that spot. He then chipped in for a birdie two.

All of this was under the discerning eyes of both the walking Rules official and a Rules rover, who was monitoring the group's pace of play. Parnevik and Jones finished the hole, and the players went to the 7th tee.

See Rule 21 on page 111 for a continuation of this incident.

Frequently asked questions

Q Is it permissible for two fellow-competitors in stroke play to agree to leave the ball of one of the players near the hole to assist the other player in playing his ball from just off the putting green?

A No. If the fellow-competitors agree not to lift a ball that might assist another player, they are disqualified – Rule 22-1.

Q In match play, the player has requested for the opponent to leave his ball near the hole. Is this request permissible? Is there a penalty if the opponent does lift the ball?

A Except while a ball is in motion, the opponent has the right under Rule 22-1 to mark the position of and lift his ball before the player plays his stroke, if he believes that his ball will assist the player in his play of the hole. Therefore, in this case, the player's opponent may mark the position of and lift his ball under Rule 22-1. There's no penalty for making this request, however the player can not deny the opponent of his right to lift the ball.

RULE **23** LOOSE IMPEDIMENTS

DEFINITIONS

All defined terms are in *italics* and are listed alphabetically in the Definitions section – see pages 9–20.

See **incident** involving Rule 23-1 on pages 116–117.

23-1. RELIEF

Except when both the *loose impediment* and the ball lie in or touch the same *hazard*, any *loose impediment* may be removed without penalty.

If the ball lies anywhere other than on the *putting green* and the removal of a *loose impediment* by the player causes the ball to *move*, Rule 18-2a applies.

On the *putting green*, if the ball or ball-marker is accidentally *moved* in the process removing a *loose impediment*, the ball or ball-marker must be replaced. There is no penalty, provided the movement of the ball or ball-marker is directly attributable to the removal of the *loose impediment*. Otherwise, if the player causes the ball to *move*, **he incurs a penalty of one stroke under Rule 18-2a**.

When a ball is in motion, a *loose impediment* that might influence the movement of the ball must not be removed.

Note: If the ball lies in a *hazard*, the player must not touch or move any *loose impediment* lying in or touching the same *hazard* – see Rule 13-4c.

PENALTY FOR BREACH OF RULE:
Match play – Loss of hole; Stroke play – Two strokes.

(Searching for ball in hazard – see Rule 12-1.)
(Touching line of putt – see Rule 16-1a.)

RULE 23-1. RELIEF

A player is entitled to remove any loose impediment without penalty, except when both the loose impediment and the player's ball lie in or touch the same hazard.

Loose impediments are natural objects that come in all shapes and sizes. At the 1999 Phoenix Open, Tiger Woods learned that a player can receive assistance in removing a large loose impediment. Details of the incident can be read below.

RULE 23 INCIDENT

Consistency lies at the heart of the Rules of Golf even when rulings are made that superficially or visually seem inconsistent. Except when both the loose impediment and a player's ball lie in or touch the same hazard, any loose impediment may be removed without penalty.

When Tiger Woods was permitted to gain assistance from his substantial gallery in order to move a boulder lying on the desert floor, it did not look appropriate, but it was – and it was consistent within the Rules.

During the final round of 1999 Phoenix Open, Woods's drive from the 13th tee traveled 360 yards before finishing in the desert just off the left side of the fairway. The ball stopped about two feet directly behind a boulder that was roughly four feet wide, two feet high, and two feet thick. The rock was too heavy for Woods to move by himself, and his ball was too close to it to play over or around. With the rock in place, Woods's best option was to play sideways onto the fairway.

With 225 yards left to reach the putting green, Woods was not enamored with the idea of pitching out to the fairway and then playing his approach to the green. PGA Tour Rules Official Orlando Pope appeared on the scene, and Woods inquired as to his options. With a glimmer of a smile, Woods kicked the rock and asked, "It's not a pebble, but is it a loose impediment?"

The definition within the Rules states that loose impediments are natural objects that are not fixed or growing, not solidly embedded, and do not adhere to the ball. There is no restriction for size or weight.

Decision 23-1/2 states that stones of any size are loose impediments and may be removed as long as they are not solidly embedded and their removal does not unduly delay play.

Pope replied to Woods, "It's readily movable if you have people who can move it real quick."

"Really?" Woods responded to the revelation quietly.

Then Pope added in an inquiring tone, "But it kind of looks embedded to me."

"It's embedded?" Woods asked as they both stepped back to look.

Pope then decided that the rock was simply lying on the desert floor and was not solidly embedded. He also knew that Decision 23-1/3 specifically permits spectators, caddies, fellow-competitors, essentially anyone to assist in removing a large, loose impediment.

Several men rolled the stone out of Woods' line of play as others watched and cheered. Following the removal, Woods shook each man's hand and then played his shot on a direct line to the green.

Golf's leading players have always enjoyed and suffered the effects of their large galleries. Bob Jones had to be protected by Marines when he completed his Grand Slam at Merion in 1930. Sam Snead, Arnold Palmer and Jack Nicklaus often had errant shots stopped by those who followed them.

In addition to situations in which they may have been helped, imagine the number of times those same stars have been distracted by a movement or noise from the spectators, photographers, reporters, and security officers that follow them. It has never been the function of the Rules of Golf to attempt to equalize such variations.

Frequently asked question

Q What is the status of stones in bunkers?

A Stones are by definition loose impediments regardless of their location. Thus, when the ball and the stone lie in or touch the same hazard, the stone must not be removed. However, a Committee may adopt a Local Rule stating that stones in bunkers are movable obstructions. Unless this Local Rule is put into effect by the Committee, players may not remove stones in bunkers without penalty.

RULE **24** OBSTRUCTIONS

DEFINITIONS

All defined terms are in *italics* and are listed alphabetically in the Definitions section – see pages 9–20.

See **incident** involving Rule 24-1 on page 125.

24-1. MOVABLE OBSTRUCTION

A player may take relief, without penalty, from a movable *obstruction* as follows:

a. If the ball does not lie in or on the *obstruction*, the *obstruction* may be removed. If the ball *moves*, it must be replaced, and there is no penalty, provided that the movement of the ball is directly attributable to the removal of the *obstruction*. Otherwise, Rule 18-2a applies.

117

BALL AGAINST RAKE ROLLS INTO BUNKER WHEN RAKE REMOVED

Yes, and if it will not come to rest on the correct spot when replaced a second time, you must place it at the nearest spot, not nearer the hole nor in the bunker, where it can be placed at rest.

If I move the rake my ball is likely to roll into the bunker. If it does, may I replace it?

b.   If the ball lies in or on the *obstruction*, the ball may be lifted and the *obstruction* removed. The ball must *through the green* or in a *hazard* be dropped, or on the *putting green* be placed, as near as possible to the spot directly under the place where the ball lay in or on the *obstruction*, but not nearer the *hole*.

The ball may be cleaned when lifted under this Rule.

When a ball is in motion, an *obstruction* that might influence the movement of the ball, other than *equipment* of any player or the *flagstick* when attended, removed or held up, must not be moved.

(Exerting influence on ball – see Rule 1-2.)

Note: If a ball to be dropped or placed under this Rule is not immediately recoverable, another ball may be *substituted*.

24-2. IMMOVABLE OBSTRUCTION
a. Interference

Interference by an immovable *obstruction* occurs when a ball lies in or on the *obstruction*, or when the *obstruction* interferes with the player's *stance* or the area of his intended swing. If the player's ball lies on the *putting green*, interference also occurs if an immovable *obstruction* on the *putting green* intervenes on his *line of putt*. Otherwise, intervention on the *line of play* is not, of itself, interference under this Rule.

FLAGSTICK REMOVED WHEN BALL IN MOTION

When a ball is in motion it is permissible to move a flagstick that has been removed and that might influence the movement of the ball.

BALL BEHIND IMMOVABLE OBSTRUCTION

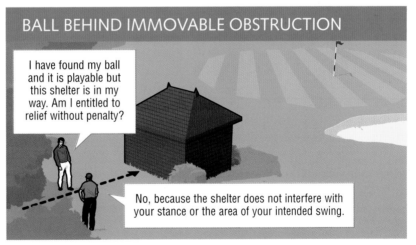

I have found my ball and it is playable but this shelter is in my way. Am I entitled to relief without penalty?

No, because the shelter does not interfere with your stance or the area of your intended swing.

See **incident** involving Rule 24-2b on pages 124–25.

b. Relief

Except when the ball is in a *water hazard* or a *lateral water hazard*, a player may take relief from interference by an immovable *obstruction* as follows:

(i) Through the Green: If the ball lies *through the green*, the player must lift the ball and drop it, without penalty, within one club-length of and not nearer the *hole* than the *nearest point of relief*. The *nearest point of relief* must not be in a *hazard* or on a *putting green*. When the ball is dropped within one club-length of the *nearest point of relief*, the ball must first strike a part of the *course* at a spot that avoids interference by the immovable *obstruction* and is not in a *hazard* and not on a *putting green*.

(ii) In a Bunker: If the ball is in a *bunker*, the player must lift the ball and drop it either:

119

(a) Without penalty, in accordance with Clause (i) above, except that the *nearest point of relief* must be in the *bunker* and the ball must be dropped in the *bunker*; or

(b) **Under penalty of one stroke**, outside the *bunker* keeping the point where the ball lay directly between the *hole* and the spot on which the ball is dropped, with no limit to how far behind the *bunker* the ball may be dropped.

(iii) On the Putting Green: If the ball lies on the *putting green*, the player must lift the ball and place it, without penalty, at the *nearest point of relief* that is not in a *hazard*. The *nearest point of relief* may be off the *putting green*.

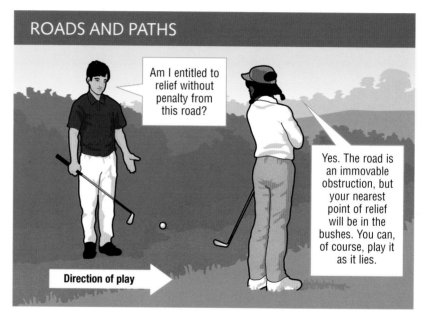

ROADS AND PATHS

Am I entitled to relief without penalty from this road?

Yes. The road is an immovable obstruction, but your nearest point of relief will be in the bushes. You can, of course, play it as it lies.

Direction of play

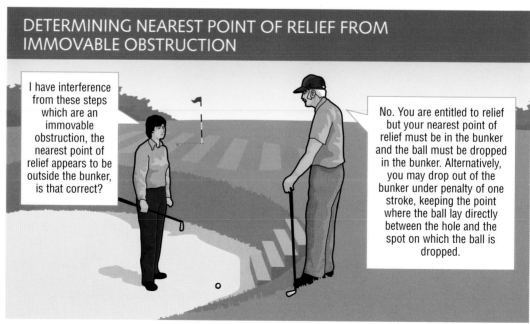

DETERMINING NEAREST POINT OF RELIEF FROM IMMOVABLE OBSTRUCTION

I have interference from these steps which are an immovable obstruction, the nearest point of relief appears to be outside the bunker, is that correct?

No. You are entitled to relief but your nearest point of relief must be in the bunker and the ball must be dropped in the bunker. Alternatively, you may drop out of the bunker under penalty of one stroke, keeping the point where the ball lay directly between the hole and the spot on which the ball is dropped.

RELIEF FOR SIDEWAYS STROKE

(iv) On the Teeing Ground: If the ball lies on the *teeing ground*, the player must lift the ball and drop it, without penalty, in accordance with Clause (i) above.

The ball may be cleaned when lifted under this Rule.

(Ball rolling to a position where there is interference by the condition from which relief was taken – see Rule 20-2c(v).)

Exception: A player may not take relief under this Rule if (a) it is clearly unreasonable for him to make a *stroke* because of interference by anything other than an immovable *obstruction* or (b) interference by an immovable *obstruction* would occur only through use of an unnecessarily abnormal *stance*, swing or direction of play.

Note 1: If a ball is in a *water hazard* (including a *lateral water hazard*), the player may not take relief from interference by an immovable *obstruction*. The player must play the ball as it lies or proceed under Rule 26-1.

Note 2: If a ball to be dropped or placed under this Rule is not immediately recoverable, another ball may be *substituted*.

Note 3: The *Committee* may make a Local Rule stating that the player must determine the *nearest point of relief* without crossing over, through or under the *obstruction*.

(iii) In a Water Hazard (including a Lateral Water Hazard): If the ball last crossed the outermost limits of the immovable *obstruction* at a spot in a *water hazard*, the player is not entitled to relief without penalty. The player must proceed under Rule 26-1.

(iv) On the Putting Green: If the ball last crossed the outermost limits of the immovable *obstruction* at a spot on the *putting green*, the player may *substitute* another ball, without penalty, and take relief as prescribed in Rule 24-2b(iii).

PENALTY FOR BREACH OF RULE:
Match play – Loss of hole; Stroke play – Two strokes.

RULE 24 INCIDENTS

The size of an obstruction does not alter the fact that it is what it is under the Rules. A bottle cap and a building are both obstructions – it's just that one is movable and one is immovable.

The clubhouse behind the 18th green at Pinehurst No. 2 is in bounds and, therefore, to be treated as an immovable obstruction should a ball find its way to a spot where the building interferes with a player's stance or the area of his intended swing.

During the second round of the 2005 U.S. Open, Nick Jones was playing the 18th hole as his 9th because his group started the round at the 10th tee. Jones drive finished in the right rough near some pine trees that interfered on a direct line to the flagstick. He decided to play a full shot toward the green and then deal with whatever circumstances resulted – a greenside bunker, the rough, or interference from the massive grand stand.

His approach shot went high into the clear, morning sky on a direct line to the far right corner of the grandstand located at the left of the green. In the bright sunlight, both Jones and the walking Rules official lost sight of the ball as it approached the seated spectators. A clearly discernible metal noise was then reported followed by laughter and murmuring from the crowd.

Arriving at the grandstand, Jones was informed that his ball had struck a metal railing and rebounded 20 yards or so to a resting position on the flat roof of the clubhouse. Several television cameras were positioned on the roof. It being early in the day, only one cameraman was on duty, but he was able to confirm that Jones ball was indeed near him and at rest on the roof.

In the heat of the moment, it seemed most logical to Jones to take the relief from the obstruction (the clubhouse) to which he was entitled, get the ball back down on the ground, and finish play of the hole. However, another option available to him under the Rules was to play the ball as it lay from its flat, unobstructed position on the roof. In hindsight, this would probably have produced a better score.

However, Jones chose to take relief. The cameraman tossed the ball down from the roof. The relief point from the clubhouse resulted in interference from the grandstand, which was a temporary immovable obstruction. Relief was then determined from that temporary immovable obstruction and Jones put his ball back in play at a point to the left of the green between the grandstand and a greenside bunker. He took five more to complete the hole.

During the 1949 British Open's second round, Harry Bradshaw was faithful to the tenet of doing what seems to be fair when you are unsure how to proceed under the Rules. Having recorded a stunning first round 68 over Royal St. George's on the southeast coast of England, Bradshaw was tied with Robert De Vincenzo and just one stroke off the lead. Playing the 5th hole, Bradshaw's ball rolled into a beer bottle with a broken neck that had been littered in the rough.

Rather than requesting a ruling for the relief to which he was entitled, Bradshaw determined on his own that he must play the ball as it lay. He selected a sand wedge and made a stroke that shattered the bottle and moved his ball slightly forward. He score for the hole was a double bogey six.

The consequence of his having played out of this movable obstruction was that Bradshaw ultimately tied Bobby Locke of South Africa at 283. In the resulting 36-hole playoff, Locke bested Bradshaw, 136 to 147, to win the first of Locke's four British Open titles.

Under Rule 24-1, because Bradshaw's ball was in a movable obstruction, it could have been lifted and cleaned without penalty, the bottle removed, and the ball dropped as nearly as possible to the spot directly under the place where the ball lay when it was in the bottle.

An obstruction can be declared by the Committee to be an integral part of the golf course. When that has been done, relief is not available under Rule 24. The ball must be played as it lies, and the player must simply deal with it.

The most famous hole in the world derives its name from the obstruction that is an integral part of the golf course and runs beside the putting green. The Road Hole, the penultimate at St. Andrews' Old Course, has been the scene of much demise and success through the years, just as it was on the final afternoon of the 1995 British Open.

Costantino Rocca struggled tenaciously over the closing holes that afternoon in hope of overcoming John Daly. Tied with Daly, Rocca missed an opportunity for birdie at the 16th, and then missed the 17th green with his approach shot. According to the 1995 Open Annual, Rocca's ball "skirted the front of the (17th) green, shot across the road, slammed into the stone wall, then rebounded back onto the road and sat in a small depression."

The depression made it impossible for a lofted club to move under the ball, and Rocca was forced to putt. Putting from asphalt produces inexact results. After being struck with the putter, Rocca's ball popped into the air, "carried over the road, caught a piece of turf that shot it forward, climbed the bank, jumped onto the green, and rolled within four feet of the cup (sic)." He holed his putt for par.

At the 18th, following a disastrous pitch, the Italian holed a 60 foot birdie putt from the Valley of Sin to force a play-off with Daly, which Daly ultimately won.

The location of the ball, rather than that of the obstruction, is of primary importance when determining relief from an obstruction. While that may sound perfectly obvious, it is not always, as Nick Dougherty realized at the 2005 Caltex Masters in Singapore.

Dougherty's drive from the 16th tee on the final day was pulled to the left and appeared to have finished in a bunker next to some large, wooden cross ties that bordered the hazard. However, the ball had run through the bunker coming to rest on grass-covered ground just in front of the wooden obstructions.

By definition, such grass-covered ground is not part of a bunker. Therefore, because his ball was lying outside the bunker, Dougherty was entitled to take relief from the obstruction within one club-length of and not nearer the hole than the nearest point of relief – and that point must not be in a hazard or on a putting green.

Had his ball been in the bunker, his options would have been to take relief in the bunker without penalty or, at the cost of one penalty stroke, to drop outside the bunker keeping the point where the ball lay directly between the hole and the spot on which the ball is dropped, with no limit to how far behind the bunker the ball may be dropped.

As can be the case in free relief situations, Dougherty's drop put him in a much more favorable position from which he played to within three feet of the hole. With Colin Montgomerie just one shot back, Dougherty's good fortune allowed him to maintain a one-shot lead and go on to win the tournament.

Because Nick Dougherty's ball was lying just in front of some wooden cross ties that bordered a hazard just outside the bunker, he was instructed to drop the ball within one-club length of his nearest point of relief, under Rule 24-2(i). Read a description of this incident above.

Frequently asked questions

Q A course has installed bushes that serve as 150-yard markers. Are players entitled to relief from these bushes?

A No. A bush is a natural object, not artificial, thus it is not an obstruction (Definition of "Obstruction"). The answer is the same regardless of whether it is used to indicate yardage.

Q A ball lies in a water hazard. The player also has interference from an immovable obstruction. Is she entitled to relief without penalty from the obstruction?

A No. When a ball is in a water hazard, a player is not entitled to relief without penalty from an immovable obstruction that is in or out of the water hazard. The ball must be played as it lies or the player may proceed under Rule 26-1. However, if the ball lies outside the water hazard and the immovable obstruction lies in the water hazard, a player may take relief under Rule 24-2. (See Note 1 under Rule 24-2).

RULE **25**

ABNORMAL GROUND CONDITIONS, EMBEDDED BALL AND WRONG PUTTING GREEN

DEFINITIONS All defined terms are in *italics* and are listed alphabetically in the Definitions section – see pages 9–20.

25-1. ABNORMAL GROUND CONDITIONS
a. Interference

Interference by an *abnormal ground condition* occurs when a ball lies in or touches the condition or when the condition interferes with the player's *stance* or the area of his intended swing. If the player's ball lies on the *putting green*, interference also occurs if an *abnormal ground condition*

GROUND UNDER REPAIR DECLARED BY COMMITTEE

A rut made by a tractor is not ground under repair, but the Committee would be justified in declaring a deep rut to be ground under repair (far left).

A fallen tree still attached to its stump is not ground under repair, but it can be so declared by the Committee (left).

127

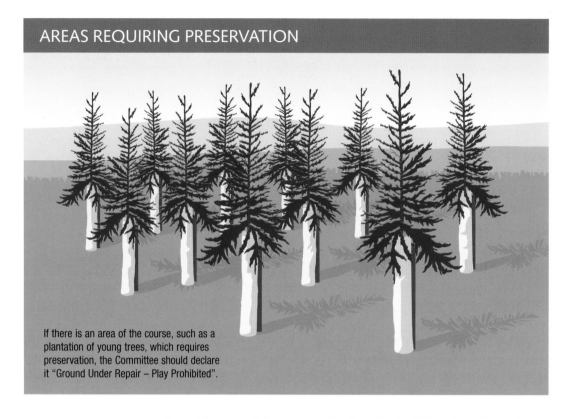

AREAS REQUIRING PRESERVATION

If there is an area of the course, such as a plantation of young trees, which requires preservation, the Committee should declare it "Ground Under Repair – Play Prohibited".

on the *putting green* intervenes on his *line of putt*. Otherwise, intervention on the *line of play* is not, of itself, interference under this Rule.

Note: The *Committee* may make a Local Rule stating that interference by an *abnormal ground condition* with a player's *stance* is deemed not to be, of itself, interference under this Rule.

b. Relief
Except when the ball is in a *water hazard* or a *lateral water hazard*, a player may take relief from interference by an *abnormal ground condition* as follows:

(i)   Through the Green: If the ball lies *through the green*, the player must lift the ball and drop it, without penalty, within one club-length of and not nearer the *hole* than the *nearest point of relief*. The *nearest point of relief* must not be in a *hazard* or on a *putting green*. When the ball is dropped within one club-length of the *nearest point of relief*, the ball must first strike a part of the *course* at a spot that avoids interference by the condition and is not in a *hazard* and not on a *putting green*.

(ii) In a Bunker: If the ball is in a *bunker*, the player must lift the ball and drop it either:

(a) Without penalty, in accordance with Clause (i) above, except that the *nearest point of relief* must be in the *bunker* and the ball must be dropped in the *bunker*, or if complete relief is impossible, as near as possible to the spot where the ball lay, but not nearer the *hole*, on a part of the *course* in the *bunker* that affords maximum available relief from the condition; or

(b) **Under penalty of one stroke**, outside the *bunker*, keeping the point where the ball lay directly between the *hole* and the spot on which the ball is dropped, with no limit to how far behind the *bunker* the ball may be dropped.

(iii) On the Putting Green: If the ball lies on the *putting green*, the player must lift the ball and place it, without penalty, at the *nearest point of relief* that is not in a *hazard*, or if complete relief is impossible, at the nearest position to where it lay that affords maximum available relief from the condition, but not nearer the *hole* and not in a *hazard*. The *nearest point of relief* or maximum available relief may be off the *putting green*.

(iv) On the Teeing Ground: If the ball lies on the *teeing ground*, the player must lift the ball and drop it, without penalty, in accordance with Clause (i) above.

The ball may be cleaned when lifted under Rule 25-1b.

(Ball rolling to a position where there is interference by the condition from which relief was taken – see Rule 20-2c(v).)

Exception: A player may not take relief under this Rule if (a) it is clearly unreasonable for him to make a stroke because of interference by anything other than an abnormal ground condition or (b) interference by an abnormal ground condition would occur only through use of an unnecessarily abnormal stance, swing or direction of play.

CASUAL WATER ON PUTTING GREEN

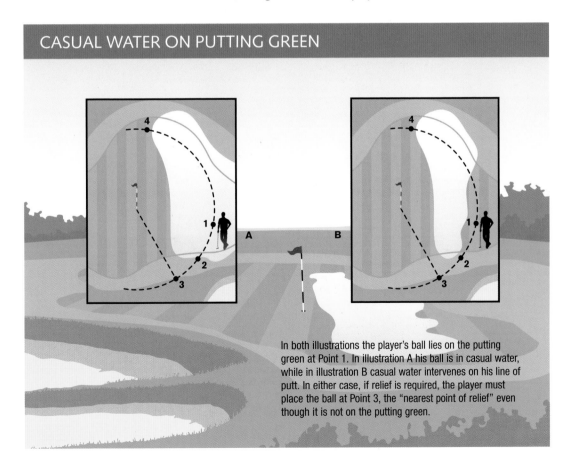

In both illustrations the player's ball lies on the putting green at Point 1. In illustration A his ball is in casual water, while in illustration B casual water intervenes on his line of putt. In either case, if relief is required, the player must place the ball at Point 3, the "nearest point of relief" even though it is not on the putting green.

BALL CLOSE TO CASUAL WATER: LEFT-HANDED STROKE NOT REASONABLE

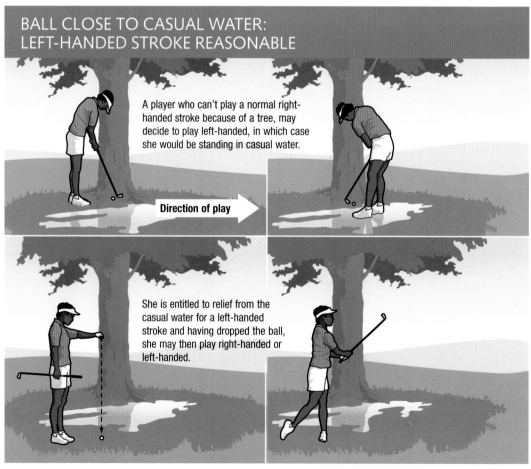

BALL CLOSE TO CASUAL WATER: LEFT-HANDED STROKE REASONABLE

Note 1: If a ball is in a *water hazard* (including a *lateral water hazard*), the player is not entitled to relief without penalty from interference by an *abnormal ground condition*. The player must play the ball as it lies (unless prohibited by Local Rule) or proceed under Rule 26-1.

Note 2: If a ball to be dropped or placed under this Rule is not immediately recoverable, another ball may be *substituted*.

c. Ball in Abnormal Ground Condition Not Found

It is a question of fact whether a ball that has not been found after having been struck toward an *abnormal ground condition* is in such a condition. In order to apply this Rule, it must be known or virtually certain that the ball is in the *abnormal ground condition*. In the absence of such knowledge or certainty, the player must proceed under Rule 27-1.

If it is known or virtually certain that a ball that has not been found is in an *abnormal ground condition*, the player may take relief under this Rule. If he elects to do so, the spot where the ball last crossed the outermost limits of the *abnormal ground condition* must be determined and, for the purpose of applying this Rule, the ball is deemed to lie at this spot and the player must proceed as follows:

BALL IN CASUAL WATER IN BUNKER

I am taking relief from this casual water. Must I drop the ball at the nearest point of relief or may I drop it within one club-length of the nearest point of relief not nearer the hole?

As you are able to take complete relief from the casual water, you are allowed to drop within one club-length of the nearest point of relief. However, if complete relief had been impossible and you were taking maximum available relief, the ball would have to be dropped on the spot which gave maximum available relief.

(i) Through the Green: If the ball last crossed the outermost limits of the *abnormal ground condition* at a spot *through the green*, the player may *substitute* another ball, without penalty, and take relief as prescribed in Rule 25-1b(i).

(ii) In a Bunker: If the ball last crossed the outermost limits of the *abnormal ground condition* at a spot in a *bunker*, the player may *substitute* another ball, without penalty, and take relief as prescribed in Rule 25-1b(ii).

(iii) In a Water Hazard (including a Lateral Water Hazard): If the ball last crossed the outermost limits of the *abnormal ground condition* at a spot in a *water hazard*, the player is not entitled to relief without penalty. The player must proceed under Rule 26-1.

(iv) On the Putting Green: If the ball last crossed the outermost limits of the *abnormal ground condition* at a spot on the *putting green*, the player may *substitute* another ball, without penalty, and take relief as prescribed in Rule 25-1b(iii).

25-2. Embedded Ball

A ball embedded in its own pitch-mark in the ground in any closely mown area *through the green* may be lifted, cleaned and dropped, without penalty, as near as possible to the spot where it lay but not nearer the *hole*. The ball when dropped must first strike a part of the *course through the green*. "Closely mown area" means any area of the *course*, including paths through the rough, cut to fairway height or less.

EMBEDDED BALL

My ball is plugged in the ground on the face of this bunker. What should I do?

Because the face is grass-covered it is not part of the bunker. It is not "closely mown" so you will have to play it as it lies or deem it unplayable. But at least you won't have to drop it in the bunker.

See **incident** involving Rule 25-3 on page 134.

25-3. WRONG PUTTING GREEN
a. Interference

Interference by a *wrong putting green* occurs when a ball is on the *wrong putting green*.

Interference to a player's *stance* or the area of his intended swing is not, of itself, interference under this Rule.

b. Relief

If a player's ball lies on a *wrong putting green* he must not play the ball as it lies. He must take relief, without penalty, as follows:

The player must lift the ball and drop it within one club-length of and not nearer the *hole* than the *nearest point of relief*. The *nearest point of relief* must not be in a *hazard* or on a *putting green*. When dropping the ball within one club-length of the *nearest point of relief*, the ball must first strike a part of the *course* at a spot that avoids interference by the *wrong putting green* and is not in a *hazard* and not on a *putting green*. The ball may be cleaned when lifted under this Rule.

PENALTY FOR BREACH OF RULE:
Match play – Loss of hole; Stroke play – Two strokes.

133

RELIEF FROM A WRONG PUTTING GREEN

I am going to be standing on this wrong putting green to play my stroke. Must I take relief?

No. Relief must be taken if your ball lies on a wrong putting green, but relief is not available for interference to your stance.

RULE 25 INCIDENT

A rare infraction for playing from a wrong putting green took place at the 1990 U.S. Senior Open at Ridgewood C.C. in Paramus, New Jersey.

Ridgewood has 27 holes. For the championship, the third nine was out of play but not out of bounds. From the second tee, a competitor hooked his drive onto a putting green that is part of the third nine. From that green, the competitor played back to the second hole of the competition course.

An observant marshal queried a Rules official about the player's procedure, and the player was subsequently penalized two strokes under Rule 25-3. It is important to note that had the player's ball been on the fringe of the wrong putting green, the player would have been required to play the ball as it lay and no penalty would be incurred.

Frequently asked question

Q A player steps all around his ball to force up water on the surface. He then claims his ball lies in casual water. What is the ruling?

A Casual water does not exist in this case. The Definition of "Casual Water" states that it is water that is visible before or after the player takes his stance.

RULE 26 WATER HAZARDS (INCLUDING LATERAL WATER HAZARDS)

DEFINITIONS

All defined terms are in *italics* and are listed alphabetically in the Definitions section – see pages 9–20.

See **incident** involving Rules 26-1 on pages 138–140.

26-1. RELIEF FOR BALL IN WATER HAZARD

It is a question of fact whether a ball that has not been found after having been struck toward a *water hazard* is in the *hazard*. In order to apply this Rule, it must be known or virtually certain that the ball is in the *hazard*. In the absence of such knowledge or certainty, the player must proceed under Rule 27-1.

If a ball is in a *water hazard* or if it is known or virtually certain that a ball that has not been found is in a *water hazard* (whether the ball lies in water or not), the player may **under penalty of one stroke**:

a. Play a ball as nearly as possible at the spot from which the original ball was last played (see Rule 20-5); or

b. Drop a ball behind the *water hazard*, keeping the point at which the original ball last crossed the margin of the *water hazard* directly between the *hole* and the spot on which the ball is dropped, with no limit to how far behind the *water hazard* the ball may be dropped; or

c. As additional options available only if the ball last crossed the margin of a *lateral water hazard*, drop a ball outside the *water hazard* within two club-lengths of and not nearer the *hole* than (i) the point where the original ball last crossed the margin of the *water hazard* or (ii) a point on the opposite margin of the *water hazard* equidistant from the *hole*.

When proceeding under this Rule, the player may lift and clean his ball or *substitute* a ball.

(Prohibited actions when ball is in hazard – see Rule 13-4.)

(Ball moving in water in a water hazard – see Rule 14-6.)

RULE 26-1. RELIEF FOR BALL IN WATER HAZARD

Jean Van de Velde's difficulty with the Barry Burn at the 72nd hole of the 1999 British Open resulted in a three-way playoff for the championship. See the details of his unfortunate brush with Rule 26-1 in the incident on pages 139–140.

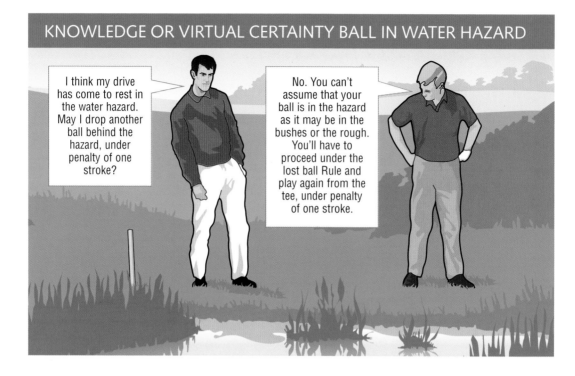

26-2. BALL PLAYED WITHIN WATER HAZARD
a. Ball Comes to Rest in Same or Another Water Hazard
If a ball played from within a *water hazard* comes to rest in the same or another *water hazard* after the stroke, the player may:

(i) proceed under Rule 26-1a. If, after dropping in the *hazard*, the player elects not to play the dropped ball, he may:

    (a) proceed under Rule 26-1b, or if applicable Rule 26-1c, **adding the additional penalty of one stroke prescribed by that Rule** and using as the reference point the point where the original ball last crossed the margin of this *hazard* before it came to rest in this *hazard*; or

    (b) **add an additional penalty of one stroke** and play a ball as nearly as possible at the spot from which the last *stroke* from outside a *water hazard* was made (see Rule 20-5); or

(ii) proceed under Rule 26-1b, or if applicable Rule 26-1c; or

(iii) **under penalty of one stroke**, play a ball as nearly as possible at the spot from which the last *stroke* from outside a *water hazard* was made (see Rule 20-5).

b. Ball Lost or Unplayable Outside Hazard or Out of Bounds
If a ball played from within a *water hazard* is *lost* or deemed unplayable outside the *hazard* or is *out of bounds*, the player may, after taking a **penalty of one stroke under Rule 27-1 or 28a**:

(i) play a ball as nearly as possible at the spot in the *hazard* from which the original ball was last played (see Rule 20-5); or

(ii) proceed under Rule 26-1b, or if applicable Rule 26-1c, **adding the additional penalty of one stroke prescribed by the Rule** and using as the reference point the point where the original ball last crossed the margin of the *hazard* before it came to rest in the *hazard*; or

(iii) **add an additional penalty of one stroke** and play a ball as nearly as possible at the spot from which the last *stroke* from outside a *water hazard* was made (see Rule 20-5).

Note 1: When proceeding under Rule 26-2b, the player is not required to drop a ball under Rule 27-1 or 28a. If he does drop a ball, he is not required to play it. He may alternatively proceed under Rule 26-2b(ii) or (iii).

Note 2: If a ball played from within a *water hazard* is deemed unplayable outside the *hazard*, nothing in Rule 26-2b precludes the player from proceeding under Rule 28b or c.

PENALTY FOR BREACH OF RULE:
Match play – Loss of hole; Stroke play – Two strokes.

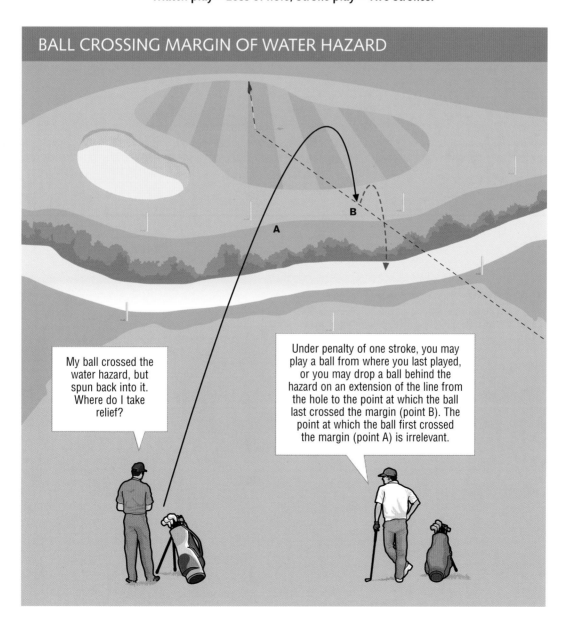

RULE 26 INCIDENTS

During the first round of the 2005 Masters Tournament, Tiger Woods used his options under Rule 26 to their logical advantage after putting into Rae's Creek at Augusta National's 13th hole.

The lightning-fast speed of the green helped to propel Woods' ball past the hole and down the closely-mown bank of the creek that runs immediately in front of the green. Woods was completely aware of his available options which were 1) without penalty, to play his ball from where it lay in the hazard; or 2) for a one-stroke penalty, to drop his ball on the fairway side of the creek and pitch back to the green; or 3) for a one-stroke penalty, to play again from where he last played.

Woods chose to play again from where he last played, i.e., to putt again. To comply with Rule 20-5, Woods was required to place his ball on the putting green, rather than drop it. He also used his option under

RELIEF FROM LATERAL WATER HAZARD

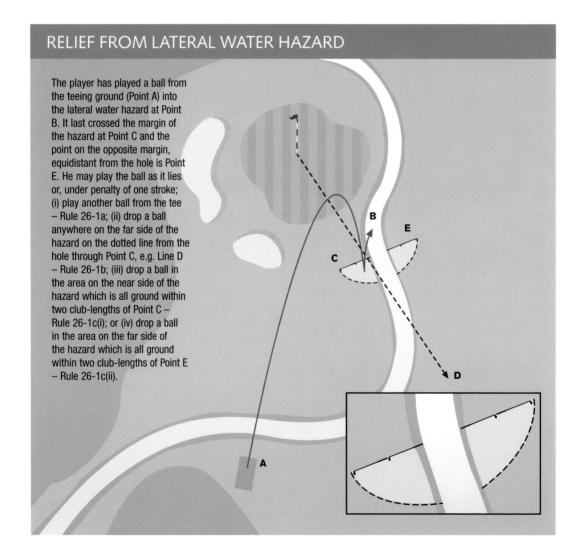

The player has played a ball from the teeing ground (Point A) into the lateral water hazard at Point B. It last crossed the margin of the hazard at Point C and the point on the opposite margin, equidistant from the hole is Point E. He may play the ball as it lies or, under penalty of one stroke; (i) play another ball from the tee – Rule 26-1a; (ii) drop a ball anywhere on the far side of the hazard on the dotted line from the hole through Point C, e.g. Line D – Rule 26-1b; (iii) drop a ball in the area on the near side of the hazard which is all ground within two club-lengths of Point C – Rule 26-1c(i); or (iv) drop a ball in the area on the far side of the hazard which is all ground within two club-lengths of Point E – Rule 26-1c(ii).

Rule 26 to substitute a ball rather than retrieving the ball he had played into the hazard. Putting again was by far his best option. Woods went on to win three days later.

One of the most remorseful Rules incidents of the past decade involved Jean Van de Velde playing the 72nd hole of the 1999 British Open. The Frenchman needed only a bogey at Carnoustie's home hole to become the first from his country to win the championship since 1907.

A short time after playing from the tee, he was standing in the Barry Burn, his navy blue trousers rolled to his knees, contemplating his fate and his options under Rule 26.

Having played a driver from the 18th tee, Van de Velde's ball finished well right but safely on a peninsula created by a bend in the burn. Instead of laying up with his second, the Frenchman attempted to play a 2-iron to the distant green. His shot was a bit wayward, and it

BALL PLAYED FROM WITHIN WATER HAZARD

The player's tee shot at a par 3 hole comes to rest in a water hazard. He plays from the hazard, but fails to get his ball out. He may play the ball as it lies or, under penalty of one stroke: (i) drop a ball at the spot from which he's just played his second stroke and play again from there; (ii) drop a ball behind the hazard, anywhere on the dotted line, and play from there; or (iii) play another ball from the tee.

ricocheted off a grandstand railing, a stone wall and finally settled behind the second crossing of the burn into some heavy rough.

Attempting to chop his ball out of the rough and over the burn, Van de Velde instead chunked it badly, and the ball finished in the shallow water of the burn. As the stream flows perpendicular to the line of play, it was marked with a yellow line indicating a water hazard – not the red line of a lateral water hazard.

His options were three: He could play the ball without penalty as it lay. For a one-stroke penalty he could play again from where he last played, or he could drop behind the hazard keeping the point at which his ball last crossed the margin of the hazard directly between the hole and the spot on which the ball would be dropped, with no limit to how far behind the hazard he might want to go.

Three in the water, Van de Velde needed a six to win the British Open. He contemplated avoiding a penalty stroke by playing the ball from the water. To assess his chances, he decided to step into the water to see what the shot required. Having removed his shoes and socks, Van de Velde rolled up his trouser legs and lowered himself down the stone wall and into the water.

There he stood in the dark water, wedge in hand, assessing his ability to play the submerged ball out of the hazard. After several minutes, discretion became the better part of valor and the Frenchman chose option b under Rule 26-1. He dropped a ball behind the hazard on the stipulated line, suffered a penalty stroke, and played his fifth shot to the right greenside bunker. His up-and-down from the bunker resulted in a score of seven, as well as a play-off between Paul Lawrie, Justin Leonard and Van de Velde, which Lawrie won.

Frequently asked question

Q The ball landed on the putting green side of a pond in front of the green, but rolled back into the pond. Where does the player drop to play the next stroke?

A The answer depends on the type of hazard the ball rolled into. Under penalty of one stroke, if the ball entered into a water hazard, (yellow stakes and/or lines) or a lateral water hazard (red stakes and/or lines), the player may play a ball from as near as possible to where the original was last played (Rule 26-1a), or drop a ball behind the hazard keeping the point where the ball last crossed the margin of the hazard between himself and the hole (Rule 26-1b). Under this option, the player must drop the ball behind the water hazard. An additional option available only for a ball in a lateral water hazard is to drop the ball within two club-lengths of the point where the ball last crossed the margin of the lateral water hazard or a point equidistant from the hole on the opposite margin of the hazard from where the ball last crossed into the hazard. However, it may not be dropped nearer the hole. If the player can drop the ball meeting the conditions of this last option, it may be dropped on the putting green side of the water hazard. Decision 26-1/15 illustrates the options under this Rule.

RULE **27** **BALL LOST OR OUT OF BOUNDS; PROVISIONAL BALL**

DEFINITIONS

All defined terms are in *italics* and are listed alphabetically in the Definitions section – see pages 9–20.

27-1. STROKE AND DISTANCE; BALL OUT OF BOUNDS; BALL NOT FOUND WITHIN FIVE MINUTES

a. Proceeding Under Stroke and Distance

At any time, a player may, **under penalty of one stroke**, play a ball as nearly as possible at the spot from which the original ball was last played (see Rule 20-5), i.e., proceed under penalty of stroke and distance.

Except as otherwise provided in the *Rules*, if a player makes a *stroke* at a ball from the spot at which the original ball was last played, he is deemed to have proceeded **under penalty of stroke and distance**.

b. Ball Out of Bounds

If a ball is *out of bounds*, the player must play a ball, **under penalty of one stroke**, as nearly as possible at the spot from which the original ball was last played (see Rule 20-5).

c. Ball Not found Within Five Minutes

If a ball is *lost* as a result of not being found or identified as his by the player within five minutes after the player's *side* or his or their *caddies* have begun

PLAYERS UNABLE TO IDENTIFY THEIR BALLS

141

BALL FOUND WITHIN FIVE MINUTES

to search for it, the player must play a ball, **under penalty of one stroke**, as nearly as possible at the spot from which the original ball was last played (see Rule 20-5).

Exceptions:
1. If it is known or virtually certain that the original ball that has not been found is in an *obstruction* (Rule 24-3) or is in an *abnormal ground condition* (Rule 25-1c), the player may proceed under the applicable *Rule*.
2. If it is known or virtually certain that the original ball that has not been found has been moved by an *outside agency* (Rule 18-1) or is in a *water hazard* (Rule 26-1), the player must proceed under the applicable *Rule*.

PENALTY FOR BREACH OF RULE 27-1:
Match play – Loss of hole;
Stroke play – Two strokes.

27-2. PROVISIONAL BALL
a. Procedure
If a ball may be *lost* outside a *water hazard* or may be *out of bounds*, to save time the player may play another ball provisionally in accordance with Rule 27-1. The player must inform his opponent in match play or his *marker* or a *fellow-competitor* in stroke play that he intends to play a *provisional ball*, and he must play it before he or his *partner* goes forward to search for the original ball.

PROVISIONAL BALL BECOMES BALL IN PLAY

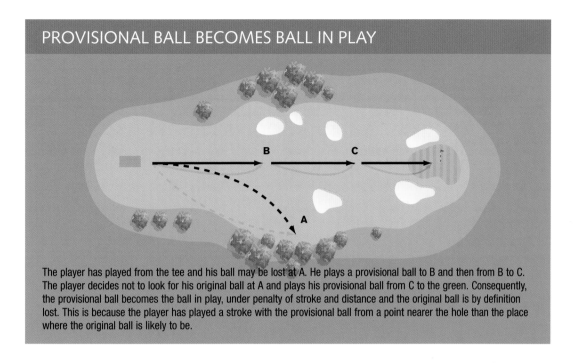

The player has played from the tee and his ball may be lost at A. He plays a provisional ball to B and then from B to C. The player decides not to look for his original ball at A and plays his provisional ball from C to the green. Consequently, the provisional ball becomes the ball in play, under penalty of stroke and distance and the original ball is by definition lost. This is because the player has played a stroke with the provisional ball from a point nearer the hole than the place where the original ball is likely to be.

PROVISIONAL BALL PLAYED: ORIGINAL BALL FOUND UNPLAYABLE

A player plays a provisional ball as his ball may be lost. The original ball is found within five minutes and before the provisional ball has become the ball in play, but the ball is unplayable. The player must abandon the provisional ball and proceed with the original ball.

If he fails to do so and plays another ball, that ball is not a *provisional ball* and becomes the *ball in play* **under penalty of stroke and distance (Rule 27-1)**; the original ball is *lost*.

(Order of play from teeing ground – see Rule 10-3.)

Note: If a *provisional ball* played under Rule 27-2a might be *lost* outside a *water hazard* or *out of bounds*, the player may play another *provisional ball*. If another *provisional ball* is played, it bears the same relationship to the previous *provisional ball* as the first *provisional ball* bears to the original ball.

b. When Provisional Ball Becomes Ball in Play

The player may play a *provisional ball* until he reaches the place where the original ball is likely to be. If he makes a *stroke* with the *provisional ball* from the place where the original ball is likely to be or from a point nearer the *hole* than that place, the original ball is *lost* and the *provisional ball* becomes the *ball in play* **under penalty of stroke and distance (Rule 27-1)**.

If the original ball is lost outside a *water hazard* or is *out of bounds*, the *provisional ball* becomes the *ball in play*, **under penalty of stroke and distance** (Rule 27-1).

If it is known or virtually certain that the original ball is *lost* in a *water hazard*, the player must proceed in accordance with Rule 26-1.

Exception: If it is known or virtually certain that the original ball is *lost* in an *obstruction* (Rule 24-3) or an *abnormal ground condition* (Rule 25-1c) the player may proceed under the applicable *Rule*.

See **incident** involving Rule 27-2c below.

c. When Provisional Ball to Be Abandoned

If the original ball is neither *lost* nor *out of bounds*, the player must abandon the *provisional ball* and continue playing the original ball. If he makes any further *strokes* at the *provisional ball*, he is playing a *wrong ball* and the provisions of Rule 15-3 apply.

Note: If a player plays a *provisional ball* under Rule 27-2a, the *strokes* made after this Rule has been invoked with a *provisional ball* abandoned under Rule 27-2c and *penalty strokes* incurred solely by playing that ball are disregarded.

RULE 27 INCIDENTS

While the Rules allot five minutes to search for a lost ball, sometimes it is to a player's advantage not to find his original ball. Phil Mickelson would have been at a distinct advantage had a diligent gallery marshal not found his ball during the third play-off hole of the 2001 Buick Invitational at Torrey Pines.

From the tee, first Mickelson and then Frank Lickliter played their drives into a rough canyon to the left of the 17th hole. Each then played a provisional ball in case his original ball turned out to be lost in the canyon.

Lickliter's first ball was soon found, requiring him to abandon his provisional ball in the fairway (Rule 27-2c). After inspecting his lie, he decided that his best course of action was to deem his ball unplayable and replay from the tee, as was his option under the unplayable ball Rule (Rule 28).

Watching the events unfold and preferring his chances lying three in the fairway with his provisional ball, Mickelson asked that the search stop for his original ball in the canyon. "Don't find it," directed

Mickleson. "I don't want to find it." He clearly understood that under the Rules a ball cannot be declared lost.

A well-intended marshal in the canyon never heard Mickelson's request, continued his search, and was successful in finding Mickelson's original ball. Fuming at the turn of events, Mickelson could be heard to say, "Did I not ask him to get out of there?"

The marshal informed Mickelson that his ball was found even though Mickelson preferred to continue play with this provisional ball. By Decision 27/13, Mickelson was obligated to have a look at the found ball and, by Rule 27-2c, if the found ball was his original, abandon his provisional ball and continue play with the original.

Because Mickelson's provisional ball was nearer the hole than his original ball was likely to be, had Mickelson made a stroke with this provisional ball before his original ball was found, the provisional ball would have become the ball in play. It would not have mattered if his original was subsequently found.

However, with his original ball found, Mickelson was required to deal with its circumstances just as Lickliter had been required to deal with his. Both players' troublesome drives were found, both players' provisional balls had to be abandoned, both deemed their original balls unplayable, and both returned to the tee to play their third stroke.

Mickelson, the defending champion, ultimately won with a double bogey six.

Mark O'Meara returns to identify a ball found within the five-minute search period during the 1998 Championship.

During the third round of the 1998 British Open at Royal Birkdale, Mark O'Meara's second shot drifted too far to the right into knee high grass and scrub trees at the 480-yard 6th hole. What happened next resulted in the adoption of a new Decision that helped to clarify the Rules of Golf.

By the time O'Meara and his caddie reached the area where they thought his ball had finished, a number of spectators were already engaged in searching for it. The Rules observer with the group was Reed Mackenzie, then vice president of the USGA and chairman of the association's Rules of Golf Committee. When O'Meara arrived on the scene, Mackenzie started timing the five-minute search period allowed under the Rules.

To everyone in the immediate area of the search, O'Meara announced the type of ball he was playing and stated that it was embossed with his logo. Several balls were found, but none were his.

After searching for approximately four minutes, O'Meara suspected that his ball was lost, left the search area, took another ball from his caddie, and started back down the fairway to play again from where his original ball had last been played.

About 30 seconds later, a spectator announced, "Here it is! I have it." Someone called to O'Meara, who did not hear and continued walking. An official went to where the spectator had found the ball and saw it was the type O'Meara was using and did have his logo on it.

By this time, it was nearing the end of the five-minute search period, and it was clear that O'Meara would not be able to get back to the ball in order to identify it within the five-minute period. The Definition of "Lost Ball" states that a ball is lost if it is not "found or identified" within the five minute search. If the Definition stated "found and identified", the procedure would have been clear. A radio call was made for a roving Rules official to make a decision.

Mike Shea, senior Rules director of the PGA Tour in the U.S., was working the area and took the call. David Rickman, Rules secretary for the R&A, was also on hand. Shea arrived first and brought O'Meara in a cart to discuss the situation with Rickman. Rickman was advised that the ball had been found, but not identified by the player, within the five-minute time limit. Considering the facts, Rickman determined that the ball had been found within the five-minute search period, that O'Meara was entitled to identify it outside the stipulated five-minute period and, if it was his ball, be was entitled to play it without penalty. Everyone returned to the area where the ball had been found

However, during search, the area had become trampled and a misguided spectator, believing the ball had been abandoned, had lifted it.

O'Meara and Rickman went to the spot, the ball was not there, but the spectator was close by and returned the ball to O'Meara who identified it as his. Although the spectator said he knew exactly where the ball had been before he lifted it, his pinpointing turned out to be only an approximation.

Under Rules 18-1 and 20-3c, O'Meara was therefore required to drop as nearly as possible to the spot where the ball had been before the spectator lifted it. When O'Meara dropped the ball, it then rolled more than two club-lengths from the spot where it struck a part of the course thus requiring a re-drop. Upon re-dropping, the ball rolled nearer the hole. Therefore, O'Meara placed it on the spot where it first struck a part of the course when re-dropped. He then played his shot and continued the round, winning the championship the following day.

The ambiguity of the Definition of "Lost Ball", in this particular situation, necessitated the addition of Decision 27/5.5. The new decision clarified that if a ball is found within five minutes, the player is allowed enough time to reach the area and identify it even though the identification takes place after the five-minute search period has elapsed.

As fate would have it, a month before O'Meara's predicament, Lee Janzen was in a similar circumstance during the final round of the U.S. Open. From the 5th tee at Olympic in San Francisco, Jansen's drive came to rest in a tree. After discussing the situation with marshals in the area, Janzen assumed his ball remained up in the tree and was, therefore, lost. He headed back to the tee to put another ball into play (Rule 27).

Before a second ball could be played, Janzen's first ball fell from the tree and was identified by his caddie. Janzen was called back, and he identified the ball as his. All this took place within the five-minute search period and, therefore, there was no question that Janzen's ball was in play and no penalty was incurred.

Janzen's ball falling from the tree was propitious as he went on to record a 68 for the day, which resulted in a one-stroke win over Payne Stewart and his second U.S. Open victory in six starts.

Frequently asked questions

Q After going forward to search for his ball, may a player return to where he last played in order to play a provisional ball?

A No. If the player did so the second ball would become the ball in play and the original ball would be lost (see Rule 27-2a and Definition of "Lost Ball"). He must play a provisional ball "before going forward to search" for the original ball.

Q A player hits his ball down the middle of the fairway. He knows it is in the fairway, but can not find it, and assumes it must have embedded in the soft ground. Is the player permitted to drop a ball without penalty where he thinks it might have come to rest?

A No. If the ball can not be found, the player must proceed under Rule 27-1, incurring the stroke-and-distance penalty. There is nothing in Rule 25-2 that permits a player to take relief for a ball that is thought to be embedded without identifying it first. The soft mushy earth is not an abnormal ground condition unless casual water is present, in which case Rule 25-1c applies.

147

RULE **28** BALL UNPLAYABLE

DEFINITIONS

All defined terms are in *italics* and are listed alphabetically in the Definitions section – see pages 9–20.

See **incident** involving Rule 28 on pages 150–51.

The player may deem his ball unplayable at any place on the *course*, except when the ball is in a *water hazard*. The player is the sole judge as to whether his ball is unplayable.

If the player deems his ball to be unplayable, he must, **under penalty of one stroke**:

a.   Play a ball as nearly as possible at the spot from which the original ball was last played (see Rule 20-5); or

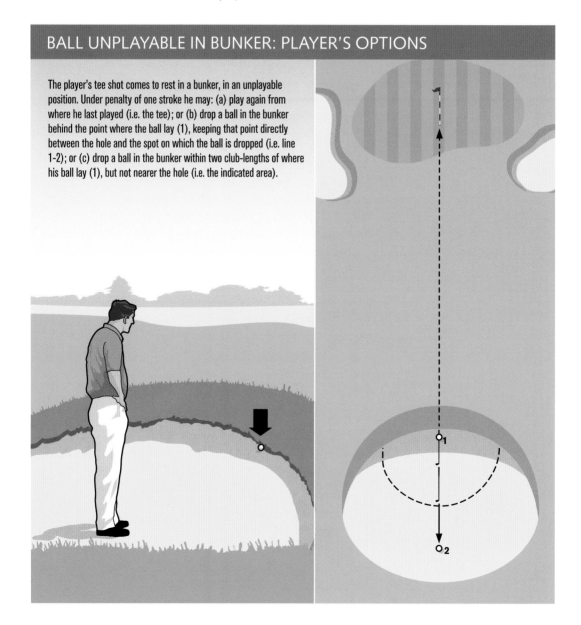

BALL UNPLAYABLE IN BUNKER: PLAYER'S OPTIONS

The player's tee shot comes to rest in a bunker, in an unplayable position. Under penalty of one stroke he may: (a) play again from where he last played (i.e. the tee); or (b) drop a ball in the bunker behind the point where the ball lay (1), keeping that point directly between the hole and the spot on which the ball is dropped (i.e. line 1-2); or (c) drop a ball in the bunker within two club-lengths of where his ball lay (1), but not nearer the hole (i.e. the indicated area).

b. Drop a ball behind the point where the ball lay, keeping that point directly between the *hole* and the spot on which the ball is dropped, with no limit to how far behind that point the ball may be dropped; or

c. Drop a ball within two club-lengths of the spot where the ball lay, but not nearer the *hole*.

If the unplayable ball is in a *bunker*, the player may proceed under Clause a, b or c. If he elects to proceed under Clause b or c, a ball must be dropped in the *bunker*.

When proceeding under this Rule, the player may lift and clean his ball or *substitute* a ball.

PENALTY FOR BREACH OF RULE:
Match play – Loss of hole; Stroke play – Two strokes.

BALL UNPLAYABLE IN BUSH: PLACE FOR DROPPING

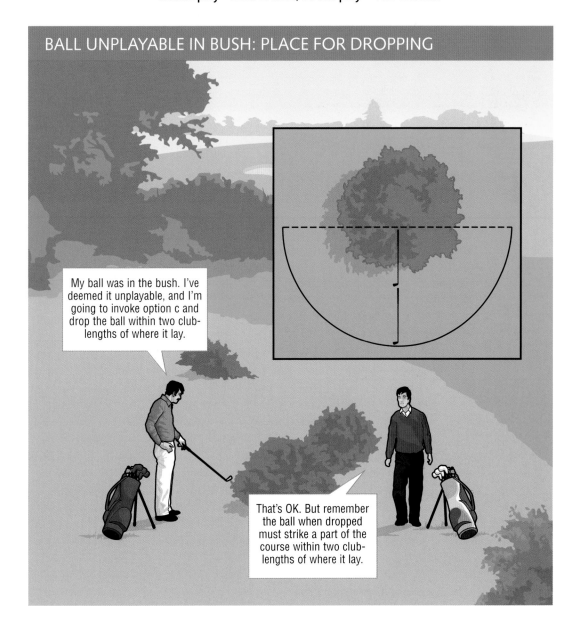

My ball was in the bush. I've deemed it unplayable, and I'm going to invoke option c and drop the ball within two club-lengths of where it lay.

That's OK. But remember the ball when dropped must strike a part of the course within two club-lengths of where it lay.

Michelle Wie plays from a wrong place after dropping improperly from an unplayable lie. Unaware of the two-stroke penalty for her infraction, she failed to include it in her third round score and was ultimately disqualified for returning a score lower than she actually made.

RULE 28 INCIDENT

It is the responsibility of every player to know the Rules, and it is incumbent upon the Committee to enforce them. In stroke play, the Committee's primary responsibility is the protection of the entire field. This responsibility lasts throughout all rounds of the competition. If there is an infraction in the first round that does not come to light until play of the fourth round, the Committee is authorized to respond retroactively. This ensures the correctness of the entire competition.

An unplayable ball (Rule 28) also requires proper adherence to dropping procedures (Rule 20). While the penalty for an unplayable ball is one stroke, the violation for an improper drop that results in playing from a wrong place results in a penalty of two strokes.

During the third round of the 2005 Samsung World Championship, Michelle Wie's ball came to rest in a bush during play of the 7th hole. She deemed her ball unplayable and selected the option that required her to drop within two club-lengths of the spot on the ground immediately below the position of the ball in the bush, no nearer the hole. Wie dropped the ball, made a stroke, finished the round, and returned her score card.

The following day, the Committee became aware that Wie may have dropped improperly and, therefore, played from a wrong place. The Committee prudently sought all sources of information in making its determination. Videotape of the incident was reviewed. Following play of the fourth round and before the close of competition, Wie and her caddie were asked to recreate the drop.

The Committee concluded that Wie had indeed dropped in and played from a wrong place. The penalty for both breaches was three strokes – one for an unplayable ball, and two for playing from a wrong place.

Because she was unaware of her infractions, Wie unintentionally and regrettably failed to include the two penalty strokes for playing from a wrong place on her score card for the third round. This was an additional breach (Rule 6-6d) for returning a score for a hole lower than the score actually made. Because the competition was not yet closed, Wie was disqualified, (Decision 33-7/4.5). Wie's marker was absolved as she was unaware that an infraction had taken place.

The Committee is obligated to use all sources and methods in protecting the field for the entire competition. In this way, the propriety of the competition is preserved. Once the competition is closed, unintentional infractions that come to light are not penalized. There is, however, no time limit for penalizing an infraction that a competitor knowingly commits but fails to include in his score.

Because Wie was unaware of her improper drop and the resulting penalty, had the infraction come to light after the close of the competition, the lower score would have stood without penalty (Rule 34-1b).

Frequently asked question

Q May a player declare a ball in a hazard unplayable?

A The answer depends on the type of hazard the ball is in. If the ball is in a water hazard, the player may not declare the ball unplayable. He may play the ball as it lies, or proceed under the water hazard Rule (Rule 26-1). If the unplayable ball lies in a bunker, the player may proceed under any of the options listed in Rule 28. However, if he elects option b or c, the ball must be dropped in the bunker.

OTHER FORMS OF PLAY

RULE

THREESOMES AND FOURSOMES

DEFINITIONS

All defined terms are in *italics* and are listed alphabetically in the Definitions section – see pages 9–20.

See **incident** involving Rule 29 on pages 154.

29-1. GENERAL

In a *threesome* or a *foursome*, during any *stipulated round* the *partners* must play alternately from the *teeing grounds* and alternately during the play of each hole. *Penalty strokes* do not affect the order of play.

151

FOURSOMES: ORDER OF PLAY WHEN PARTNER DRIVES OUT OF BOUNDS

29-2. MATCH PLAY

If a player plays when his *partner* should have played, **his *side* loses the hole**.

29-3. STROKE PLAY

If the *partners* make a *stroke* or *strokes* in incorrect order, such *stroke* or *strokes* are canceled and **the *side* incurs a penalty of two strokes**. The *side* must correct the error by playing a ball in correct order as nearly as possible at the spot from which it first played in incorrect order (see Rule 20-5). If the *side* makes a *stroke* on the next *teeing ground* without first correcting the error or, in the case of the last hole of the round, leaves the *putting green* without declaring its intention to correct the error, **the *side* is disqualified**.

FOURSOMES: WHICH PARTNER DROPS BALL

We are entitled to free relief from the casual water. Do I drop the ball or do you?

It's my turn to play the next shot so I drop the ball.

See Rule 20-2a which requires a ball to be dropped by the player himself.

ORDER OF PLAY IN 36-HOLE COMPETITION

Now that we're starting the second 18 holes, are we allowed to change the order of teeing off so that you drive at the evens and I drive at the odds?

Yes, unless the Committee in charge of the competition has laid down a condition to the contrary.

Rule 29-1. See Definition of "Stipulated Round".

RULE 29 INCIDENT

The practice putting green at the Old Course in St. Andrews lies just off the course and a short distance from the 1st tee. Paired together on the second day for the morning foursomes of the 1975 Walker Cup Match, the U.S. side of veteran William C. Campbell and newcomer John Grace reported to the tee a little ahead of their starting time. They had already decided that Grace would drive at the odd numbered holes, so Campbell decided to use the extra time before the match began to hit a few putts on the practice green – some 50 yards from the 1st tee.

As the visiting team, Campbell and Grace had the honor. The wind was gusting from the west, which carried the announcement of the match's beginning beyond Campbell's earshot.

As the breeze momentarily died, Campbell heard "the click" of Grace's drive just before striking a practice putt, and he was unable to interrupt his practice stroke. Therefore, Campbell had practiced during play of the hole. Instantly and instinctively recognizing his infraction of the Rules, Campbell walked onto the fairway and reported to the referee. The U.S. had just lost the first hole (Rule 7-2).

The referee for the match, John Pasquill from the Royal and Ancient Golf Club, accepted Campbell's report but made no immediate announcement to the other players. Because play of the hole had ended with the Rules violation and the loss of hole, Campbell was free to play his side's second toward the 1st green as simply more practice. Besides, he was reluctant to chill his partner's enthusiasm.

Walking across the Swilken Burn, Campbell told Grace what had taken place. "He was incredulous, to say the least," Campbell recalls.

The fact that the practice green was off the course, beyond the out of bounds markers, gave Grace reason to believe they might have a chance on appeal, though there is no such distinction within the Rules.

Campbell reported to Pasquill that his partner wished to protest the ruling and appeal to the Committee. In a neutral voice, Pasquill appropriately replied,"On the golf course, I am the Committee." Thus, the Americans lost the first hole and eventually the match to Mark James and Richard Eyles.

Frequently asked question

Q What determines which partner tees off on the next hole in a threesome or foursome competition – the one who last played on the previous hole or the number of the hole?

A The number of the hole. In a threesome or foursome competition, one partner tees off on the odd-numbered holes and the other on the even-numbered holes. It is irrelevant who played last on the previous hole.

RULE **30** THREE-BALL, BEST-BALL AND FOUR-BALL MATCH PLAY

DEFINITIONS

All defined terms are in *italics* and are listed alphabetically in the Definitions section – see pages 9–20.

30-1. RULES OF GOLF APPLY
The Rules of Golf, so far as they are not at variance with the following specific Rules, apply to *three-ball*, *best-ball* and *four-ball matches*.

30-2. THREE-BALL MATCH PLAY
a. Ball at Rest Moved by an Opponent
Except as otherwise provided in the *Rules*, if the player's ball is touched or *moved* by an opponent, his *caddie* or *equipment* other than during search, Rule 18-3b applies. **That opponent incurs a penalty of one stroke in his match with the player**, but not in his match with the other opponent.

BREACH OF RULE BY ONE PARTNER IN MATCH PLAY

I'll just remove this twig.

I'm afraid you're disqualified from the hole for removing a loose impediment from the bunker. Fortunately, although I'm in the same bunker I'm not penalized because your breach of Rule 13-4 did not assist my play.

THREE-BALL MATCH PLAY

FOUR-BALL: ONE PLAYER MAY REPRESENT SIDE

Your partner's late. Are you disqualified, or just your partner?

Fortunately, neither of us. Because this is a four-ball match I am entitled to represent the side. Let's start. My partner is allowed to join us later, at the conclusion of a hole.

A John, my ball has struck your bag. What do I do now?
B In your match with me you may either play the ball as it lies or cancel that stroke and replay it. In your match with Jim you must play your original ball as it lies.
A That means I'm going to have two balls in play at the same time.
B That's right. Rule 30-2b.

b. Ball Deflected or Stopped by an Opponent Accidentally

If a player's ball is accidentally deflected or stopped by an opponent, his *caddie* or *equipment*, there is no penalty. In his match with that opponent the player may, before another *stroke* is made by either *side*, cancel the *stroke* and play a ball, without penalty, as nearly as possible at the spot from which the original ball was last played (see Rule 20-5) or he may play the ball as it lies.

Exception: Ball striking person attending or holding up *flagstick* or anything carried by him – see Rule 17-3b.
(Ball purposely deflected or stopped by opponent – see Rule 1-2.)

30-3. BEST-BALL AND FOUR-BALL MATCH PLAY
a. Representation of Side

A *side* may be represented by one *partner* for all or any part of a match; all *partners* need not be present. An absent *partner* may join a match between holes, but not during play of a hole.

b. Order of Play

Balls belonging to the same *side* may be played in the order the *side* considers best.

c. Wrong Ball

If a player incurs the loss of hole penalty under Rule 15-3a for making a *stroke* at a *wrong ball*, **he is disqualified for that hole**, but his *partner* incurs no penalty even if the *wrong ball* belongs to him. If the *wrong ball* belongs to another player, its owner must place a ball on the spot from which the *wrong ball* was first played.

d. Penalty to Side

A *side* **is penalized** for a breach of any of the following by any *partner*:
- Rule 4 – Clubs
- Rule 6-4 – Caddie
- Any Local Rule or Condition of Competition for which the penalty is an adjustment to the state of the match.

e. Disqualification of Side

(i) **A *side* is disqualified** if any *partner* incurs a penalty of disqualification under any of the following:
- Rule 1-3 – Agreement to Waive Rules
- Rule 4 – Clubs
- Rule 5-1 or 5-2 – The Ball
- Rule 6-2a – Handicap
- Rule 6-4 – Caddie
- Rule 6-7 – Undue Delay; Slow Play
- Rule 11-1 – Teeing
- Rule 14-3 – Artificial Devices, Unusual Equipment and Unusual Use of Equipment
- Rule 33-7 – Disqualification Penalty Imposed by Committee

(ii) **A *side* is disqualified** if all *partners* incur a penalty of disqualification under any of the following:
- Rule 6-3 – Time of Starting and Groups
- Rule 6-8 – Discontinuance of Play

(iii) In all other cases where a breach of a *Rule* would result in disqualification, **the player is disqualified for that hole only**.

f. Effect of Other Penalties

If a player's breach of a *Rule* assists his *partner's* play or adversely affects an opponent's play, **the *partner* incurs the applicable penalty in addition to any penalty incurred by the player**.

In all other cases where a player incurs a penalty for breach of a *Rule*, the penalty does not apply to his *partner*. Where the penalty is stated to be loss of hole, **the effect is to disqualify the player for that hole**.

Frequently asked question

Q A and B are playing C and D in a four-ball match. B's ball is near the hole in a position to serve as a backstop for A's ball. C requests B to lift his ball. B does not comply and A putts. What is the ruling?

A B is disqualified for the hole for failing to comply with Rule 22-1. If A's ball strikes B's ball, A would also be disqualified from the hole since B's infringement assisted A – Rule 30-3f. If the balls do not collide, A is not penalized.

RULE 31 FOUR-BALL STROKE PLAY

DEFINITIONS All defined terms are in *italics* and are listed alphabetically in the Definitions section – see pages 9–20.

31-1. GENERAL
The Rules of Golf, so far as they are not at variance with the following specific Rules, apply to *four-ball* stroke play.

31-2. REPRESENTATION OF SIDE
A *side* may be represented by either *partner* for all or any part of a *stipulated round*; both *partners* need not be present. An absent *competitor* may join his *partner* between holes, but not during play of a hole.

31-3. SCORING
The *marker* is required to record for each hole only the gross score of whichever *partner's* score is to count. The gross scores to count must be individually identifiable; otherwise, **the *side* is disqualified**. Only one of the *partners* need be responsible for complying with Rule 6-6b.
(Wrong score – see Rule 31-7a.)

31-4. ORDER OF PLAY
Balls belonging to the same *side* may be played in the order the *side* considers best.

31-5. WRONG BALL
If a *competitor* is in breach of Rule 15-3b for making a *stroke* at a *wrong ball*, **he incurs a penalty of two strokes** and must correct his mistake by playing the correct ball or by proceeding under the *Rules*. His *partner* incurs no penalty even if the *wrong ball* belongs to him.

If the *wrong ball* belongs to another *competitor*, its owner must place a ball on the spot from which the *wrong ball* was first played.

31-6. PENALTY TO SIDE
A *side* is penalized for a breach of any of the following by either *partner*:
• Rule 4 – Clubs
• Rule 6-4 – Caddie
• Any Local Rule or Condition of Competition for which there is a maximum penalty per round.

31-7. DISQUALIFICATION PENALTIES
a. Breach by One Partner
A *side* is disqualified from the competition if either *partner* incurs a penalty of disqualification under any of the following:
• Rule 1-3 – Agreement to Waive Rules
• Rule 3-4 – Refusal to Comply with a Rule
• Rule 4 – Clubs

FOUR-BALL STROKE PLAY

Date _3RD APRIL 1996_

Competition _SPRING OPEN FOUR-BALL_

PLAYER A _J. SUTHERLAND_   Handicap _16_   Strokes _12_

PLAYER B _W.B. TAYLOR_   Handicap _12_   Strokes _9_

Hole	Length Yards	Par	Stroke Index	Gross Score A	Gross Score B	Net Score A	Net Score B	Won X Lost – Half O	Mar. Score	Hole	Length Yards	Par	Stroke Index	Gross Score A	Gross Score B	Net Score A	Net Score B	Won X Lost – Half O	Mar. Score
1	437	4	4			4	3			10	425	4	3		5		4		
2	320	4	14			4	4			11	141	3	17	3		3			
3	162	3	18			4	4			12	476	5	9	6		5			
4	504	5	7	6		5				13	211	3	11		4		4		
5	181	3	16	4		4				14	437	4	5		5		4		
6	443	4	2		5	4				15	460	4	1		5		4		
7	390	4	8		5	4				16	176	3	15	4		4			
8	346	4	12	5		4				17	340	4	13	4		4			
9	340	4	10	4		3				18	435	4	6	6		5			
Out	3123	35					35			In	3101	34					37		
										Out	3123	35					35		
										T'tl	6224	69					72		

Player's Signature _J. Sutherland_

Marker's Signature _R.J. Parker_

Handicap									
Net Score									

Partner's scores to be individually identified

1 The lower score of the partners is the score for the hole (Rule 31).

2 Only one of the partners need be responsible for complying with Rule 6-6b, i.e. recording scores, checking scores, countersigning and returning the card (Rule 31-3).

3 The competitor is solely responsible for the correctness of the gross score recorded. Although there is no objection to the competitor (or his marker) entering the net score, it is the Committee's responsibility to record the better ball score for each hole, to add up the scores and to apply the handicaps recorded on the card (Rule 33-5). Thus there is no penalty for an error by the competitor (or his marker) for recording an incorrect net score.

4 Scores of the two partners must be kept in separate columns otherwise it is impossible for the Committee to apply the correct handicap. If the scores of both partners, having different handicaps, are recorded in the same column, the Committee has no alternative but to disqualify both partners (Rule 31-7 and Rule 6-6 apply).

5 The Committee is responsible for laying down the conditions under which a competition is to be played (Rule 33-1), including the method of handicapping. In the above illustration the Committee laid down that ¾ handicaps would apply.

- Rule 5-1 or 5-2 – The Ball
- Rule 6-2b – Handicap
- Rule 6-4 – Caddie
- Rule 6-6b – Signing and Returning Score Card
- Rule 6-6d – Wrong Score for Hole
- Rule 6-7 – Undue Delay; Slow Play
- Rule 7-1 – Practice Before or Between Rounds
- Rule 11-1 – Teeing
- Rule 14-3 – Artificial Devices, Unusual Equipment and Unusual Use of Equipment
- Rule 22-1 – Ball Assisting Play
- Rule 31-3 – Gross Scores to Count Not Individually Identifiable
- Rule 33-7 – Disqualification Penalty Imposed by Committee

b. Breach by Both Partners

A *side* **is disqualified from the competition**:

(i) if each *partner* incurs a penalty of disqualification for a breach of Rule 6-3 (Time of Starting and Groups) or Rule 6-8 (Discontinuance of Play), or

(ii) if, at the same hole, each *partner* is in breach of a *Rule* the penalty for which is disqualification from the competition or for a hole.

c. For the Hole Only

In all other cases where a breach of a *Rule* would result in disqualification, **the** *competitor* **is disqualified only for the hole at which the breach occurred**.

31-8. EFFECT OF OTHER PENALTIES

If a *competitor's* breach of a *Rule* assists his *partner's* play, **the** *partner* **incurs the applicable penalty in addition to any penalty incurred by the** *competitor*.

In all other cases where a *competitor* incurs a penalty for breach of a *Rule*, the penalty does not apply to his *partner*.

Frequently asked question

Q In four-ball stroke play, what score must be recorded on the score card?

A Only the gross score of whichever partner's score is to count for the hole must be recorded on the card. The score of the other player does not need to be recorded. Additionally, the scores must be individually identifiable so the Committee can determine which partner's score is recorded.

RULE **32** BOGEY, PAR AND STABLEFORD COMPETITIONS

DEFINITIONS

All defined terms are in *italics* and are listed alphabetically in the Definitions section – see pages 9–20.

32-1. CONDITIONS

Bogey, par and Stableford competitions are forms of stroke play in which play is against a fixed score at each hole. The *Rules* for stroke play, so far as they are not at variance with the following specific Rules, apply.

In handicap bogey, par and Stableford competitions, the *competitor* with the lowest net score at a hole takes the *honor* at the next *teeing ground*.

a. Bogey and Par Competitions

The scoring for bogey and par competitions is made as in match play. Any hole for which a *competitor* makes no return is regarded as a loss. The winner is the *competitor* who is most successful in the aggregate of holes.

The *marker* is responsible for marking only the gross number of *strokes* for each hole where the *competitor* makes a net score equal to or less than the fixed score.

Note 1: The *competitor's* score is adjusted by **deducting a hole or holes under the applicable *Rule*** when a penalty other than disqualification is incurred under any of the following:
• Rule 4 – Clubs
• Rule 6-4 – Caddie
• Any Local Rule or Condition of Competition for which there is a maximum penalty per round.

The *competitor* is responsible for reporting the facts regarding such a breach to the *Committee* before he returns his score card so that the *Committee* may apply the penalty. If the *competitor* fails to report his breach to the *Committee*, **he is disqualified**.

Note 2: If the *competitor* is in breach of Rule 6-7 (Undue Delay; Slow Play), the *Committee* will **deduct one hole** from the aggregate of holes. For a repeated offense, see Rule 32-2a.

b. Stableford Competitions

The scoring in Stableford competitions is made by points awarded in relation to a fixed score at each hole as follows:

Hole Played In	Points	Hole Played In	Points
More than one over fixed score or no score returned	0	One under fixed score	3
		Two under fixed score	4
One over fixed score	1	Three under fixed score	5
Fixed score	2	Four under fixed score	6

The winner is the *competitor* who scores the highest number of points.

161

The *marker* is responsible for marking only the gross number of *strokes* at each hole where the *competitor's* net score earns one or more points.

Note 1: If a *competitor* is in breach of a *Rule* for which there is a maximum penalty per round, he must report the facts to the *Committee* before returning his score card; if he fails to do so, **he is disqualified**. The *Committee* will, from the total points scored for the round, **deduct two points for each hole at which any breach occurred, with a maximum deduction per round of four points for each Rule breached.**

Note 2: If the *competitor* is in breach of Rule 6-7 (Undue Delay; Slow Play), the *Committee* will **deduct two points from the total points scored for the round.** For a repeated offense, see Rule 32-2a.

32-2. DISQUALIFICATION PENALTIES
a. From the Competition
A *competitor* **is disqualified** from the competition if he incurs a penalty of disqualification under any of the following:
- Rule 1-3 – Agreement to Waive Rules
- Rule 3-4 – Refusal to Comply with Rule
- Rule 4 – Clubs
- Rule 5-1 or 5-2 – The Ball
- Rule 6-2b – Handicap
- Rule 6-3 – Time of Starting and Groups
- Rule 6-4 – Caddie
- Rule 6-6b – Signing and Returning Score Card
- Rule 6-6d – Wrong Score for Hole, i.e., when the recorded score is lower than actually taken, except that no penalty is incurred when a breach of this Rule does not affect the result of the hole
- Rule 6-7 – Undue Delay; Slow Play
- Rule 6-8 – Discontinuance of Play
- Rule 7-1 – Practice Before or Between Rounds
- Rule 11-1 – Teeing
- Rule 14-3 – Artificial Devices, Unusual Equipment and Unusual Use of Equipment
- Rule 22-1 – Ball Assisting Play
- Rule 33-7 – Disqualification Penalty Imposed by Committee

b. For a Hole
In all other cases where a breach of a *Rule* would result in disqualification, **the *competitor* is disqualified only for the hole at which the breach occurred**.

ADMINISTRATION

RULE **33** **THE COMMITTEE**

DEFINITIONS

All defined terms are in *italics* and are listed alphabetically in the Definitions section – see pages 9–20.

See **incident** involving Rule 33-1 on pages 166–67.

33-1. CONDITIONS; WAIVING RULE

The *Committee* must establish the conditions under which a competition is to be played.

The *Committee* has no power to waive a Rule of Golf.

Certain specific *Rules* governing stroke play are so substantially different from those governing match play that combining the two forms of play is not practicable and is not permitted. The result of a match played in these circumstances is null and void and, in the stroke-play competition, **the competitors are disqualified.**

In stroke play the *Committee* may limit a *referee's* duties.

33-2. THE COURSE
a. Defining Bounds and Margins
The *Committee* must define accurately:
(i)   the *course* and *out of bounds*,
(ii) the margins of *water hazards* and *lateral water hazards*,
(iii) *ground under repair*, and
(iv) *obstructions* and integral parts of the *course*.

b. New Holes
New *holes* should be made on the day on which a stroke-play competition begins and at such other times as the *Committee* considers necessary, provided all *competitors* in a single round play with each *hole* cut in the same position.

Exception: When it is impossible for a damaged *hole* to be repaired so that it conforms with the Definition, the *Committee* may make a new *hole* in a nearby similar position.

Note: Where a single round is to be played on more than one day, the *Committee* may provide, in the conditions of a competition (Rule 33-1), that the *holes* and *teeing grounds* may be differently situated on each day of the competition, provided that, on any one day, all *competitors* play with each *hole* and each *teeing ground* in the same position.

c. Practice Ground
Where there is no practice ground available outside the area of a competition *course*, the *Committee* should establish the area on which players may practice on any day of a competition, if it is practicable to do so. On any day of a stroke-play competition, the *Committee* should not normally permit practice on or to a *putting green* or from a *hazard* of the competition *course*.

163

RULE 33-2d. COURSE UNPLAYABLE

If the course is not in a playable condition, the Committee may have to temporarily suspend play. In stroke play only, if further play becomes impossible, the Committee may have to declare play null and void.

d. Course Unplayable

If the *Committee* or its authorized representative considers that for any reason the *course* is not in a playable condition or that there are circumstances that render the proper playing of the game impossible, it may, in match play or stroke play, order a temporary suspension of play or, in stroke play, declare play null and void and cancel all scores for the round in question. When a round is canceled, all penalties incurred in that round are canceled.

(Procedure in discontinuing and resuming play – see Rule 6-8.)

33-3. TIMES OF STARTING AND GROUPS

The *Committee* must establish the times of starting and, in stroke play, arrange the *groups* in which *competitors* must play.

When a match-play competition is played over an extended period, the *Committee* establishes the limit of time within which each round must be completed. When players are allowed to arrange the date of their match within these limits, the *Committee* should announce that the match must be played at a stated time on the last day of the period, unless the players agree to a prior date.

33-4. HANDICAP STROKE TABLE

The *Committee* must publish a table indicating the order of holes at which handicap strokes are to be given or received.

33-5. SCORE CARD

In stroke play, the *Committee* must provide each *competitor* with a score card containing the date and the *competitor's* name or, in *foursomes* or *four-ball* stroke play, the *competitors'* names.

In stroke play, the *Committee* is responsible for the addition of scores and the application of the handicap recorded on the score card.

In *four-ball* stroke play, the *Committee* is responsible for recording the better-ball score for each hole and in the process applying the handicaps recorded on the score card, and adding the better-ball scores.

In bogey, par and Stableford competitions, the *Committee* is responsible for applying the handicap recorded on the score card and determining the result of each hole and the overall result or points total.

Note: The *Committee* may request that each *competitor* record the date and his name on his score card.

33-6. DECISION OF TIES

The *Committee* must announce the manner, day and time for the decision of a halved match or of a tie, whether played on level terms or under handicap.

A halved match must not be decided by stroke play. A tie in stroke play must not be decided by a match.

33-7. DISQUALIFICATION PENALTY; COMMITTEE DISCRETION

A penalty of disqualification may in exceptional individual cases be waived, modified or imposed if the *Committee* considers such action warranted.

Any penalty less than disqualification must not be waived or modified.

If a *Committee* considers that a player is guilty of a serious breach of etiquette, it may impose a penalty of disqualification under this Rule.

See **incident** involving Rule 33-8 on pages 166–167.

33-8. LOCAL RULES
a. Policy

The *Committee* may establish Local Rules for local abnormal conditions if they are consistent with the policy set forth in Appendix I.

b. Waiving or Modifying a Rule

A Rule of Golf must not be waived by a Local Rule. However, if a *Committee* considers that local abnormal conditions interfere with the proper playing of the game to the extent that it is necessary to make a Local Rule that modifies the Rules of Golf, the Local Rule must be authorized by the USGA.

RULE 33 INCIDENTS

Rule 33 states that the Committee must establish the conditions under which a competition is to be played and lists very specific areas that require attention, such as starting times, score cards, definition of the bounds and margins of the course, and what to do in case of a tie.

Each of the four major championships uses a different method for settling a tie. Each is also very specific in delineating exactly what will take place:

Masters Tournament If there is a tie after 72 holes of play, a hole-by-hole play-off commences at Hole No.18. Hole nos. 18 and 10 are played alternatively until a champion is decided.

U.S. Open In the case of a tie after 72 holes, an 18-hole play-off is held on the Monday following. If this play-off results in a tie, the tied players immediately continue to play-off hole by hole until the winner is determined.

British Open In the event of a tie after four rounds, the winner is decided by a play-off by stroke play over the four holes to be chosen by the Committee. The play-off starts as soon as practicable after the last players have finished their round.

The player with the lowest aggregate over the four extra holes is declared the winner. If the players are still tied having played these four holes, a hole by hole play-off is played immediately over the 18th hole only until a winner emerges. If the play-off involves more than 2 players, those other than the winner are deemed to have tied for 2nd place regardless of their scores in the play-off.

PGA Championship In the event of a tie for first place after 72 holes, there is a three-hole aggregate score play-off over three holes to be chosen by the Committee. If a tie still remains, there is a sudden-death play-off beginning on Hole No. 18, and if a tie remains, the progression of play-off holes is in the same play-off order determined by the Committee orginally until a winner is determined.

Prior to the opening round of the second U.S. Open, the USGA's first president, Theodore Havemeyer, made what is arguably the most important ruling in the championship's long history.

The championship was to be held during July 1896 at Shinnecock Hills on Long Island and was precluded by a situation which led Havemeyer to establish the Committee's unequivocal authority, as stated in Rule 33, to lay down the conditions under which a competition is to be played.

Gathering before the opening round, a group of competitors, comprised of proficient or professional players mostly from Scotland, England, and private clubs in New York, New England and Chicago, objected to John Shippen being accepted into the competitive field. Shippen's mother was a Shinnecock Indian and his father was a black, Presbyterian minister on the nearby Shinnecock Indian Reservation.

The objectors threatened that if forced to play with Shippen they would withdraw from the competition, thereby leaving a weaker field and a dubious U.S. Open Champion. At this early point in the game's American history, those less knowledgeable of the game generally deferred to those proficient in its playing to help mold competitive policies and procedures. Such a dilemma extended to golf in the 1890s. Fortunately, Havemeyer provided insight and direction on his side of the equation.

He met with the objectors and made the USGA's argument succinctly: An open competition was to be held; in order to be an open competition, applications had been accepted from all qualified individuals; to limit the field on any basis other than proficiency would invalidate the open nature of the competition and, in turn, the identification of the national open champion.

Havemeyer emphasized that it was the objectors' unquestioned right to withdraw. However, as far as the national championship was concerned, if Shippen chose to play and he were the only competitor in the field, he would be the national champion.

Feeling the intransigence of Havemeyer's argument and his irrefutable logic, those objecting reversed themselves and chose to compete. James Foulis, a Scottish professional playing out of the Chicago Golf Club was the champion with a score of 152. Shippen tied for fifth place.

Frequently asked questions

Q Our group has a season long match play competition. Some of the players want to play in our weekly stroke play competition, and play their match at the same time. Is this permissible?

A No. Rule 33-1 states that certain special Rules governing stroke play are so substantially different from those governing match play that combining the two forms of play is not practicable and is not permitted. The results of matches played and the scores returned in these circumstances must not be accepted.

Q The Committee issued one card for our group for the day. Must all players sign the card?

A The Rules of Golf do not provide an answer to the question. Rule 33-5 requires that the Committee provide a score card for each competitor.

RULE **34** DISPUTES AND DECISIONS

DEFINITIONS   All defined terms are in *italics* and are listed alphabetically in the Definitions section – see pages 9–20.

34-1. CLAIMS AND PENALTIES
a. Match Play
If a claim is lodged with the *Committee* under Rule 2-5, a decision should be given as soon as possible so that the state of the match may, if necessary, be

adjusted. If a claim is not made in accordance with Rule 2-5, it must not be considered by the *Committee*.

There is no time limit on applying the disqualification penalty for a breach of Rule 1-3.

b. Stroke Play

In stroke play, a penalty must not be rescinded, modified or imposed after the competition has closed. A competition is closed when the result has been officially announced or, in stroke-play qualifying followed by match play, when the player has teed off in his first match.

Exceptions: **A penalty of disqualification** must be imposed after the competition has closed if a *competitor*:

(i)   was in breach of Rule 1-3 (Agreement to Waive Rules); or

(ii) returned a score card on which he had recorded a handicap that, before the competition closed, he knew was higher than that to which he was entitled, and this affected the number of strokes received (Rule 6-2b); or

(iii) returned a score for any hole lower than actually taken (Rule 6-6d) for any reason other than failure to include a penalty that, before the competition closed, he did not know he had incurred; or

(iv) knew, before the competition closed, that he had been in breach of any other *Rule* for which the penalty is disqualification.

34-2. REFEREE'S DECISION

If a *referee* has been appointed by the *Committee*, his decision is final.

34-3. COMMITTEE'S DECISION

In the absence of a *referee*, any dispute or doubtful point on the *Rules* must be referred to the *Committee*, whose decision is final.

If the *Committee* cannot come to a decision, it may refer the dispute or doubtful point to the Rules of Golf Committee of the United States Golf Association, whose decision is final.

If the dispute or doubtful point has not been referred to the Rules of Golf Committee, the player or players may request that an agreed statement be referred through a duly authorized representative of the *Committee* to the Rules of Golf Committee for an opinion as to the correctness of the decision given. The reply will be sent to this authorized representative.

If play is conducted other than in accordance with the Rules of Golf, the Rules of Golf Committee will not give a decision on any question.

APPENDIX I

CONTENTS

APPENDIX I

LOCAL RULES; CONDITIONS OF THE COMPETITION

Definitions

All defined terms are in *italics* and are listed alphabetically in the Definitions section – see pages 9–20.

APPENDIX 1 INCIDENTS

Appendix I is where you will find very specific instructions about Local Rules and Conditions of Competition. Many of the nuances reflected here are useful when employing the Rules for situations that arise at all levels of competition. Environmentally-sensitive areas, protection of young trees, mud, stones in bunkers, deciding ties, etc. are all addressed.

In many national competitions, motorized transportation is prohibited under a Local Rule. Unless provided or sanctioned by a Rules official, a competitor is never allowed to ride. At the 2003 U.S. Women's Amateur at Philadelphia C.C., Maru Martinez was 2-up in her match with Michelle Wie after the first nine holes of the first round.

At the turn, Martinez made a quick stop in the clubhouse. Emerging from the building, she was offered a ride to the 10th tee by a well-meaning volunteer. A violation of the transportation rule does not trigger an immediate loss of hole penalty, but rather a "state of the match" penalty. In other words, the hole where the infraction took place or is discovered is played out and, following that, the state of the match is altered accordingly.

Both Martinez and Wie were misled in thinking that there was an automatic loss of hole. Both players picked up there balls in the 10th fairway and headed for the 11th tee. Before reaching the tee, they were corrected and returned to the spots where they had lifted their respective balls. Play of the 10th hole was completed. Wie won with a conceded birdie. The state of the match was then adjusted with one up being taken from Martinez. The match was now all square. Martinez went on to win 1-up.

"I was very mad," she sad later, "but I just said I've got to start all over again. It was my responsibility."

Temporary Immovable Obstruction (TIO) is the term used to describe the various obstructions that are specific to national championships. Grandstands, concession stands, score boards, television booths, camera stands, cables, and cranes can all fall into this category. They are unusual to the normal playing of the course and for that reason relief is granted. Although the logic is consistent, many times the relief appears to favor a wayward shot that would otherwise have the player playing from a more penal place.

During the second round of the 2006 WGC-Bridgestone Invitational, Tiger Woods's 167-yard second shot to the 9th green bounced off a concrete walkway near the clubhouse, onto and over the roof, and into a cart of a kitchen employee. Unaware of where the ball had come from, the employee put it into one of the cup holders and drove off. Once it became known where the ball had finished before the kitchen hand drove off with it, it was decided that Woods' line to hole was interfered with by the grandstands near the clubhouse. This entitled him to free relief under the Local Rule for TIOs. The resulting drop gave Woods an unobstructed line to the hole. He was able to make a bogey five when superficially it appeared his score would be much greater.

PART A: LOCAL RULES

As provided in Rule 33-8a, the *Committee* may make and publish Local Rules for local abnormal conditions if they are consistent with the policy established in this Appendix. In addition, detailed information regarding acceptable and prohibited Local Rules is provided in "Decisions on the Rules of Golf" under Rule 33-8 and in "How to Conduct a Competition."

If local abnormal conditions interfere with the proper playing of the game and the *Committee* considers it necessary to modify a Rule of Golf, authorization from the United States Golf Association must be obtained.

1. Defining Bounds and Margins

Specifying means used to define *out of bounds*, *water hazards*, *lateral water hazards*, *ground under repair*, *obstructions* and integral parts of the *course* (Rule 33-2a).

2. Water Hazards

a. Lateral Water Hazards

Clarifying the status of *water hazards* that may be *lateral water hazards* (Rule 26).

b. Ball Played Provisionally Under Rule 26-1

Permitting play of ball provisionally under Rule 26-1 for a ball that may be in a *water hazard* (including a *lateral water hazard*) of such character that, if the original ball is not found, it is known or virtually certain that it is in the *water hazard* and it would be impracticable to determine whether the ball is in the *hazard* or to do so would unduly delay play.

3. Areas of the Course Requiring Preservation; Environmentally-Sensitive Areas

Assisting preservation of the *course* by defining areas, including turf nurseries, young plantations and other parts of the course under cultivation, as *ground under repair* from which play is prohibited.

When the *Committee* is required to prohibit play from environmentally-sensitive areas that are on or adjoin the *course*, it should make a Local Rule clarifying the relief procedure.

4. Course Conditions – Mud, Extreme Wetness, Poor Conditions and Protection of Course

a. Lifting an Embedded Ball; Cleaning

Course conditions that might interfere with proper playing of the game, including mud and extreme wetness, warranting relief for an embedded ball anywhere *through the green* or permitting lifting, cleaning and replacing a ball anywhere *through the green* or on a closely mown area *through the green*.

b. "Preferred Lies" and "Winter Rules"

Adverse conditions, including the poor condition of the *course* or the existence of mud, are sometimes so general, particularly during winter months, that the *Committee* may decide to grant relief by temporary Local Rule either to protect the *course* or to promote fair and pleasant play. The Local Rule should be withdrawn as soon as the conditions warrant.

5. Obstructions

a. General

Clarifying the status of objects that may be *obstructions* (Rule 24).

Declaring any construction to be an integral part of the *course* and, accordingly, not an *obstruction*, e.g., built-up sides of *teeing grounds*, *putting greens* and *bunkers* (Rules 24 and 33-2a).

b. Stones in Bunkers

Allowing the removal of stones in *bunkers* by declaring them to be movable *obstructions* (Rule 24-1).

c. Roads and Paths

(i)   Declaring artificial surfaces and sides of roads and paths to be integral parts of the *course*, or

(ii) Providing relief of the type afforded under Rule 24-2b from roads and paths not having artificial surfaces and/or sides, if they could unfairly affect play.

d. Immovable Obstructions Close to Putting Green

Providing relief from intervention by immovable *obstructions* on or within two club-lengths of the

171

putting green when the ball lies within two club-lengths of the immovable *obstruction*.

e. Protection of Young Trees
Providing relief for the protection of young trees.

f. Temporary Obstructions
Providing relief from interference by temporary *obstructions* (e.g., grandstands, television cables and equipment, etc.).

6. Dropping Zones
Establishing special areas on which balls may or must be dropped when it is not feasible or practicable to proceed exactly in conformity with Rule 24-2b (Immovable Obstruction), Rule 24-3 (Ball in Obstruction Not Found), Rule 25-1b or 25-1c (Abnormal Ground Conditions), Rule 25-3 (Wrong Putting Green), Rule 26-1 (Water Hazards and Lateral Water Hazards) or Rule 28 (Ball Unplayable).

PART B:
SPECIMEN LOCAL RULES

Within the policy established in Part A of this Appendix, the *Committee* may adopt a Specimen Local Rule by referring, on a score card or notice board, to the examples given below. However, Specimen Local Rules of a temporary nature should not be printed or referred to on a score card.

1. Water Hazards; Ball Played Provisionally Under Rule 26-1
If a *water hazard* (including a *lateral water hazard*) is of such size and shape and/or located in such a position that:
(i) it would be impracticable to determine whether the ball is in the *hazard* or to do so would unduly delay play, and
(ii) if the original ball is not found, it is known or virtually certain that it is in the *water hazard*,
the *Committee* may introduce a Local Rule permitting the play of a ball provisionally under Rule 26-1. The ball is played provisionally under any of the applicable options under Rule 26-1 or any applicable Local Rule. In such a case, if a ball is

played provisionally and the original ball is in a *water hazard*, the player may play the original ball as it lies or continue with the ball played provisionally, but he may not proceed under Rule 26-1 with regard to the original ball.

In these circumstances, the following Local Rule is recommended:

"If there is doubt whether a ball is in or is *lost* in the *water hazard* (specify location), the player may play another ball provisionally under any of the applicable options in Rule 26-1.

If the original ball is found outside the *water hazard*, the player must continue play with it.

If the original ball is found in the *water hazard*, the player may either play the original ball as it lies or continue with the ball played provisionally under Rule 26-1.

If the original ball is not found or identified within the five-minute search period, the player must continue with the ball played provisionally.

PENALTY FOR BREACH OF LOCAL RULE:
Match play – Loss of hole;
Stroke play – Two strokes."

2. Areas of the Course Requiring Preservation; Environmentally-Sensitive Areas

a. Ground Under Repair; Play Prohibited

If the *Committee* wishes to protect any area of the *course*, it should declare it to be *ground under repair* and prohibit play from within that area. The following Local Rule is recommended:

"The _____(defined by _____) is *ground under repair* from which play is prohibited. If a player's ball lies in the area, or if it interferes with the player's *stance* or the area of his intended swing, the player must take relief under Rule 25-1.

PENALTY FOR BREACH OF LOCAL RULE:
Match play – Loss of hole;
Stroke play – Two strokes."

b. Environmentally-Sensitive Areas

If an appropriate authority (i.e., a government agency or the like) prohibits entry into and/or play from an area on or adjoining the *course* for environmental reasons, the *Committee* should make a Local Rule clarifying the relief procedure.

ENVIRONMENTALLY-SENSITIVE AREAS

The Links course at Spanish Bay in California has areas of sand dunes which have been declared environmentally-sensitive. A player may not play from or enter these areas.

The *Committee* has some discretion in terms of whether the area is defined as *ground under repair*, a *water hazard* or *out of bounds*. However, it may not simply define such an area to be a *water hazard* if it does not meet the Definition of a *"Water Hazard"* and it should attempt to preserve the character of the hole.

The following Local Rule is recommended:

"I. Definition

An environmentally-sensitive area (ESA) is an area so declared by an appropriate authority, entry into and/or play from which is prohibited for environmental reasons. These areas may be defined as *ground under repair*, a *water hazard*, a *lateral water hazard* or *out of bounds* at the discretion of the *Committee* provided that, in the case of an ESA that has been defined as a *water hazard* or a *lateral water hazard*, the area is, by Definition, a *water hazard*.

Note: The *Committee* may not declare an area to be environmentally-sensitive.

II. Ball in Environmentally-Sensitive Area

a. Ground Under Repair

If a ball is in an ESA defined as *ground under repair*, a ball must be dropped in accordance with Rule 25-1b.

If it is known or virtually certain that a ball that has not been found is in an ESA defined as *ground under repair*, the player may take relief, without penalty, as prescribed in Rule 25-1c.

b. Water Hazards and Lateral Water Hazards

If it is known or virtually certain that a ball that has not been found is in an ESA defined as a *water hazard* or *lateral water hazard*, the player must, **under penalty of one stroke**, proceed under Rule 26-1.

Note: If a ball dropped in accordance with Rule 26 rolls into a position where the ESA interferes with the player's *stance* or the area of his intended swing, the player must take relief as provided in Clause III of this Local Rule.

c. Out of Bounds

If a ball is in an ESA defined as *out of bounds*, the player must play a ball, **under penalty of one stroke**, as nearly as possible at the spot from which the original ball was last played (see Rule 20-5).

III. Interference with Stance or Area of Intended Swing

Interference by an ESA occurs when the ESA interferes with the player's *stance* or the area of his intended swing. If interference exists, the player must take relief as follows:

(a) **Through the Green:** If the ball lies *through the green*, the point on the *course* nearest to where the ball lies must be determined that (a) is not nearer the *hole*, (b) avoids interference by the ESA and (c) is not in a *hazard* or on a *putting green*. The player must lift the ball and drop it, without penalty, within one club-length of the point so determined on a part of the *course* that fulfills (a), (b) and (c) above.

(b) **In a Hazard:** If the ball is in a *hazard*, the player must lift the ball and drop it either:

   (i) Without penalty, in the *hazard*, as near as possible to the spot where the ball lay, but not nearer the *hole*, on a part of the *course* that provides complete relief from the ESA; or

   (ii) **Under penalty of one stroke**, outside the *hazard*, keeping the point where the ball lay directly between the *hole* and the spot on which the ball is dropped, with no limit to how far behind the *hazard* the ball may be dropped. Additionally, the player may proceed under Rule 26 or 28, if applicable.

(c) **On the Putting Green:** If the ball lies on the *putting green*, the player must lift the ball and place it, without penalty, in the nearest position to where it lay that affords complete relief from the ESA, but not nearer the *hole* or in a *hazard*.

The ball may be cleaned when lifted under Clause III of this Local Rule.

Exception: A player may not take relief under Clause III of this Local Rule if (a) it is clearly unreasonable for him to play a *stroke* because of interference by anything other than an ESA or (b) interference by the ESA would occur only through use of an unnecessarily abnormal *stance*, swing or direction of play.

PENALTY FOR BREACH OF LOCAL RULE:
Match play – Loss of hole;
Stroke play – Two strokes.

Note: In the case of a serious breach of this Local Rule, the *Committee* may impose a penalty of disqualification."

3. Protection of Young Trees

When it is desired to prevent damage to young trees, the following Local Rule is recommended:

"Protection of young trees identified by _____ – If such a tree interferes with a player's *stance* or the area of his intended swing, the ball must be lifted, without penalty, and dropped in accordance with the procedure prescribed in Rule 24-2b (Immovable Obstruction). If the ball lies in a *water hazard*, the player must lift and drop the ball in accordance with Rule 24-2b(i), except that the *nearest point of relief* must be in the *water hazard* and the ball must be dropped in the *water hazard* or the player may proceed under Rule 26. The ball may be cleaned when lifted under this Local Rule.

Exception: A player may not take relief under this Local Rule if (a) it is clearly unreasonable for him to make a *stroke* because of interference by anything other than the tree or (b) interference by the tree would occur only through use of an unnecessarily abnormal *stance*, swing or direction of play.

PENALTY FOR BREACH OF LOCAL RULE:
Match play – Loss of hole;
Stroke play – Two strokes."

4. Course Conditions – Mud, Extreme Wetness, Poor Conditions and Protection of the Course

a. Relief for Embedded Ball

Rule 25-2 provides relief, without penalty, for a ball embedded in its own pitch-mark in any closely mown area *through the green*. On the *putting green,* a ball may be lifted and damage caused by the impact of a ball may be repaired (Rules 16-1b and c). When permission to take relief for an embedded ball anywhere *through the green* would be warranted, the following Local Rule is recommended:

"*Through the green*, a ball that is embedded in its own pitch-mark in the ground may be lifted, without penalty, cleaned and dropped as near as possible to where it lay but not nearer the *hole*. The ball when dropped must first strike a part of the *course through the green*.

Exceptions:

1. A player may not take relief under this Local Rule if the ball is embedded in sand in an area that is not closely mown.

2. A player may not take relief under this Local Rule if it is clearly unreasonable for him to make a *stroke* because of interference by anything other than the condition covered by this Local Rule.

PENALTY FOR BREACH OF LOCAL RULE:
Match play – Loss of hole;
Stroke play – Two strokes."

b. Cleaning Ball

Conditions, such as extreme wetness causing significant amounts of mud to adhere to the ball, may be such that permission to lift, clean and replace the ball would be appropriate. In these circumstances, the following Local Rule is recommended:

"(Specify area) a ball may be lifted, cleaned and replaced without penalty.

Note: The position of the ball must be marked before it is lifted under this Local Rule – see Rule 20-1.

PENALTY FOR BREACH OF LOCAL RULE:
Match play – Loss of hole;
Stroke play – Two strokes."

c. "Preferred Lies" and "Winter Rules"

Ground under repair is provided for in Rule 25, and, occasional local abnormal conditions that might interfere with fair play and are not widespread should be defined as *ground under repair*.

However, adverse conditions, such as heavy snows, spring thaws, prolonged rains or extreme heat can make fairways unsatisfactory and sometimes prevent use of heavy mowing equipment. When these conditions are so general throughout a *course* that the *Committee* believes "preferred lies" or "winter rules" would promote fair play or help protect the *course*, the following Local Rule is recommended:

175

"A ball lying on a closely mown area *through the green* [or specify a more restricted area, e.g., at the 6th hole] may be lifted without penalty and cleaned. Before lifting the ball, the player must mark its position. Having lifted the ball, he must place it on a spot within [specify area, e.g., six inches, one club-length, etc.] of and not nearer the *hole* than where it originally lay, that is not in a *hazard* and not on a *putting green*.

A player may place his ball only once, and it is *in play* when it has been placed (Rule 20-4). If the ball fails to come to rest on the spot on which it was placed, Rule 20-3d applies. If the ball when placed comes to rest on the spot on which it is placed and it subsequently *moves*, there is no penalty and the ball must be played as it lies, unless the provisions of any other *Rule* apply.

If the player fails to mark the position of the ball before lifting it or *moves* the ball in any other manner, such as rolling it with a club, **he incurs a penalty of one stroke**.

Note: "Closely mown area" means any area of the *course*, including paths through the rough, cut to fairway height or less.

*PENALTY FOR BREACH OF LOCAL RULE:
Match play – Loss of hole;
Stroke play – Two strokes
*If a player incurs the general penalty for a breach of this Local Rule, no additional penalty under the Local Rule is applied."

d. Aeration Holes

When a *course* has been aerated, a Local Rule permitting relief, without penalty, from an aeration hole may be warranted. The following Local Rule is recommended:

"*Through the green*, a ball that comes to rest in or on an aeration hole may be lifted without penalty, cleaned and dropped, as near as possible to the spot where it lay but not nearer the *hole*. The ball when dropped must first strike a part of the *course through the green*.

On the *putting green*, a ball that comes to rest in or on an aeration hole may be placed at the nearest spot not nearer the *hole* that avoids the situation.

PENALTY FOR BREACH OF LOCAL RULE:
Match play – Loss of hole;
Stroke play – Two strokes."

e. Seams of Cut Turf

If a *Committee* wishes to allow relief from seams of cut turf, but not from the cut turf itself, the following Local Rule is recommended:

"*Through the green*, seams of cut turf (not the turf itself) are deemed to be *ground under repair*. However, interference by a seam with the player's *stance* is deemed not to be, of itself, interference under Rule 25-1. If the ball lies in or touches the seam or the seam interferes with the area of intended swing, relief is available under Rule 25-1. All seams within the cut turf area are considered the same seam."

PENALTY FOR BREACH OF LOCAL RULE:
Match play – Loss of hole;
Stroke play – Two strokes."

5. Stones in Bunkers

Stones are, by definition, *loose impediments* and, when a player's ball is in a *hazard*, a stone lying in or touching the *hazard* may not be touched or moved (Rule 13-4). However, stones in *bunkers* may represent a danger to players (a player could be injured by a stone struck by the player's club in an attempt to play the ball) and they may interfere with the proper playing of the game.

When permission to lift a stone in a *bunker* is warranted, the following Local Rule is recommended:

"Stones in *bunkers* are movable *obstructions* (Rule 24-1 applies)."

6. Immovable Obstructions Close to Putting Green

Rule 24-2 provides relief, without penalty, from interference by an immovable *obstruction*, but also provides that, except on the *putting green*, intervention on the *line of play* is not, of itself, interference under this Rule.

However, on some courses, the aprons of the *putting greens* are so closely mown that players may wish to putt from just off the green. In such conditions, immovable *obstructions* on the apron may interfere with the proper playing of the game and the introduction of the following Local Rule providing additional relief, without penalty, from intervention by an immovable *obstruction* would be warranted:

"Relief from interference by an immovable *obstruction* may be taken under Rule 24-2. In addition, if a ball lies off the *putting green* but not in a *hazard* and an immovable *obstruction* on or within two club-lengths of the *putting green* and within two club-lengths of the ball intervenes on the *line of play* between the ball and the *hole*, the player may take relief as follows:

The ball must be lifted and dropped at the nearest point to where the ball lay that (a) is not nearer the *hole*, (b) avoids intervention and (c) is not in a *hazard* or on a *putting green*. The ball may be cleaned when lifted.

Relief under this Local Rule is also available if the player's ball lies on the *putting green* and an immovable *obstruction* within two club-lengths of the *putting green* intervenes on his *line of putt*. The player may take relief as follows:

The ball must be lifted and placed at the nearest point to where the ball lay which (a) is not nearer the *hole*, (b) avoids intervention and (c) is not in a *hazard*. The ball may be cleaned when lifted.

PENALTY FOR BREACH OF LOCAL RULE:
Match play – Loss of hole;
Stroke play – Two strokes."

7. Temporary Obstructions

When temporary obstructions are installed on or adjoining the *course*, the *Committee* should define the status of such obstructions as movable, immovable or temporary immovable obstructions.

a. Temporary Immovable Obstructions

If the *Committee* defines these obstructions as temporary immovable obstructions, the following Local Rule is recommended:

"I. Definition

A temporary immovable obstruction (TIO) is a non-permanent artificial object that is often erected in conjunction with a competition and is fixed or not readily movable.

Examples of TIOs include, but are not limited to, tents, scoreboards, grandstands, television towers and lavatories.

Supporting guy wires are part of the TIO, unless the *Committee* declares that they are to be treated as elevated power lines or cables.

RULE 24-2. IMMOVABLE OBSTRUCTION

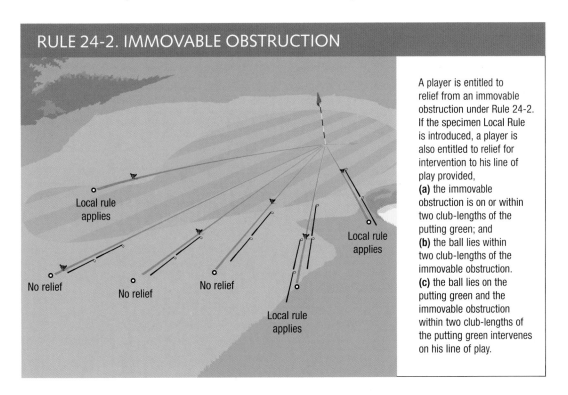

Local rule applies

No relief

No relief

No relief

Local rule applies

Local rule applies

A player is entitled to relief from an immovable obstruction under Rule 24-2. If the specimen Local Rule is introduced, a player is also entitled to relief for intervention to his line of play provided,
(a) the immovable obstruction is on or within two club-lengths of the putting green; and
(b) the ball lies within two club-lengths of the immovable obstruction.
(c) the ball lies on the putting green and the immovable obstruction within two club-lengths of the putting green intervenes on his line of play.

II. Interference

Interference by a TIO occurs when (a) the ball lies in front of and so close to the TIO that the TIO interferes with the player's *stance* or the area of his intended swing, or (b) the ball lies in, on, under or behind the TIO so that any part of the TIO intervenes directly between the player's ball and the *hole* and on his *line of play*; interference also exists if the ball lies within one club-length of a spot equidistant from the *hole* where such intervention would exist.

Note: A ball is under a TIO when it is below the outermost edges of the TIO, even if these edges do not extend downward to the ground.

III. Relief

A player may obtain relief from interference by a TIO, including a TIO that is *out of bounds*, as follows:

(a) **Through the Green:** If the ball lies *through the green*, the point on the *course* nearest to where the ball lies must be determined that (a) is not nearer the *hole*, (b) avoids interference as defined in Clause II and (c) is not in a *hazard* or on a *putting green*. The player must lift the ball and drop it, without penalty, within one club-length of the point so determined on a part of the *course* that fulfills (a), (b) and (c) above.

(b) **In a Hazard:** If the ball is in a *hazard*, the player must lift and drop the ball either:

(i) Without penalty, in accordance with Clause III(a) above, except that the nearest part of the *course* affording complete relief must be in the *hazard* and the ball must be dropped in the *hazard*, or, if complete relief is impossible, on a part of the *course* within the *hazard* that affords maximum available relief; or

(ii) **Under penalty of one stroke**, outside the *hazard* as follows: the point on the *course* nearest to where the ball lies must be determined that (a) is not nearer the *hole*, (b) avoids interference as defined in Clause II and (c) is not in a *hazard*. The player must drop the ball within one club-length of the point so determined on a part of the *course* that fulfills (a), (b) and (c) above.

The ball may be cleaned when lifted under Clause III.

Note 1: If the ball lies in a *hazard*, nothing in this Local Rule precludes the player from proceeding under Rule 26 or Rule 28, if applicable.

Note 2: If a ball to be dropped under this Local Rule is not immediately recoverable, another ball may be *substituted*.

Note 3: A *Committee* may make a Local Rule (a) permitting or requiring a player to use a Dropping Zone when taking relief from a TIO or (b) permitting a player, as an additional relief option, to drop the ball on the opposite side of the TIO from the point established under Clause III, but otherwise in accordance with Clause III.

Exceptions: If a player's ball lies in front of or behind the TIO (not in, on or under the *obstruction*) he may not obtain relief under Clause III if:

1. It is clearly unreasonable for him to make a *stroke* or, in the case of intervention, to make a *stroke* such that the ball could finish on a direct line to the *hole*, because of interference by anything other than the TIO;

2. Interference by the TIO would occur only through use of an unnecessarily abnormal *stance*, swing or direction of play; or

3. In the case of intervention, it would be clearly unreasonable to expect the player to be able to strike the ball far enough toward the *hole* to reach the TIO.

A player not entitled to relief due to these exceptions may proceed under Rule 24-2, if applicable.

IV. Ball in TIO Not Found

If it is known or virtually certain that a ball that has not been found is in, on or under a TIO, a ball may be dropped under the provisions of Clause III or Clause V, if applicable. For the purpose of applying Clauses III and V, the ball is deemed to lie at the spot where it last crossed the outermost limits of the TIO (Rule 24-3).

V. Dropping Zones

If the player has interference from a TIO, the *Committee* may permit or require the use of a Dropping Zone. If the player uses a Dropping Zone in taking relief, he must drop the ball in the

TEMPORARY IMMOVABLE OBSTRUCTIONS

If there are temporary immovable obstructions, such as TV towers, on the course, the Committee should introduce a Local Rule providing for relief from such temporary immovable obstructions.

Dropping Zone nearest to where his ball originally lay or is deemed to lie under Clause IV (even though the nearest dropping zone may be nearer the *hole*).

Note: A *Committee* may make a Local Rule prohibiting the use of a Dropping Zone that is nearer the *hole*.

PENALTY FOR BREACH OF LOCAL RULE:
Match play – Loss of hole;
Stroke play – Two strokes.*"*

b. Temporary Power Lines and Cables

When temporary power lines, cables or telephone lines are installed on the *course*, the following Local Rule is recommended:

"Temporary power lines, cables, telephone lines and mats covering or stanchions supporting them are *obstructions*:

1. If they are readily movable, Rule 24-1 applies.
2. If they are fixed or not readily movable, the player may, if the ball lies *through the green* or in a *bunker*, obtain relief as provided in Rule 24-2b. If the ball lies in a *water hazard*, the player may obtain relief under Rule 24-2b(i), except that the *nearest point of relief* must be in the *water hazard* and the ball must be dropped in the *water hazard* or the player may proceed under Rule 26.

3. If a ball strikes an elevated power line or cable, the *stroke* must be canceled and replayed, without penalty (see Rule 20-5). If the ball is not immediately recoverable, another ball may be *substituted*.

Note: Guy wires supporting a temporary immovable obstruction are part of the temporary immovable obstruction, unless the *Committee*, by Local Rule, declares that they are to be treated as elevated power lines or cables.

Exception: A *stroke* that results in a ball striking an elevated junction section of cable rising from the ground must not be replayed.

4. Grass-covered cable trenches are *ground under repair*, even if not marked, and Rule 25-1b applies."

8. Dropping Zones

If the *Committee* considers that it is not feasible or practicable to proceed in accordance with a Rule providing relief, it may establish Dropping Zones in which balls may or must be dropped when taking relief. Generally, such Dropping Zones should be provided as an additional relief option to those available under the Rule itself, rather than being mandatory.

Using the example of a Dropping Zone for a *water hazard*, when such a Dropping Zone is established, the following Local Rule is recommended:

"If a ball is in or it is known or virtually certain that a ball that has not been found is in the *water hazard* (specify location), the player may:

(i) proceed under Rule 26; or

(ii) as an additional option, drop a ball, under penalty of one stroke, in the Dropping Zone.

PENALTY FOR BREACH OF LOCAL RULE:
Match play – Loss of hole;
Stroke play – Two strokes."

Note: When using the Dropping Zone the following provisions apply regarding the dropping and re-dropping of the ball:

(a) The player does not have to stand within the Dropping Zone when dropping the ball.

(b) The dropped ball must first strike a part of the *course* within the Dropping Zone.

(c) If the Dropping Zone is defined by a line, the line is within the Dropping Zone.

(d) The dropped ball does not have to come to rest within the Dropping Zone.

(e) The dropped ball must be re-dropped if it rolls and comes to rest in a position covered by Rule 20-2c(i-vi).

(f) The dropped ball may roll nearer the hole than the spot where it first struck a part of the *course* provided it comes to rest within two club-lengths of that spot and not into any of the positions covered by (e).

(g) Subject to the provisions of (e) and (f), the dropped ball may roll and come to rest nearer the *hole* than:

- its original position or estimated position (see Rule 20-2b);
- the *nearest point of relief* or maximum available relief (Rule 24-2, 24-3, 25-1 or 25-3); or
- the point where the original ball last crossed the margin of the *water hazard* or *lateral water hazard* (Rule 26-1).

9. Distance-Measuring Devices

If the *Committee* wishes to act in accordance with the Note under Rule 14-3, the following wording is recommended:

"**Distance-Measuring Devices:** [Specify as appropriate, e.g., In this competition, or For all play at this *course*, etc.], a player may obtain distance information by using a device that measures distance only. If, during a *stipulated round,* a player uses a distance-measuring device that is designed to gauge or measure other conditions that might affect his play (e.g., gradient, wind-speed, temperature, etc.), the player is in breach of Rule 14-3, for which the penalty is disqualification, regardless of whether any such additional function is actually used."

PART C: CONDITIONS OF THE COMPETITION

Rule 33-1 provides, "The *Committee* must establish the conditions under which a competition is to be played." These conditions should include many matters such as method of entry, eligibility, number of rounds to be played, etc., that it is not appropriate to deal with in the Rules of Golf or this Appendix. Detailed information regarding these conditions is provided in "Decisions on the Rules of Golf" under Rule 33-1 and in "How to Conduct a Competition."

However, there are a number of matters that might be covered in the Conditions of the Competition to which the *Committee's* attention is specifically drawn. These are:

1. Specifications of Clubs and the Ball
The following conditions are recommended only for competitions involving expert players:

a. List of Conforming Driver Heads
On its Web site (http://www.usga.org) the USGA periodically issues a List of Conforming Driver Heads that lists driving clubheads that have been evaluated and found to conform to the Rules of Golf. If the *Committee* wishes to limit players to drivers that have a clubhead, identified by model and loft, that is on the List, the List should be made available and the following condition of competition used:

"Any driver the player carries must have a clubhead, identified by model and loft, that is named on the current List of Conforming Driver Heads issued by the USGA.

Exception: A driver with a clubhead that was manufactured prior to 1998 is exempt from this condition.

PENALTY FOR CARRYING, BUT NOT MAKING STROKE WITH, CLUB OR CLUBS IN BREACH OF CONDITION:
Match Play – At the conclusion of the hole at which the breach is discovered, the state of the match is adjusted by deducting one hole for each hole at which a breach occurred; maximum deduction per round – Two holes.
Stroke Play – Two strokes for each hole at which any breach occurred; maximum penalty per round – Four strokes.
Match or Stroke Play – In the event of a breach between the play of two holes, the penalty applies to the next hole.
Bogey and par competitions – See Note 1 to Rule 32-1a.
Stableford competitions – See Note 1 to Rule 32-1b.
*Any club or clubs carried in breach of this condition must be declared out of play by the player to his opponent in match play or his *marker* **or a** *fellow-competitor* **in stroke play immediately upon discovery that a breach has occurred. If the player fails to do so, he is disqualified.**
PENALTY FOR MAKING STROKE WITH CLUB IN BREACH OF CONDITION:
Disqualification."

b. List of Conforming Golf Balls

On its Web site (http://www.usga.org) the USGA periodically issues a List of Conforming Golf Balls that lists balls that have been tested and found to conform with the Rules of Golf. If the *Committee* wishes to require players to play a brand and model of golf ball on the List, the List should be posted and the following condition of competition used:

"The ball the player plays must be named on the current List of Conforming Golf Balls issued by the United States Golf Association.

PENALTY FOR BREACH OF CONDITION:
Disqualification."

c. One Ball Condition

If it is desired to prohibit changing brands and models of golf balls during a *stipulated round*, the following condition is recommended:

"Limitation on Balls Used During Round (Note to Rule 5-1):

(i) **One Ball Condition** During a *stipulated round*, the balls a player plays must be of the same brand and model as detailed by a single entry on the current List of Conforming Golf Balls.

Note: If a ball of a different brand and/or model is dropped or placed, it may be lifted, without penalty, and the player must then proceed by dropping or placing a proper ball (Rule 20-6).

PENALTY FOR BREACH OF CONDITION:
Match Play – At the conclusion of the hole at which the breach is discovered, the state of the match is adjusted by deducting one hole for each hole at which a breach occurred; maximum deduction per round – Two holes.
Stroke Play – Two strokes for each hole at which any breach occurred; maximum penalty per round – Four strokes.

(ii) **Procedure When Breach Discovered** When a player discovers that he has played a ball in breach of this condition, he must abandon that ball before playing from the next *teeing ground* and complete the round with a proper ball; otherwise, **the player is disqualified**. If discovery is made during play of a hole and the player elects to *substitute* a proper ball before completing that hole, the player must place a proper ball on the spot where the ball used in breach of the condition lay."

2. Time of Starting (Note to Rule 6-3a)

If the *Committee* wishes to act in accordance with the Note, the following wording is recommended:

"If the player arrives at his starting point, ready to play, within five minutes after his starting time, in the absence of circumstances that warrant waiving the penalty of disqualification as provided in Rule 33-7, **the penalty for failure to start on time is loss of the first hole to be played in match play or two strokes in stroke play. Penalty for lateness beyond five minutes is disqualification.**"

3. Caddie (Note to Rule 6-4)

Rule 6-4 permits a player to use a *caddie*, provided he has only one *caddie* at any one time. However, there may be circumstances where a *Committee*

181

may wish to prohibit *caddies* or restrict a player in his choice of *caddie*, e.g., professional golfer, sibling, parent, another player in the competition, etc. In such cases, the following wording is recommended:

Use of Caddie Prohibited

"A player is prohibited from using a *caddie* during the *stipulated round*."

Restriction on Who May Serve as Caddie

"A player is prohibited from having _____ serve as his *caddie* during the *stipulated round*.

PENALTY FOR BREACH OF CONDITION:

Match play – At the conclusion of the hole at which the breach is discovered, the state of the match is adjusted by deducting one hole for each hole at which a breach occurred; maximum deduction per round – Two holes.

Stroke play – Two strokes for each hole at which any breach occurred; maximum penalty per round – Four strokes.

Match or stroke play – In the event of a breach between the play of two holes, the penalty applies to the next hole.

A player having a *caddie* in breach of this condition must immediately upon discovery that a breach has occurred ensure that he conforms with this condition for the remainder of the *stipulated round*. Otherwise, the player is disqualified."

4. Pace of Play (Note 2 to Rule 6-7)

The *Committee* may establish pace of play guidelines to help prevent slow play, in accordance with Note 2 to Rule 6-7.

5. Suspension of Play Due to a Dangerous Situation (Note to Rule 6-8b)

As there have been many deaths and injuries from lightning on golf courses, all clubs and sponsors of golf competitions are urged to take precautions for

SUSPENSION OF PLAY DUE TO A DANGEROUS SITUATION

the protection of persons against lightning. Attention is called to Rules 6-8 and 33-2d. If the *Committee* desires to adopt the condition in the Note under Rule 6-8b, the following wording is recommended:

"When play is suspended by the *Committee* for a dangerous situation, if the players in a match or group are between the play of two holes, they must not resume play until the *Committee* has ordered a resumption of play. If they are in the process of playing a hole, they must discontinue play immediately and not resume play until the *Committee* has ordered a resumption of play. If a player fails to discontinue immediately, **he is disqualified,** unless circumstances warrant waiving the penalty as provided in Rule 33-7.

The signal for suspending play due to a dangerous situation will be a prolonged note of the siren."

The following signals are generally used and it is recommended that all *Committees* do similarly:

- **Discontinue Play Immediately:** One prolonged note of siren.
- **Discontinue Play:** Three consecutive notes of siren, repeated.
- **Resume Play:** Two short notes of siren, repeated.

6. Practice
a. General
The *Committee* may make regulations governing practice in accordance with the Note to Rule 7-1, Exception (c) to Rule 7-2, Note 2 to Rule 7 and Rule 33-2c.

b. Practice Between Holes (Note 2 to Rule 7)
If the *Committee* wishes to act in accordance with Note 2 to Rule 7-2, the following wording is recommended:

"Between the play of two holes, a player must not make any practice *stroke* on or near the *putting green* of the hole last played and must not test the surface of the *putting green* of the hole last played by rolling a ball.

PENALTY FOR BREACH OF CONDITION:
Match play – Loss of next hole.
Stroke play – Two strokes at the next hole.

Match or stroke play – In the case of a breach at the last hole of the *stipulated round*, the player incurs the penalty at that hole."

7. Advice in Team Competitions (Note to Rule 8)
If the *Committee* wishes to act in accordance with the Note under Rule 8, the following wording is recommended:

"In accordance with the Note to Rule 8 of the Rules of Golf, each team may appoint one person (in addition to the persons from whom *advice* may be asked under that *Rule*) who may give *advice* to members of that team. Such person **(if it is desired to insert any restriction on who may be nominated insert such restriction here)** must be identified to the *Committee* before giving *advice*."

8. New Holes (Note to Rule 33-2b)
The *Committee* may provide, in accordance with the Note to Rule 33-2b, that the *holes* and *teeing grounds* for a single round competition, being held on more than one day, may be differently situated on each day.

9. Transportation
If it is desired to require players to walk in a competition, the following condition is recommended:

"Players must not ride on any form of transportation during a *stipulated round* unless authorized by the *Committee*.

PENALTY FOR BREACH OF CONDITION:
Match play – At the conclusion of the hole at which the breach is discovered, the state of the match is adjusted by deducting one hole for each hole at which a breach occurred. Maximum deduction per round: Two holes.
Stroke play – Two strokes for each hole at which any breach occurred; maximum penalty per round: Four strokes.
Match or stroke play – In the event of a breach between the play of two holes, the penalty applies to the next hole. Use of any unauthorized form of transportation must be discontinued immediately upon discovery that a breach has occurred. Otherwise, the player is disqualified."

10. Anti-Doping

The *Committee* may require, in the conditions of competition, that players comply with an anti-doping policy.

11. How to Decide Ties

In both match play and stroke play a tie can be an acceptable result. However, when it is desired to have a sole winner, the *Committee* has the authority, under Rule 33-6, to determine how and when a tie is decided. The decision should be published in advance.

The USGA recommends:

Match Play

A match that ends all square should be played off hole by hole until one *side* wins a hole. The play-off should start on the hole where the match began. In a handicap match, handicap strokes should be allowed as in the *stipulated round*.

Stroke Play

(a) In the event of a tie in a scratch stroke-play competition, a play-off is recommended. The play-off may be over 18 holes or a smaller number of holes as specified by the *Committee*. If that is not feasible or there is still a tie, a hole-by-hole play-off is recommended.

(b) In the event of a tie in a handicap stroke-play competition, a play-off with handicaps is recommended. The play-off may be over 18 holes or a smaller number of holes as specified by the *Committee*. It is recommended that any such play-off consist of at least three holes.

In competitions where the handicap stroke allocation table is not relevant, if the play-off is less than 18 holes the percentage of 18 holes played should be applied to the players' handicaps to determine their play-off handicaps. Handicap stroke fractions of one-half stroke or more should count as a full stroke and any lesser fraction should be disregarded.

In competitions where the handicap stroke table is relevant, such as four-ball stroke play and bogey, par and Stableford competitions, handicap strokes should be taken as they were assigned for the competition using the players' respective stroke allocation table(s).

(c) If a play-off of any type is not feasible, matching score cards is recommended. The method of matching cards should be announced in advance and should also provide what will happen if this procedure does not produce a winner. An acceptable method of matching the cards is to determine the winner on the basis of the best score for the last nine holes. If the tying players have the same score for the last nine, determine the winner on the basis of the last six holes, last three holes and finally the 18th hole. If this method is used in a competition with a multiple tee start, it is recommended that the "last nine holes, last six holes, etc." is considered to be holes 10-18, 13-18, etc.

For competitions where the handicap stroke table is not relevant, such as individual stroke play, if the last nine, last six, last three holes scenario is used, one-half, one-third, one-sixth, ec. of the handicaps should be deducted from the score for those holes. In terms of the use of fractions in such deductions, the *Committee* should act in accordance with the recommendations of the relevant handicapping authority.

In competitions where the handicap stroke table is relevant, such as *four-ball* stroke play and bogey, par and Stableford competitions, handicap strokes should be taken as they were assigned for the competition, using the players' respective stroke allocation table(s).

12. Draw for Match Play

Although the draw for match play may be completely blind or certain players may be distributed through different quarters or eighths, the General Numerical Draw is recommended if matches are determined by a qualifying round.

General Numerical Draw

For purposes of determining places in the draw, ties in qualifying rounds other than those for the last qualifying place are decided by the order in which scores are returned, with the first score to be returned receiving the lowest available number, etc. If it is impossible to determine the order in which scores are returned, ties are determined by a blind draw.

UPPER HALF	LOWER HALF	UPPER HALF	LOWER HALF
64 QUALIFIERS		**32 QUALIFIERS**	
1 vs. 64	2 vs. 63	1 vs. 32	2 vs. 31
32 vs. 33	31 vs. 34	16 vs. 17	15 vs. 18
16 vs. 49	15 vs. 50	8 vs. 25	7 vs. 26
17 vs. 48	18 vs. 47	9 vs. 24	10 vs. 23
8 vs. 57	7 vs. 58	4 vs. 29	3 vs. 30
25 vs. 40	26 vs. 39	13 vs. 20	14 vs. 19
9 vs. 56	10 vs. 55	5 vs. 28	6 vs. 27
24 vs. 41	23 vs. 42	12 vs. 21	11 vs. 22
4 vs. 61	3 vs. 62	**16 QUALIFIERS**	
29 vs. 36	30 vs. 35	1 vs. 16	2 vs. 15
13 vs. 52	14 vs. 51	8 vs. 9	7 vs. 10
20 vs. 45	19 vs. 46	4 vs. 13	3 vs. 14
5 vs. 60	6 vs. 59	5 vs. 12	6 vs. 11
28 vs. 37	27 vs. 38	**8 QUALIFIERS**	
12 vs. 53	11 vs. 54	1 vs. 8	2 vs. 7
21 vs. 44	22 vs. 43	4 vs. 5	3 vs. 6

Frequently asked questions

Q What does the "One Ball Condition" mean?

A The Rules of Golf do not require a player to use the same brand and type of golf ball throughout the stipulated round. A player may use a different ball to start each hole. However, the Committee may adopt as a Condition of a Competition, the "One Ball Condition." When this condition is adopted, players are required to use the same brand and type of golf ball throughout the stipulated round. Please refer to Appendix 1; Part C; 1 (Specification of the Ball).

Q Is there a penalty if, when playing "Preferred Lies", the player simply rolls the ball to prefer his lie?

A The Committee in charge of a competition or golf course may adopt a Local Rule allowing players to lift, clean and place their ball when conditions warrant such a Local Rule – see Appendix I; Part B; Item 3b. Before lifting the ball, the position of the ball must be marked. If the player fails to mark the position of the ball before lifting it, he incurs a penalty of one stroke.

APPENDICES II AND III

The USGA reserves the right, at any time, to change the Rules relating to clubs and balls and make or change the interpretations relating to these Rules. For up-to-date information, please contact the USGA or refer to *www.usga.org*.

Any design in a club or ball which is not covered by the Rules, which is contrary to the purpose and intent of the Rules or which might significantly change the nature of the game, will be ruled on by the USGA.

The dimensions and limits contained in Appendices II and III are given in the units by which conformance is determined. An equivalent imperial/metric conversion is also referenced for information, calculated using a conversion rate of 1 inch = 25.4 mm.

APPENDIX II

DESIGN OF CLUBS

A player in doubt as to the conformity of a club should consult the USGA.

A manufacturer should submit to the USGA a sample of a club to be manufactured for a ruling as to whether the club conforms with the *Rules*. The sample becomes the property of the USGA for reference purposes. If a manufacturer fails to submit a sample or, having submitted a sample, fails to await a ruling before manufacturing and/or marketing the club, the manufacturer assumes the risk of a ruling that the club does not conform with the *Rules*.

The following paragraphs prescribe general regulations for the design of clubs, together with specifications and interpretations. Further information relating to these regulations and their proper interpretation is provided in "A Guide to the Rules on Clubs and Balls."

Where a club, or part of a club, is required to meet a specification within the *Rules*, it must be designed and manufactured with the intention of meeting that specification.

1. Clubs
a. General
A club is an implement designed to be used for striking the ball and generally comes in three forms: woods, irons and putters distinguished by shape and intended use. A putter is a club with a loft not exceeding ten degrees designed primarily for use on the putting green.

The club must not be substantially different from the traditional and customary form and make. The club must be composed of a shaft and a head and it may also have material added to the shaft to enable the player to obtain a firm hold (see 3 below). All parts of the club must be fixed so that the club is one unit, and it must have no external attachments. Exceptions may be made for attachments that do not affect the performance of the club.

b. Adjustability
All clubs may incorporate mechanisms for weight adjustment. Other forms of adjustability may also be permitted upon evaluation by the USGA. The following requirements apply to all permissible methods of adjustment:
(i)   the adjustment cannot be readily made;
(ii) all adjustable parts are firmly fixed and there is no reasonable likelihood of them working loose during a round; and
(iii) all configurations of adjustment conform with the Rules.

During a stipulated round, the playing characteristics of a club must not be purposely changed by adjustment or by any other means (see Rule 4-2a).

c. Length
The overall length of the club must be at least 18 inches (0.457 m) and, except for putters, must not exceed 48 inches (1.219 m). For woods and irons, the measurement of length is taken when the club is lying on a horizontal plane and the sole is set against a 60 degree plane as

CLUB LENGTH AND ALIGNMENT; SHAFT STRAIGHTNESS

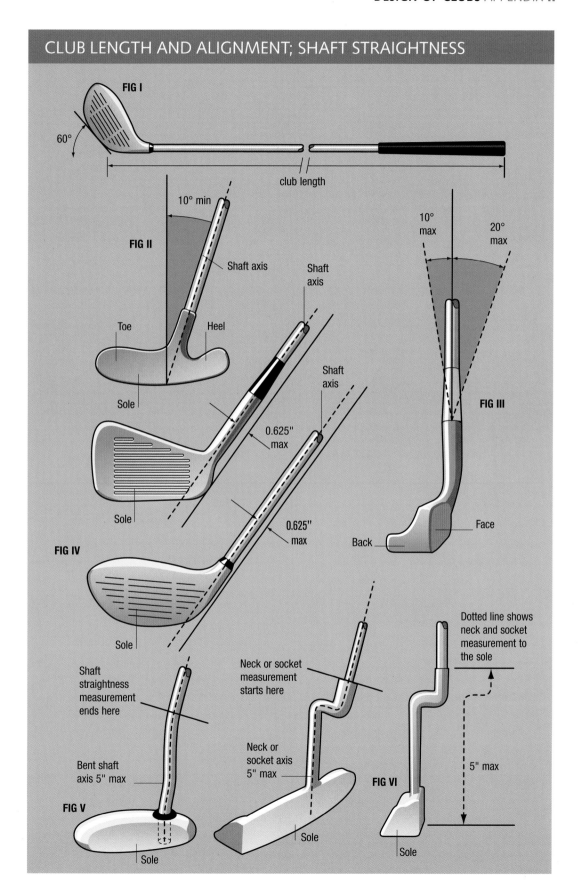

FIG I

60°

club length

FIG II

10° min

Shaft axis

Toe

Heel

Sole

Shaft axis

Shaft axis

0.625" max

Sole

FIG IV

0.625" max

Sole

10° max

20° max

FIG III

Face

Back

Shaft straightness measurement ends here

Bent shaft axis 5" max

FIG V

Sole

Neck or socket measurement starts here

Neck or socket axis 5" max

Sole

Dotted line shows neck and socket measurement to the sole

FIG VI

5" max

Sole

GRIP AND CLUB FACE

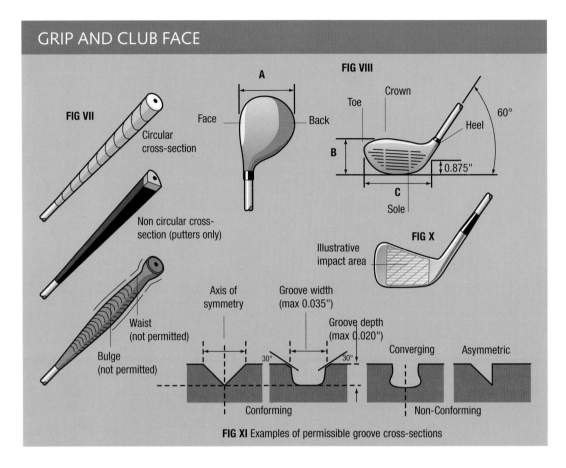

FIG VII Circular cross-section

Non circular cross-section (putters only)

Waist (not permitted)

Bulge (not permitted)

A

Face — Back

FIG VIII

Crown
Toe
Heel
60°
B
0.875"
C
Sole

FIG X
Illustrative impact area

Axis of symmetry

Groove width (max 0.035")

Groove depth (max 0.020")

30° 30°

Converging Asymmetric

Conforming Non-Conforming

FIG XI Examples of permissible groove cross-sections

shown in Fig. I. The length is defined as the distance from the point of the intersection between the two planes to the top of the grip. For putters, the measurement of length is taken from the top of the grip along the axis of the shaft or a straight line extension of it to the sole of the club.

d. Alignment

When the club is in its normal address position the shaft must be so aligned that:

(i) the projection of the straight part of the shaft on to the vertical plane through the toe and heel must diverge from the vertical by at least 10 degrees (see Fig. II). If the overall design of the club is such that the player can effectively use the club in a vertical or close-to-vertical position, the shaft may be required to diverge from the vertical in this plane by as much as 25 degrees;

(ii) the projection of the straight part of the shaft on to the vertical plane along the intended line of play must not diverge from the vertical by

more than 20 degrees forward or 10 degrees backward (see Fig. III).

Except for putters, all of the heel portion of the club must lie within 0.625 inches (15.88 mm) of the plane containing the axis of the straight part of the shaft and the intended (horizontal) *line of play* (see Fig. IV).

2. Shaft

a. Straightness

The shaft must be straight from the top of the grip to a point not more than 5 inches (127 mm) above the sole, measured from the point where the shaft ceases to be straight along the axis of the bent part of the shaft and the neck and/or socket (see Fig. V).

b. Bending and Twisting Properties

At any point along its length, the shaft must:

(i) bend in such a way that the deflection is the same regardless of how the shaft is rotated about its longitudinal axis; and

(ii) twist the same amount in both directions.

c. Attachment to Clubhead

The shaft must be attached to the clubhead at the heel either directly or through a single plain neck and/or socket. The length from the top of the neck and/or socket to the sole of the club must not exceed 5 inches (127 mm), measured along the axis of, and following any bend in, the neck and/or socket (see Fig. VI).

Exception for Putters: The shaft or neck or socket of a putter may be fixed at any point in the head.

3. Grip (see Fig. VII)

The grip consists of material added to the shaft to enable the player to obtain a firm hold. The grip must be fixed to the shaft, must be straight and plain in form, must extend to the end of the shaft and must not be molded for any part of the hands. If no material is added, that portion of the shaft designed to be held by the player must be considered the grip.

(i)   For clubs other than putters the grip must be circular in cross-section, except that a continuous, straight, slightly raised rib may be incorporated along the full length of the grip, and a slightly indented spiral is permitted on a wrapped grip or a replica of one.

(ii) A putter grip may have a non-circular cross-section, provided the cross-section has no concavity, is symmetrical and remains generally similar throughout the length of the grip. (See Clause (v), below.)

(iii) The grip may be tapered but must not have any bulge or waist. Its cross-sectional dimensions measured in any direction must not exceed 1.75 inches (44.45 mm).

(iv) For clubs other than putters the axis of the grip must coincide with the axis of the shaft.

(v)   A putter may have two grips, provided each is circular in cross-section, the axis of each coincides with the axis of the shaft, and they are separated by at least 1.5 inches (38 mm).

4. Clubhead
a. Plain in Shape

The clubhead must be generally plain in shape. All parts must be rigid, structural in nature and functional. The clubhead or its parts must not be designed to resemble any other object. It is not practicable to define plain in shape precisely and comprehensively. However, features which are deemed to be in breach of this requirement and are therefore not permitted include, but are not limited to:

(i)   All Clubs
  • holes through the face;
  • holes through the head (some exceptions may be made for putters and cavity back irons);
  • facsimiles of golf balls or actual golf balls incorporated into the head;
  • features that are for the purpose of meeting dimensional specifications;
  • features that extend into or ahead of the face;
  • features that extend significantly above the top line of the head;
  • furrows in or runners on the head that extend into the face (some exceptions may be made for putters); and
  • optical or electronic devices.

(ii) Woods and Irons
  • all features listed in (i) above;
  • cavities in the outline of the heel and/or the toe of the head that can be viewed from above;
  • severe or multiple cavities in the outline of the back of the head that can be viewed from above;
  • transparent material added to the head with the intention of rendering conforming a feature that is not otherwise permitted; and
  • features that extend beyond the outline of the head when viewed from above.

b. Dimensions, Volume and Moment of Inertia

(i)   Woods
  When the club is in a 60 degree lie angle, the dimensions of the clubhead must be such that:
  • the distance from the heel to the toe of the clubhead is greater than the distance from the face to the back;
  • the distance from the heel to the toe of the clubhead is not greater than 5 inches (127 mm); and
  • the distance from the sole to the crown of the clubhead including any permitted features, is not greater than 2.8 inches (71.12 mm).

These dimensions are measured on horizontal lines between vertical projections of the outermost points of:

- the heel and the toe; and
- the face and the back (see Fig. VIII, dimension A); and on vertical lines between the horizontal projections of the outermost points of the sole and the crown (see Fig. VIII, dimension B). If the outermost point of the heel is not clearly defined, it is deemed to be 0.875 inches (22.23 mm) above the horizontal plane on which the club is lying (see Fig. VIII, dimension C).

The volume of the clubhead must not exceed 460 cubic centimeters (28.06 cubic inches), plus a tolerance of 10 cubic centimeters (0.61 cubic inches).

When the club is in a 60 degree lie angle, the moment of inertia component around the vertical axis through the clubhead's center of gravity must not exceed 5900 g cm^2 (32.259 oz in^2), plus a test tolerance of 100 g cm^2 (0.547 oz in^2).

(ii) Irons

When the clubhead is in its normal address position, the dimensions of the head must be such that the distance from the heel to the toe is greater than the distance from the face to the back.

(iii) Putters (see Fig. IX)

When the clubhead is in its normal address position, the dimensions of the head must be such that:

- the distance from the heel to the toe is greater than the distance from the face to the back;
- the distance from the heel to the toe of the head is less than or equal to 7 inches (177.8 mm);
- the distance from the heel to the toe of the face is greater than or equal to two thirds of the distance from the face to the back of the head;
- the distance from the heel to the toe of the face is greater than or equal to half of the distance from the heel to the toe of the head;
- the distance from the sole to the top of the head, including any permitted features, is less than or equal to 2.5 inches (63.5 mm).

For traditionally shaped heads, these dimensions will be measured on horizontal lines between vertical projections of the outermost points of:

- the heel and the toe of the head;
- the heel and the toe of the face;
- the face and the back;

and on vertical lines between the horizontal projections of the outermost points of the sole and the top of the head.

For unusually shaped heads, the heel to toe measurement may be made at the face.

c. Spring Effect and Dynamic Properties

The design, material and/or construction of, or any treatment to, the clubhead (which includes the club face) must not:

(i) have the effect of a spring which exceeds the limit set forth in the Pendulum Test Protocol on file with the USGA, or

(ii) incorporate features or technology, including, but not limited to separate springs or spring features, that have the intent of, or the effect of, unduly influencing the clubhead's spring effect, or

(iii) unduly influence the movement of the ball.

Note: (i) above does not apply to putters.

d. Striking Faces

The clubhead must have only one striking face, except that a putter may have two such faces if their characteristics are the same, and they are opposite each other.

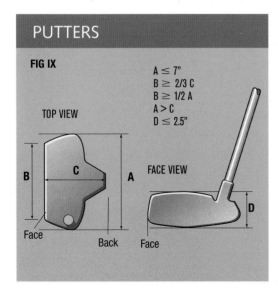

PUTTERS

FIG IX

A ≤ 7"
B ≥ 2/3 C
B ≥ 1/2 A
A > C
D ≤ 2.5"

TOP VIEW

FACE VIEW

B   C   A

Face   Back   Face

D

5. Club Face

a. General

The face of the club must be hard and rigid and must not impart significantly more or less spin to the ball than a standard steel face (some exceptions may be made for putters). Except for such markings listed below, the club face must be smooth and must not have any degree of concavity.

b. Impact Area Roughness and Material

Except for markings specified in the following paragraphs, the surface roughness within the area where impact is intended (the "impact area") must not exceed that of decorative sandblasting, or of fine milling (see Fig. X).

The whole of the impact area must be of the same material (exceptions may be made for clubheads made of wood).

c. Impact Area Markings

If a club has grooves and/or punch marks in the impact area, they must be designed and manufactured to meet the following specifications:

(i) Grooves
- Grooves must not have sharp edges or raised lips (test on file).
- Grooves must be straight and parallel.
- Grooves must have a symmetrical cross-section and have sides which do not converge (see Fig. XI).
- The width, spacing and cross-section must be consistent throughout the impact area.
- Any rounding of groove edges must be in the form of a radius which does not exceed 0.020 inches (0.508 mm).
- The width of each groove must not exceed 0.035 inches (0.9 mm), using the 30 degree method of measurement on file with the USGA.
- The distance between edges of adjacent grooves must not be less than three times the width of the grooves, and not less than 0.075 inches (1.905 mm).
- The depth of a groove must not exceed 0.020 inches (0.508 mm).

(ii) Punch Marks
- The area of any such mark must not exceed 0.0044 square inches (2.84 sq. mm).
- The distance between adjacent punch marks (or between punch marks and grooves) must not be less than 0.168 inches (4.27 mm), measured from center to center.
- The depth of a punch mark must not exceed 0.040 inches (1.02 mm).
- Punch marks must not have sharp edges or raised lips (test on file).

d. Decorative Markings

The center of the impact area may be indicated by a design within the boundary of a square whose sides are 0.375 inches (9.53 mm) in length. Such a design must not unduly influence the movement of the ball. Decorative markings are permitted outside the impact area.

e. Non-metallic Club Face Markings

The above specifications do not apply to clubheads made of wood on which the impact area of the face is of a material of hardness less than the hardness of metal and whose loft angle is 24 degrees or less, but markings which could unduly influence the movement of the ball are prohibited.

f. Putter Face Markings

Any markings on the face of a putter must not have sharp edges or raised lips. The specifications with regard to roughness, material and markings in the impact area do not apply.

APPENDIX III
THE BALL

1. General
The ball must not be substantially different from the traditional and customary form and make. The material and construction of the ball must not be contrary to the purpose and the intent of the Rules.

2. Weight
The weight of the ball must not be greater than 1.620 ounces avoirdupois (45.93 gm).

3. Size
The diameter of the ball must not be less than 1.680 inches (42.67 mm). This specification will be satisfied if, under its own weight, a ball falls through a 1.680 inches diameter ring gauge in fewer than 25 out of 100 randomly selected positions, the test being carried out at a temperature of 23 ± 1°C.

4. Spherical Symmetry
The ball must not be designed, manufactured or intentionally modified to have properties which differ from those of a spherically symmetrical ball.

5. Initial Velocity
The initial velocity of the ball must not exceed the limit specified (test on file) when measured on apparatus approved by the USGA.

6. Overall Distance Standard
The combined carry and roll of the ball, when tested on apparatus approved by the United States Golf Association, must not exceed the distance specified under the conditions set forth in the Overall Distance Standard for golf balls on file with the USGA.

Photographic acknowledgments:

Peter Dazeley 127 right. **Getty Images** 99, 127 left;/ David Cannon 18, 42, 91, 115, 145;/ Phil Cole 164;/ Richard Heathcote 126;/ Hulton Archive 26;/ Craig Jones 116;/ Robert Laberge 150;/ Donald Miralle 35;/ Stephen Munday 13. **Royal & Ancient** 11. **Phil Sheldon Golf Picture Library** 12, 67, 76, 135, 173, 179;. **PA Photos**/Simon Barber/Jam Media 109;/ David James 48. **USGA Archives**/John Mummert 71.

Illustration by Sudden Impact Media

An Hachette UK Company
www.hachette.co.uk

First published in Great Britain in 2003

This revised and updated edition published in 2008 by Hamlyn a division of Octopus Publishing Group Ltd
2–4 Heron Quays, London E14 4JP.
www.octopusbooks.co.uk.

Distributed in the United States and Canada by Sterling Publishing Co., Inc.
387 Park Avenue South, New York, NY 10016–8810

ISBN: 978-0-600-61788-4

A CIP catalogue record of this book is available from the British Library.

Printed and bound in China

10 9 8 7 6 5 4